IMAGE AND AUDIENCE

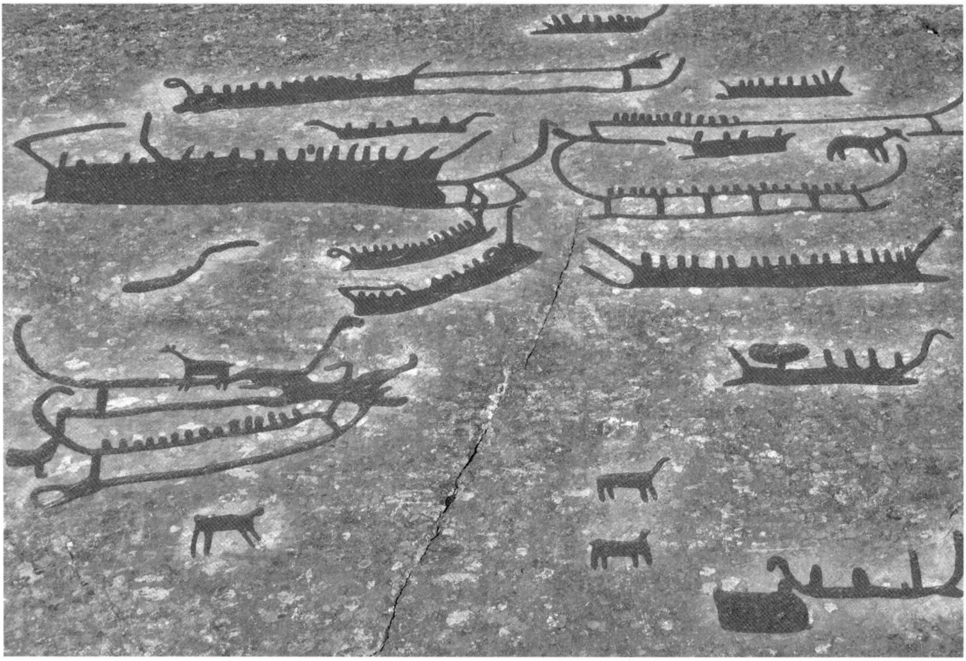

Frontispiece. Carvings of ships and animals at Himmelstalund, Sweden. As in other illustrations of Scandinavian rock art, the images have been painted in order to display them to the public

Image and Audience

Rethinking Prehistoric Art

RICHARD BRADLEY

OXFORD
UNIVERSITY PRESS

OXFORD
UNIVERSITY PRESS

Great Clarendon Street, Oxford OX2 6DP

Oxford University Press is a department of the University of Oxford.
It furthers the University's objective of excellence in research, scholarship,
and education by publishing worldwide in

Oxford New York

Auckland Cape Town Dar es Salaam Hong Kong Karachi
Kuala Lumpur Madrid Melbourne Mexico City Nairobi
New Delhi Shanghai Taipei Toronto

With offices in

Argentina Austria Brazil Chile Czech Republic France Greece
Guatemala Hungary Italy Japan Poland Portugal Singapore
South Korea Switzerland Thailand Turkey Ukraine Vietnam

Oxford is a registered trade mark of Oxford University Press
in the UK and in certain other countries

Published in the United States
by Oxford University Press Inc., New York

First published 2009

British Library Cataloguing in Publication Data
Data available

Library of Congress Control Number: 2008942644

Typeset by SPI Publisher Services, Pondicherry, India
Printed in Great Britain
on acid-free paper by
the MPG Books Group

ISBN 978–0–19–953385–5

1 3 5 7 9 10 8 6 4 2

For Mark Edmonds

Preface

I wrote my first article about prehistoric 'art' in 1989 and others have followed over more recent years. In 1997, I brought some of my ideas together in a book *Rock Art and the Prehistory of Atlantic Europe*. During almost two decades my research has led me from Britain and Ireland to the Iberian Peninsula and then to Scandinavia, but during this time my interests have broadened from an initial concern with rock carvings and megalithic tombs to the decorated artefacts of the same periods. I have never felt comfortable with the use of the term 'art' to describe so many different phenomena and have become increasingly aware of the difficulties involved in their study. Both those difficulties and some of the ways of resolving them are considered here.

Although there have been many accounts of prehistoric art, nearly all of them begin by making the assumption that the concept is a useful one. Because they take the existence of ancient artworks for granted, these studies pay little attention to the contexts in which they were made and used. It is only in accounts of Palaeolithic painted caves that a more rounded approach has been taken, yet even here there is a tendency to publish catalogues of attractive images without much discussion of their wider significance. Either the painted or carved designs are treated as sufficient in themselves, or they are studied for the light they might shed on early cognition. Perhaps that is understandable because the archaeological evidence from this period is otherwise quite limited.

The problem becomes more serious in accounts of later prehistory. This is rather surprising, for not only were natural places embellished in the ways that had already happened during the Palaeolithic period, the earliest architecture seems to have developed at this time. Again there has been a tendency to treat certain objects or images as a self-contained field of research. The academic and popular literature is dominated by catalogues of drawings and photographs and by analyses of individual artefacts which take little account of their contexts. Again that has happened because it is assumed that prehistoric artefacts can be treated as works of art. Such studies take place in a vacuum, and as a result archaeologists scarcely use this evidence in their interpretations of the past.

There are several ways in which to break the impasse. The first is to question whether *art* is a useful term in studies of prehistory and whether the methods of modern art historians have much to contribute to accounts of such a remote period. There are two reasons for adopting this position. We can investigate the circumstances in which prehistoric art was first identified and the ways in which it emerged as a distinct field of study. That happened during the nineteenth and twentieth centuries through the activities of museums and private collectors. Its recognition followed a similar process to that of 'primitive art', and in each case it seems possible that particular artefacts only assumed the status of artworks once they had been removed from their original settings. The kinds of material culture treated as prehistoric art are normally those that were made with considerable virtuosity, yet there is no justification for selecting the most complex examples from what was really a continuum. The same applies to decorated monuments or rock formations. Again those with the most arresting visual patterns have dominated the discussion, and superficially simpler designs have been overlooked.

Another approach is to integrate this material into a more ambitious contextual archaeology in which these phenomena are studied in relation to the places and circumstances in which they were used in prehistory. Thus decorated metalwork can be studied in relation to funeral rites and votive offerings, and decorated monuments in relation to the people who performed their rituals there. It is rarely possible to infer the meanings of ancient images without the help of written evidence, but it may be possible to investigate the relationship between the designs that were created and displayed and the audiences who encountered them. That is the premise of this book. It seeks to redirect studies of prehistoric art so that they can be better integrated into the methods of contemporary archaeology.

The book is concerned with later prehistoric art rather than the well researched images of the Palaeolithic period. It is divided into four parts, each of which is directly related to the approaches taken in an influential publication. It is also structured around two substantial case studies, one of which considers a tradition which includes some non-figurative or 'abstract' designs (megalithic art), whilst the other considers the more naturalistic images of the Scandinavian Bronze Age. The introduction and conclusion also draw on the well-known evidence of Celtic art, but it does not provide a major focus for this account. The text is not limited to the complex artefacts that are usually described as prehistoric art but also discusses the evidence of ancient architecture, rock paintings, rock carvings, sculptures, and even geoglyphs, as well as the designs on ceramics, metalwork, and other artefacts. Although the detailed case studies consider the period between about 4000 BC and the mid first millennium BC, the text will include material created over an even longer period of time. It will be concerned primarily with the prehistory of Western and Northern Europe, from Portugal to Finland, but will draw more selectively on examples from Central Europe and the Mediterranean. The concluding chapter will also consider the relationship between current approaches to prehistory and some of the concepts employed by contemporary artists.

The book is in four parts. The first is divided into two chapters and introduces the main theme of the book. Chapter 1 questions the basic notion of prehistoric art and discusses the circumstances in which it became a separate field of study in Europe. It discusses the arbitrary manner in which certain kinds of material were included within the canon whilst others were rejected. It also suggests that particular objects have been treated as prehistoric art because they have been divorced from their original contexts. That theme is developed in Chapter 2 which discusses the approach proposed in Alfred Gell's influential book *Art and Agency*. Rather than discussing the aesthetics of artworks, he emphasized their effects upon the viewer. Gell's study was a contribution to social anthropology and documented the active role that art plays in non-Western society. Prehistorians cannot do this, but they can study the interplay between the kinds of images that were created in the past and the audiences that are likely to have encountered them. That idea is developed in the remaining sections of the book.

Part II is a study of megalithic art. This material is distinctive for two reasons. This tradition of painting and stone-carving is defined not by stylistic criteria but by the contexts in which those images occur. It is partly abstract. The starting point for Part II is the recent book *Inside the Neolithic Mind* by David Lewis-Williams and David Pearce which reconstructs a prehistoric cosmology on the basis of stone-built tombs and the images found within them. By treating megalithic art as a distinctive phenomenon archaeologists have failed to appreciate its broader context in prehistoric society. Chapter 3 introduces Lewis-Williams's and Pearce's hypothesis through a discussion of the origins of megalithic tombs. It pays particular attention to their controversial hypothesis that some of the imagery associated with these monuments referred to altered states of consciousness. Chapter 4 considers the evidence that certain of the decorated stones found inside these monuments originated as statues in the open air. When they were broken up and built into the tombs their significance changed, and so did the audiences who could have viewed them. Chapter 5 compares the nature and distribution of the images found inside megalithic tombs with those on exposed surfaces within the wider landscape. To what extent were some images regarded as 'public' and others as 'private'? Did the audience for paintings and carvings change during the currency of megalithic art, and how far did some of those designs extend into the domestic domain through the embellishment of portable objects and even the decoration of houses? These studies bring together the results of new research on chambered tombs from the West Mediterranean, the Iberian Peninsula, France, Britain, Ireland, and Scandinavia.

Part III considers images which are united by a common style but which were created in several different media. In contrast to the main groups of designs in megalithic art, the visual culture of the Scandinavian Bronze Age is predominately figurative. It extends from decorated metalwork to the embellishment of burial cists and the drawings on rock outcrops. Here the starting point is Flemming Kaul's book *Ships on Bronze* which proposes a new reading of the designs on the metalwork of this period which show boats, horses, fish, snakes, and the sun. Chapter 6 introduces the images that were created in three different media during the Scandinavian Bronze Age: decorated metalwork, rock carvings, and stone settings. Chapter 7 summarizes Kaul's interpretations of these pictures in relation to the movement of the sun through the sky during the day and its passage beneath the sea at night. It extends his analysis to the carved rocks of South Scandinavia and discusses the extent to which the same concerns were expressed in that medium. It also considers the organization of cemeteries containing stone ships and other monuments. Chapter 8 suggests some new ways of thinking about this evidence in relation to more general ideas about fertility and death. It attempts to integrate the results of artefact analysis with studies of the ancient landscape, and in doing so it considers who was making the rock carvings and the ways in which these images were used during prehistory.

Part IV, which consists of one long chapter, discusses the interpretations put forward in the book and reflects on their implications for prehistoric archaeology. It suggests that the most productive way of studying the images described as prehistoric 'art' is to consider how they differed from the artworks of the twentieth century which they helped to inspire. Although the meanings of ancient designs will often remain elusive, the contexts in which they were effective are sometimes ones that archaeologists can reconstruct. Chapter 9 reviews the argument in Colin Renfrew's book *Figuring it Out: The Parallel Visions of Artists and Archaeologists*, which considers the relationship between archaeology and contemporary art. The notion of artefact biographies which has had so much influence on prehistorians has its counterpart in Conceptual Art. Installation Art is founded on similar principles to the displays of ancient objects like those associated with Iron Age burials, sanctuaries and votive deposits. They are among the contexts in which 'prehistoric art' has been discovered.

So the discussion returns to some of the ancient objects introduced at the beginning of the book. If the argument has any merit, they will have taken on a new significance.

Acknowledgements

Although I wrote this book in a year, I have been thinking about it for more than a decade. During that time I have been influenced by many people who have talked about their ideas, discussed my research in conferences and seminars, and have shown me many fascinating sites and artefacts. They are too numerous to mention individually, but I thank them all. I owe a further debt to the archaeologists who have already worked in this difficult field. Most of them feature in the bibliography, although I have been able to cite only a small proportion of the books and articles I have read in recent years. That I have been able to study sources that are not widely available is due to the kindness of their authors who have sent me copies of their publications. At certain points the text also draws on the results of fieldwork I have undertaken with other people, and it is right to name them here: Ramón Fábregas Valcarce, Aaron Watson, and Dag Widholm. Most important of all, I could not have written this without Katherine's patience and support.

I have been helped by many people in bringing this project to completion. A number of colleagues have read all, or part of, the text and have provided very useful suggestions, many of which I have adopted here. I wish to thank: Dr Lara Bacelar Alves, Professor Bob Chapman, Professor Ramón Fábregas Valcarce, Dr Sara Fairén Jiménez, Dr Joakim Goldhahn, and Dr Peter Skoglund. Dr Tony Mathews, Emilio Rodríguez Alvarez, and Evi Riikonen helped with the bibliography, and Elise Fraser played a major part in the preparation of the text. The figure drawings were prepared by Frances Taylor, Margaret Mathews, and Aaron Watson. Unless otherwise stated, the photographs are my own. The sources of the other figures are noted in the list on pp. xii–xv. Every attempt has been made to seek the permission of the copyright holders, but in a few cases this has not been possible. The omission will rectified if more information becomes available.

Lastly, the dedication. Not many archaeologists share an interest in contemporary art, ancient artefacts, and the prehistoric landscape. One of the few is Mark Edmonds, who has influenced my work and been a source of encouragement ever since we worked together in the field over twenty years ago. This book is dedicated to him and celebrates his recent appointment to a chair at the University of York.

Contents

Figures

Tables

Part I

The Problem with Prehistoric Art

1

The Division of the Spoils

THAT SENSATION OF ACCORD

The category of 'prehistoric art' has seldom been defined. It is a task that inhibits even the most confident writer. Consider this passage from one of the best books on the subject. The author is obviously uneasy about the relationship between Western art and ancient material culture, but, as he begins his account, he puts the problem from his mind:

Art is a term too readily borrowed in archaeology to explain things from the far past that are not obviously utilitarian. But every scratch and mark is not art any more than need be the most elaborate, costly, or curious, objects of devotion and display. On the other hand, many straightforward appliances of daily life, mere tools and vessels, by virtue of their stark simplicity, their aptness for use, positively draw out *that sensation of accord* which is the recognition of art uniting the modern beholder with the maker however far apart in time and space. No closer approach to a definition of art will be made here. (Powell 1966: 7; my emphasis)

Similar sentiments can be found in a book published two years later:

The study of prehistoric art allows, if it does not actually demand, a much greater freedom than does prehistory itself. There is in the nature of the subject and the monuments an absence of classificatory machinery, a lack of definition, a something ambivalent, in addition to the usual, and quite shocking, barrier of distance and decay. (Sandars 1968: xxvii–xxviii)

Such uncertainly is not confined to these pioneering accounts. Thirty years after Sandars's study was published, Paul Bahn made another attempt to characterize prehistoric art. Although his style is more assertive, the hesitation remains:

Art can be a deliberate communication through visual form, a message expressed in durable form, an expression of group mentality and of an artist's inner world. Art is art, regardless of the difference and variety of its meaning and function, regardless of qualitative or aesthetic appreciation, and whether it be prehistoric, Greek, Assyrian or anything else. (Bahn 1998: xiii)

It remained for Colin Renfrew to offer another definition, but, he warned, it was one that might have little relevance to the past. For Renfrew a work of art was:

> Any painting or sculpture or material object that is produced to be the focus of our visual contemplation or enjoyment. It is implicit in such a definition that the work does not at the same time fulfil some other primary purpose . . . We are ethnocentric if we apply our own concept of 'art' to the products of other cultures and eras. (Renfrew 2002: 66)

It follows that if the word *art* is to be used at all, it must be treated with caution. Since no alternative is available, from here on the reader must imagine that it is enclosed by inverted commas.

There can be no dispassionate view of prehistoric art, because the choice of this term already makes assumptions about the past. That has always been true. It raises a number of questions which are considered later in this chapter. How was prehistoric art first identified? Which categories were admitted to the corpus, and which were excluded? How were ancient artefacts treated by archaeologists, collectors, galleries and museums? Why was there so little interest in their original contexts?

Perhaps the most important discussion of ancient art took place in Palaeolithic archaeology over a hundred years ago. It is with those arguments that my account begins.

AUTHENTICITY AND ART

Nineteenth-century discoveries of what has become known as Palaeolithic art took two different forms. There were the paintings and engravings found on cave walls, and there were smaller objects that had been embellished in the same style. In each case the most common elements were drawings of animals. These discoveries also happened in two countries, France and Spain, which had rather different traditions of archaeological research. According to Oscar Moro Abadía (2006), that distinction is crucial for it accounts for significant contrasts in the reception and interpretation of this evidence.

When these images were first identified, there were several problems to consider. The first was a factual issue. Were the drawings ancient or modern? That question was the easiest one to answer, as some of the small decorated objects came from stratified contexts, while a number of painted or engraved surfaces extended below the floors of the caves or were masked by more recent mineral deposits. A second matter was harder to resolve, for it concerned the definition of prehistoric art itself. It was here that the views of French and

Spanish scholars diverged. The issues that their disagreement raised have implications even today.

The nature of this debate has sometimes been misrepresented. It is true that French scholars like Gabriel de Mortillet were reluctant to accept that the phenomenon extended to another country, but that superficial contrast conceals a more fundamental difference of opinion. French researchers were committed to an evolutionary model of the emergence of human society. This went back to the conjectural histories favoured during the Enlightenment and received an important stimulus from the work of Charles Darwin. Similar beliefs were common during the nineteenth century, from the writings of Lewis Henry Morgan to those of Sir John Lubbock, and involved direct comparisons between prehistoric evidence and what was known about non-Western societies. They remained influential for a long time. It is often forgotten that little over fifty years ago Gordon Childe wrote a book discussing Morgan's notions of 'savagery', 'barbarism', and 'civilization' (Childe 1951).

If societies could be organized like biological organisms along a scale from simple to complex, so could the visual images that they produced. For nineteenth-century scholars this view was reinforced by collections of non-Western artefacts that were being introduced to Europe by travellers, soldiers and colonial administrators. If these objects were artworks, then they were 'primitive art', just as the people who made them lived in 'primitive societies'. Again it is surprising how long both these terms remained in use. The problem for French archaeologists was that sophisticated paintings were coming to light in caves where they were apparently associated with the remains of extinct animals. This violated the principles of social evolution, for cave art showed a disquieting resemblance to the accepted conventions of nineteenth-century painting. For that reason it was difficult to accommodate these findings in a broader understanding of the past.

Although it is sometimes argued that similar problems were experienced in Spain, there is actually some evidence that the antiquity and authenticity of cave paintings were accepted with less hesitation. Researchers were not so troubled by its apparent sophistication, or by the uncanny way in which certain of the paintings seemed to anticipate visual techniques invented in the Renaissance (Moro Abadía 2006). The fact that some of those scholars were priests seems to be particularly relevant, for among them were people who believed the biblical account of the creation. If the world had come into being fully formed, the idea of progressive social evolution would be ill-founded. Again that influenced the ways in which the archaeological evidence was interpreted. Human beings had not changed significantly since the world was made, and nor had their abilities or their spiritual concerns. Thus there was no objection to the discovery of sophisticated paintings and carvings dating from the remote past.

The immediate result was that 'prehistoric art' was conceived in two quite different ways, for reasons which had little to do with the material that was being studied, and everything to do with the philosophical positions of the researchers. The existence of cave paintings raised no problem for those Spanish scholars who accepted the literal truth of the Book of Genesis, but it posed real difficulties for French intellectuals who had adopted an evolutionary model. In fact another issue influenced this debate. Some of the French authorities seem to have been explicitly anti-clerical. This not only influenced their attitudes to creationist beliefs, it coloured their interpretations of the images themselves. Even when their authenticity had been accepted, de Mortillet could not accept that the paintings in French caves had any connection with prehistoric systems of belief. That was because of his personal hostility to religion. He was reluctant to concede that early humans possessed any concept of the supernatural. Like other scholars of his day, he preferred to view these drawings and paintings in wholly secular terms. They were an exemplification of the peculiarly nineteenth-century notion of 'art for art's sake'.

ARTS AND CRAFT

That idea raised yet another problem, but this time it was not specific to the Palaeolithic period. During the nineteenth century it was customary to distinguish between fine art and the 'decorative' or 'applied arts' (Moro Abadía and González Morales 2005; Moro Abadía 2006). The distinction was enshrined in the collections of the museums and galleries founded at the time, and to a large extent that institutional division retains its influence today. Fine art was created by people with extraordinary abilities. From the Renaissance onwards they enjoyed a special reputation. The privileging of certain media, in particular painting and sculpture, only increased with time, and, as it happened, the monetary value of works of art increased. Larry Shiner (2001) argues that the contemporary conception of art developed in the eighteenth century. The 'decorative arts', on the other hand, were made by skilled craft workers whose names have often been lost. They usually produced smaller items, which might include pottery, textiles or jewellery. Many of these artefacts played useful roles in daily life. It was in an attempt to break down this artificial distinction that the 'Arts and Crafts Movement' was founded.

One way in which nineteenth-century researchers were able to come to terms with the discovery of Palaeolithic images was to interpret them according to the distinction between fine art and applied art. At its simplest this could reflect the different media in which they had been made. Thus the painted panels inside some French and Spanish caves could be treated as fine art, while the portable objects, many of which were engraved in exactly the same style, were allied to the less prestigious field of the decorative arts (Moro Abadía 2006). The differences between them were emphasized by the use of language. The separate chambers inside the decorated caves were often described as 'galleries', as if they were really the equivalent of a Western art museum, while the decorated artefacts were usually referred to according to their functions, where they could be inferred.

For a while that distinction was employed by French researchers, for it was possible to combine it with the prevailing model of social evolution. They could accept the evidence for decorative arts in the Palaeolithic period more readily than the antiquity of cave paintings, especially those which featured extensive or elaborate designs. That was because it seemed consistent with an evolutionary framework to argue that small, utilitarian objects might have been embellished at an earlier date than the creation of fine painted 'panels'– again the choice of term is unconsciously revealing. For the reasons given earlier, that distinction was not so troubling for Spanish researchers. For them both kinds of images could have been used simultaneously.

There were two reasons why this disagreement was eventually resolved. The first was simply the weight of archaeological evidence that the cave paintings were not only authentic but also ancient. That should have been apparent from the outset, and the main reason for so much resistance was theoretical rather than empirical. A second factor that should not be overlooked was a change in the ways in which European artists and intellectuals viewed non-Western societies and their material culture.

ART AND THE EXOTIC

It happened that the archaeological evidence for the high antiquity of cave art was accepted at much the same time as a new academic discipline was emerging. This was social anthropology. Its distinctive feature was that it was explicitly comparative and, to an increasing extent, based on first-hand observation. The study of non-Western peoples was no longer an intellectual exercise to be conducted from a library, and, as scholars came to know these societies in more detail, it became obvious that a simple evolutionary framework was inadequate. It could not accommodate the variety that was becoming apparent in the ethnographic record. There was still a tendency to equate geographical remoteness with chronological distance (Fabian 1983), but even this simple scheme seemed less attractive. From the early years of the twentieth century more attention was paid to the characteristics of individual peoples.

That coincided with a new attitude to the material culture of the same societies. Now it was increasingly acceptable to consider it as art. That happened for two reasons. The first was that as exotic items were collected they were assimilated into the Western art market (N. Thomas 1999). When the artefacts were put in display they also attracted the attention of painters and sculptors. The work of Picasso, Brancusi or Modigliani shows the impact of the new source of inspiration (Renfrew 2002). This has been treated as a revelation which changed the visual art of the twentieth century, but a comparison between the exotic objects and the paintings and sculptures that they inspired shows how literally some of them were copied. In that sense they were co-opted not only into the art market but also into the repertoire of Modernism.

The same applied to antiquities, and those European artists who sought inspiration in 'primitive' art were just as prone to draw on archaeological material for ideas. They made no distinction between these categories and may not have been aware of them. The same was true in the salesroom where ancient artefacts were marketed alongside what became known as 'indigenous' or 'tribal art'. In fact the two classes seem to have merged in the organization of some displays. That is hardly surprising since both groups of material were equally remote from the contexts in which they had been used.

MUSEUMS AND THE 'FIRST ARTS'

Recently these problems have assumed a new prominence. This is most apparent from developments in Paris, the city in which early displays of 'tribal art' had such an impact on twentieth century painters and sculptors. As so often happens, the history of public institutions provides a subtle index of wider changes in cultural life.

Until recently the organization of Paris museums followed the conventional distinction between fine art and the decorative arts (S. Price 2007). In the same way, non-Western artefacts were generally housed in the Musée de l'Homme, and archaeological material in the chateau at Saint-Germain-en-Laye.

There were always some anomalies, and these prove highly revealing. The fine art museum of the Louvre actually includes ancient artefacts, but they are of two different kinds. Many of them are classical antiquities, but there is also a collection from Egypt, which was conquered by Napoleon. Both groups feature large and impressive items. Here the connecting link seems to be that they come from states and empires, for there is an implicit comparison with the political history of France. The displays also include small groups of objects, including fragments of pottery and worked stone of the kind which might be found in any archaeological collection. They have not been chosen for their aesthetic qualities, and at first sight they seem to be out of place. In fact there is a simple explanation for their presence. They are used to represent early human activity in regions of the world that only later came to prominence. Thus there are crude stone artefacts from Egypt and potsherds from the Mediterranean which have nothing to contribute to the historical development of fine art.

In recent years another element has diluted the idea of the Louvre as a museum of European fine art. At the instigation of President Chirac, several rooms were devoted to an attractive display of non-Western artefacts (S. Price 2007). They were selected from the ethnographic collections of the Musée de l'Homme and were intended to provide a foretaste of the contents of the Musée du quai Branly which has recently opened in Paris. In the light of the earlier discussion it was perhaps inevitable that among these objects there were antiquities from the New World which would have been more appropriate in an archaeological collection.

The small display in the Louvre was accompanied by two short texts which were intended to place the exhibition in its wider context. In each case the English language version is revealing:

> The arrival in the Louvre—or, rather the return—of art long considered, unjustly, to be primitive is the culmination of a dream shared over a period of more than a century by a wide range of people: poets, artists, scientists, collectors, Heads of States, or ordinary citizens.

This seems to suggest that the visual arts possess an essential unity that the display in the Louvre was meant to celebrate. The statement also draws attention to the role of this material as a source of inspiration for modernism, yet this passage does not mention any of the people who had made these artefacts; they have been excluded from the 'dream'. In any case these sentiments are undermined by the other text, which utilizes the very notion that the project is intended to reject:

> Place of homage to non-Western societies and the sharing of cultures still too often misunderstood, the Musée du quai Branly is the expression of the will of France to

grant their just place to *primitive arts* in the world of museums. Further, it is a witness of the fact that hierarchy no longer exists between the arts any more than it does between people. (my emphasis)

Either there is 'primitive art' or there is not. No doubt this is partly a problem of language, but the French original shows the same confusion. It is clear that similar problems beset other parts of this project. What should the new museum be called? Although it was a favourite project of Jacques Chirac, there was opposition to the idea that it should bear his name. Perhaps more revealing are other names that were rejected before the project came to fruition. Many of the objects that are now on display were originally in the Musée de l'Homme, an institution whose title makes no reference to art of any kind. If there was little support for a reference to 'primitive' art, another proposal was to refer to 'arts premiers' (the first arts). Although this idea did not find favour, it made two assumptions that remain extremely widespread. The first is that the material that it would display should properly be characterized as art. The second is that the contents of the museum would not only be exotic objects, they would also represent a formative phase in the evolution of art itself. Once again the geographically distant was confused with the chronologically remote.

In that sense the problems of displaying this material echo those associated with the first discovery of Palaeolithic art, and over a century later the evolutionary framework still seems to have supporters in the French cultural establishment. There is the same implicit equation between non-Western objects and prehistoric antiquities, as if both represented the earliest ancestors of contemporary European art. There is also an understandable hesitation as to whether the term *art* is really the right one to use. Happily, neither problem is raised by the name that was eventually chosen for the new museum.

Reviews of the Musée du quai Branly have been mixed; some commentators have been more impressed by its architecture than they have by the displays (S. Price 2007). For present purposes two observations seem particularly relevant. The artefacts are displayed in a setting which apparently represents a jungle. This attempt to provide local colour has not always been welcomed as it seems to reinforce visitors' stereotypes of distant parts of the world. At the same time, other critics have commented that the objects on display, while undoubtedly arresting, are shown entirely out of context so that it is difficult to appreciate how they would have been employed in their original settings. In that sense the Western art market seems to have colonized other areas of the globe, and the museum has even been criticized as a celebration of the private collector.

LATER PREHISTORIC ART IN EUROPE

So far the discussion has placed most emphasis on the reception of Palaeolithic art in the late nineteenth century and the academic debates that took place at that time. The major issues extend from the status of 'artworks' as part of prehistoric material culture to the problems associated with their collection and display. To some extent their treatment has run in parallel with that of ethnographic art, and there are even cases in which those categories have been confused with one another.

The same lessons are apparent from the objects that have been identified as later prehistoric art in Europe; for the purposes of this chapter the term applies to the material culture of the Neolithic, the Bronze Age and the Iron Age. Two themes are particularly apparent in accounts of these phases. The first was prefigured by the discussions in France over the relationship between fine art and decorative art during the Palaeolithic period. Even assuming that art is a useful concept in archaeology, which objects should be included in this category, and which must be excluded? What are the limits of the canon? Does the study of this material encourage researchers to make arbitrary subdivisions within what was once a continuous distribution of artefacts of greater or lesser visual elaboration? Indeed, it is worth asking how far it is the appearance of such objects that is being studied rather than the technological processes involved in making them. That is why artefacts in certain raw materials, like metalwork, seem to be privileged over others.

The second question arose in discussing the mobile art of the Palaeolithic period and applies even more obviously to the ethnographic art displayed in Western museums. To what extent can these artefacts be treated as a self-contained field of study, when the main feature that they share in common is that they have been removed from their original contexts? In some cases their roles may have been well documented and can be explained to the public, but, in others, they were lost as these objects were transformed into artworks. That is still more of a problem with archaeological material, where it is harder to decide how it had originally been deployed. The growth of the antiquities trade means that some of the most impressive artefacts surviving from the ancient world must be treated separately from the main body of archaeological evidence. That is certainly the case with finds obtained by illegal excavations and distributed through the salesroom (Renfrew 2000). Indeed, it is difficult to decide how such items can be valued when so little is known about their original significance. Quite simply, their price depends on judging them by the same criteria as more recent artworks—the materials used, the skills required to make them, their visual impact—and combining this with an estimate of the rarity of similar objects in existing collections. As much as anything else, it is their role in the market that has turned them into art.

One can recognize this tension in accounts of prehistoric Europe. Those written for the general reader are usually well illustrated and make effective use of drawings and photographs of a small selection of 'artworks'. Their role seems to be to show the level of sophistication of ancient visual culture, for otherwise they play little role in the text. More academic studies often encounter the same problem, but deal with it in a different way. The production, circulation and deposition of complex artefacts are often treated seriously, but specific objects attract less attention and the question of 'art styles' is rarely discussed in any detail. In fact certain kinds of archaeological information have been marginalized in the past. For many years the painted and decorated surfaces collectively known as rock art were largely the preserve of amateur archaeologists and were neglected by academics. Similarly, the images found inside megalithic tombs have attracted less attention than the ground plans of those monuments. That may be why prehistoric paintings and carvings are still being identified inside such structures today.

At the same time, there have been specialists who treat prehistoric images as a self-contained field of study without feeling much need to integrate their results into broader interpretations of the past. This has only encouraged the idea that ancient art can be studied in isolation. When the two approaches are brought together, the union can be difficult to sustain. Nowhere is this more obvious than in studies of Celtic art, perhaps the best known style of later prehistoric imagery in Europe.

THE CASE OF CELTIC ART

The special status of Celtic art is widely acknowledged, yet both these terms pose problems. There has been controversy over the significance of the peoples Classical writers referred to as Celts. It is obvious that they did not use the name consistently, so the Celts themselves were located in different areas of Europe. The use of the term also changed and it is perfectly possible that it was applied to different communities at different times (Collis 2003). Some writers did have a clear idea of the groups whom they called by this name. Others may have thought of *Celts* simply as a synonym for barbarians. Peter Wells (2001) has argued that it was the expansion of Roman power that encouraged previously independent groups to form alliances with one another. In that sense Celtic identity would have emerged only slowly and in response to the threat posed by Rome.

The problem is made even worse, because the adjective Celtic has been applied to a family of languages spoken along the western margin of the Continent. The links between them have been accepted for many years, but it is not known when they first developed. During the last two centuries these connections have taken on a political dimension, as nationalist movements have used both the literary and linguistic evidence to emphasize the distinctive identities of countries along the Atlantic coastline. This approach has also drawn on archaeological material, which has often been misunderstood. Among these sources were prehistoric visual images. Again the notion of Celtic art has given rise to problems.

There seems no reason to question the former existence of people who called themselves Celts. On the other hand, the term has not been much help to archaeologists and would have been better avoided. Enough confusion has been created by the identification of 'Celtic' languages (whose reality is not in any doubt). It creates still more uncertainty to apply the same adjective to a style of art.

CELTIC ART AND LA TÈNE ART

Those who are uneasy with the adjective *Celtic* because of its ethnic connotations talk of the *La Tène* style, named after a prolific find of decorated artefacts in Switzerland. At first sight that is a reasonable procedure, and an entire phase of the Iron Age is also called 'La Tène'. In its wider connotation the term is used from Eastern Europe to Ireland.

On a descriptive level it is clear what is meant by the La Tène style:

> In La Tène there is a total transformation of the natural world. The clumsily fused composite beasts of [an earlier] period give way to apparently free-form fantastic shapes and creatures and allow the effortless grafting of plant and animal motifs. Each piece of La Tène art is different, involving a unique nexus of curving lines that converge and diverge. Artists had tried sometimes maintaining and sometimes releasing the developing trajectories of edges, so as always to keep the motifs from being over-geometric, stylized or, indeed, replicable. (Taylor 1996: 122)

The problem is that the nature of the original find spot was controversial when this style was first defined and remained so until a new programme of research began in 2007 (Hummler 2007). There was no doubt that the decorated artefacts were found in a river associated with the remains of two wooden bridges and other structures. There were deposits of animal bones and human remains, but opinion was divided whether this was a rich settlement or a sanctuary associated with unusually lavish deposits. Those who advocated a mundane interpretation postulated a catastrophic flood which had overwhelmed the site and drowned some of the inhabitants. Their opponents drew attention to the unusual nature of the faunal assemblage and to the distinctive manner in which human remains had been treated at La Tène. The discovery of a similar complex on the nearby site of Cornaux did not resolve the problem: it made it still more complex. Here there was another wooden bridge associated with deposits like those at La Tène, but these structures were not contemporary with one another (Schwab 1990–2002). If the metalwork and other material had accumulated by accident, it was necessary to postulate two separate floods, both with exactly the same consequences.

Research on these sites is still in progress, but now there is more reason to accept that their contents were placed there intentionally (Reginelli Servais 2007). Even so, few of these interpretations can be entirely satisfactory since many of the artefacts from La Tène have been dispersed and the most informative fieldwork took place many years ago. That is not important for the present argument. The point is that an entire style of prehistoric art—one of the best known of all—was created around a collection of objects whose original significance was poorly understood. If it was difficult to say whether the finds from La Tène were votive offerings or chance losses, there was little justification for a more ambitious analysis. Their find spot was known and had even been investigated, but until recently the outcome of this work remained unclear. Perhaps that is why so much attention has been paid to the classification of the decorated artefacts and their counterparts in other regions of Europe. Specialists on Celtic art ran the risk of conducting an enquiry which studied only part of the evidence. All too often they used the methods of art history rather than those of archaeology. They can still do that today.

There are other questions concerning the use of the word *art* to describe a body of material whose distribution extends across much of Central and Western Europe. This is recognized in one of the best accounts of this evidence:

> In dealing with Celtic art, it is necessary to abandon post-Renaissance definitions, which are as meaningless in understanding Celts as they are for most other prehistoric or ethnographic material. Distinctions developed in our own society between 'high art', popular art, and craft are alien to most other peoples at most other times.... Much Celtic art is found on everyday objects—pottery, weapons and horse-harness. (Megaw and Megaw 2001: 16)

Despite these caveats, it is clear that the Megaws think that Celtic art is a meaningful category:

> A minimal working definition of Celtic art is that it encompasses elements of decoration beyond those necessary for functional utility, though these elements represent a form of symbolic visual communication which is only partly accessible to us. (Megaw and Megaw 2001: 19)

Their account goes on to emphasize the role played by decorated metalwork. It was made by specialists and required unusual skills. Its production was probably commissioned by members of a social elite and may have been a particular feature of regions with high levels of agricultural production.

Other scholars have shown similar uncertainty is defining the repertoire of Celtic art. Again the nineteenth-century distinction between fine art and the decorative arts has played a part in their thinking. Introducing his book *Pattern and Purpose*, published in 1958, Cyril Fox expressed the dilemma in this way:

> Early Celtic art is distinctive; technique and design in gold, bronze or iron are often masterly, but there is nothing of 'Fine Art' about it; the incised patterns of relief ornament are on purposeful things—torcs, brooches and bracelets, weapons and drinking vessels, for example. It was not only a *decorative art*; useful things were well shaped, with a sense of style, so a beautiful or well-balanced form often sufficed, satisfying the bronze-worker's critical sense, as it does ours. (emphasis in the original; Fox 1958: v)

At other points he seems more tentative:

> The character and quality of many works of Celtic art . . . are not of the first rank. . . . It will be found difficult, as in the case of other societies at the same stage of development, to distinguish between works of art and of 'craft'. (Fox 1958: vi)

Martyn Jope's great study of *Early Celtic Art in the British Isles* was published in 2000, over forty years after Fox's book, although much of the text was written earlier. He expresses the same difficulties in characterizing Celtic art, although he maintains that it is a useful term. Like Fox, he also accepts that there is considerable variation in the quality of the material being studied:

> There are degrees of quality within the material before us . . . Artist is a difficult term. It lies at the refined end of a long hierarchy, with craftsmen of varying skill and aspiration at the other. We often find need for the intermediate, more fluid terms *artificer*, or *artisan* in its older sense of one who practices or cultivates an art. (emphasis in the original; Jope 2000: 3)

Having established this point, Jope's two-volume study is concerned almost entirely with artefacts. For that reason it has not had much influence on more general studies of the Iron Age. Its findings play little part in the most recent edition of Cunliffe's *Iron Age Communities in Britain* (Cunliffe 2005) or in Harding's *The Iron Age in Northern Britain* (Harding 2004) Indeed, this evidence has been so difficult to integrate into the mainstream of prehistoric studies that three years later Harding followed it with a separate book, *The Archaeology of Celtic Art* (Harding 2007).

DEFINING THE CANON

All the writers quoted here express uncertainties over the status of Celtic 'artworks' and their relationship to the production of other Iron Age objects. Megaw and Megaw (2001) explain that the modern distinction between 'high art', popular art and handicrafts might have had no significance for people in the past. Fox (1958) makes a similar observation. He emphasizes the production of 'purposeful things', although he goes on to say that those objects often amount to more than 'decorative art'. Similarly, Jope (2000) distinguishes between artists and 'craftsman' but acknowledges that there was 'a long hierarchy' extending between the two extremes. These writers, and others, seem to accept that there was really a continuum of decorated objects, although it is not so clear at which point they felt that *art* became the appropriate term to use.

Celtic art is identified through its appearance rather than the processes by which it was made. An undecorated object, however demanding its production, is rarely admitted to the corpus. Books about Celtic art are lavishly illustrated with drawings and photographs. Another way of deciding what is included in this category is to go beyond the written definitions and to analyse the illustrations themselves. Which kinds of object are depicted as examples of Celtic art, and which do not appear? Do their proportions vary between different authors? Has the range of artefacts accepted as Celtic art changed significantly during the period in which it has been studied?

The account that follows is based on an analysis of the artefacts illustrated in a series of books whose titles include the term *Celtic art*. The areas covered extend from Central Europe to the British Isles and the publications span the course of the twentieth century. They were also aimed at a variety of different readers, so the sample includes general accounts of Celtic art, museum and exhibition catalogues, and academic studies of this material. The one limitation is that this review does not include any material earlier than the Iron Age or any artefacts dating from the post-Roman period. Roman Iron Age objects are considered, however, as the use of this style obviously extended into that phase.

For the purposes of this study the material was divided into eight categories (Tables 1 and 2). This meant that some of the rarer types were excluded and that a number of artefacts had to be treated together. They were grouped as follows: weapons; large ornaments; small ornaments; pottery; coins; sculptures; artefacts for preparing or serving food and drink; and equipment associated with horse riding and the use of wheeled vehicles. A few of these categories require some explanation. The larger personal ornaments are artefacts like torcs which can be recognized from some distance away; the smaller examples are mostly brooches. Occasionally these classes overlap. For example, lavishly decorated helmets might be treated as objects for personal adornment. Here they are classified as weapons on analogy with decorated sword scabbards.

In a few cases the contrasts between the objects illustrated in these books can be explained by regional variations in the material identified as Celtic art. Thus decorated pots feature particularly strongly in an account of the evidence from Central Europe; Iron Age sculptures are mainly depicted in books about the Continent; and horse harness plays an important role in studies of the British Isles. Much more revealing are the contrasts between different accounts of the same regions. Thus Romilly Allen's early account of metalwork in Britain places most emphasis on small ornaments such as brooches, followed (in decreasing order of frequency) by ceramics, weapons and the larger ornaments (Allen 1904). Another major study of the same material was by Cyril Fox and was published by the National Museum of Wales. Here the proportions are not dissimilar. Most of the illustrations are of small ornaments, followed by weapons, pottery, equipment associated with horses, and coins (Fox 1958). Ian Stead's introduction to Celtic art, which was published by the British Museum, puts most emphasis on weapons. There are fewer illustrations of personal ornaments of both kinds, or of equipment connected with riding. Pots scarcely feature in his review (Stead 1996). The situation is different again in Martyn Jope's major study, for here the artefacts associated with riding dominate the illustrations, followed by weapons, coins, and artefacts associated with eating and drinking. Even fewer personal ornaments are shown (Jope 2000).

Publications of Celtic art on the Continent are less diverse. Jacobstahl's monumental study includes more illustrations of small ornaments than any other artefact type. They are followed by large personal ornaments, weapons, artefacts associated with the service of food and drink, and sculptures (Jacobstahl 1944). The recent account by Megaw and Megaw (2001) observes a similar balance among its drawings and photographs. The most

Table 1. The relative quantities of different kinds of artefacts illustrated as examples of Celtic Art in Britain and Ireland. The sample is limited to objects of pre-Roman and Roman Iron Age dates and shows their distribution from 1 (the most frequent) to 8 (the least). Data from Allen (1904), Fox (1958), Finlay (1973), MacGregor (1976), Stead (1996), and Jope (2000)

	Weapons	Large ornaments	Small ornaments	Pots	Eating and drinking	Coins	Horses and vehicles	Sculptures
Allen	3	4	1	2	6	8	5	7
Fox	2	7	1	3	6	5	4	8
Finlay	3	4	7	6	8	1	5	2
MacGregor	2	3	4	6	5	–	1	–
Stead	1	4	3	7	5	–	2	6
Jope	2	6	5	7	4	3	1	8

frequent elements are weapons. Large ornaments follow, and then artefacts associated with feasting, smaller ornaments, and coins. In this case the two studies feature approximately the same kinds of material. That is also true of a more popular account of Celtic art commissioned by UNESCO (Raftery ed. 1990). Again there are some significant contrasts. Jacobstahl illustrates roughly twice as many small ornaments as these other books, while the Megaws feature significantly more weapons than had featured in his monograph fifty-seven years earlier.

Even this cursory study is sufficient to show that there is no consensus about the contents of Celtic art. Although there are regional traditions of research—and obvious contrasts in the material available for study in different parts of Europe—there are noticeable variations in the choice of illustrations between successive studies of the Iron Age archaeology of the same regions. Why is this?

Perhaps the main reason is that the authors of those studies strike a different balance between large visually arresting items such as swords, shields and helmets, and inconspicuous items like brooches. There are also differences in the amount of attention paid to pottery and coins. That is not to criticize these studies, but merely to make the observation that there is no one body of material which everyone would accept as Celtic art. The main differences follow similar lines to the distinction that has long been made between 'fine art' and the 'decorative arts'. The principal writers in this field have acknowledged this point, although they do not seem to agree on where, or how, to make the division.

The changing corpus accepted as Celtic art is also influenced by the pattern of discovery. This is clearly illustrated by the genesis of Jope's account

Table 2. The relative quantities of different kinds of artefacts illustrated as examples of Celtic Art in studies mainly concerned with Continental Europe. The table shows their distribution from 1 (the most frequent) to 8 (the least). Data from Jacobstahl (1944), Hawkes and Duval (1972), Szabo (1974), Duval and Kruta (1982), Raftery (1990), and Megaw and Megaw (2001)

	Weapons	Large ornaments	Small ornaments	Pots	Eating and drinking	Coins	Horses and vehicles	Sculptures
Jacobstahl	3	2	1	6	4	–	7	5
Hawkes and Duval	4	5	3	2	6	1	8	7
Szabo	2	5	3	1	6	4	–	–
Duval and Kruta	4	1	2	3	5	6	7	8
Raftery	2	1	3	7	4	5	8	6
Megaw and Megaw	1	2	4	7	3	5	8	6

which was composed over many years. It has three components: a substantial text concerned with the character, chronology and distribution of this style in Britain and Ireland; a large number of photographs and drawings of individual objects; and an inventory of the illustrated artefacts. The text was largely complete thirty years before the book was published and makes little reference to some of the items that feature in the catalogue. 1970 was not a good time to complete an undertaking of this kind, for the closing decades of the last century saw an increase in the amount of archaeological fieldwork necessitated by commercial development. It also saw the use of metal detectors and the large scale collection of artefacts from unexcavated sites, many of which have passed into private hands. There were a few cemetery excavations and even discoveries of river finds, but the main source of the new material was the settlements. They have always been associated with small personal artefacts and coins. The result of this activity was that the body of material available for study not only increased, it also changed its composition. The structure of Jope's monograph bears witness to this development and helps to explain why he experienced such difficulties in finishing it.

THE LOSS OF CONTEXT

If one problem in discussing prehistoric art is deciding which material comes into that category, the other is that the contexts of ancient artefacts are often lost. That is certainly true of some of the best-known examples of Celtic art.

The closing section of this chapter illustrates this point with three examples. In each case it can be argued that the appearance of ancient objects has commanded so much attention because their wider cultural connections have been overlooked.

The first of these artefacts is the Battersea Shield, which was discovered in the River Thames when a bridge was constructed in the middle of the nineteenth century. There is no doubt that this is one of the most impressive pieces of Iron Age metalwork, and it is decorated with the many of the most characteristic devices of insular Celtic art. Not only is it embellished with three raised panels which incorporate pieces of glass, the design also includes several heads which had been carefully concealed amidst the flowing imagery (Figure 1)

Ian Stead (1985) has written an important monograph on the Battersea Shield, which contains a detailed analysis of its manufacture, style and chronology, but in only one paragraph does he mention that it was found together with over a hundred human skulls. This attracted so much attention at the time that the discovery of these remains entirely overshadowed the identification of the shield. Indeed the find spot was soon described as a 'Celtic Golgotha' (Cuming 1857). Only later did the Battersea Shield become the focus of attention. It is now in the British Museum, while the skulls have been

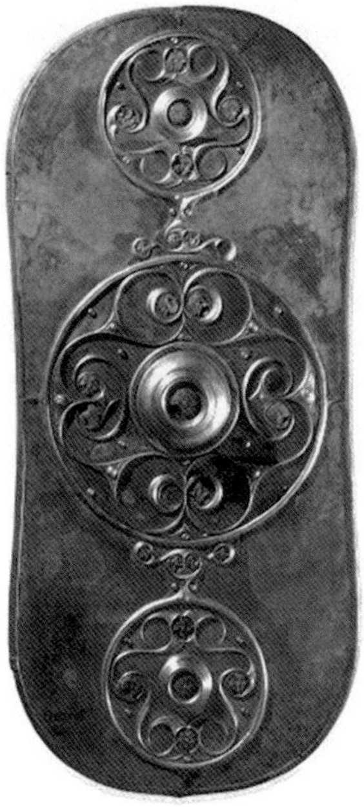

Figure 1. Iron Age shield from the River Thames at Battersea.

largely forgotten. Many years later some of them were identified in the collection of another London museum (Bradley and Gordon 1988).

Stead's book says very little about this, for, like Jope's corpus, it treats the decorated metalwork in almost complete isolation. Only on the last page does he concede that the find might be of any wider interest. His discussion is very brief:

> It is conceivable that it was lost in a riverside battle, or that it fell from a capsized boat, but is just as likely that it was deliberately consigned to the river to placate or honour a Celtic god. (1985: 47)

Another famous find of Celtic art comes from Basse-Yutz in the Moselle. Again the finds are displayed in the British Museum and have been the subject of an entire monograph (Megaw and Megaw 1990). This small collection consisted of two bronze flagons and a pair of Etruscan *stamnoi.* The flagons are among the best known of all Iron Age artefacts and have been described as 'great masterpieces of Celtic art'. They are unusually complex artefacts which feature animals and birds amidst a wealth of seemingly abstract ornament (Figure 2).

These four objects have a curious history. When they were found by workmen in 1927 they were mistaken for unexploded shells from the First World War, and even after their recovery there were numerous differences of opinion concerning their antiquity and their original place of origin. Were they really of nineteenth-century date, or were they Romanesque? They might have been ancient or modern, but were they loot buried by the German army

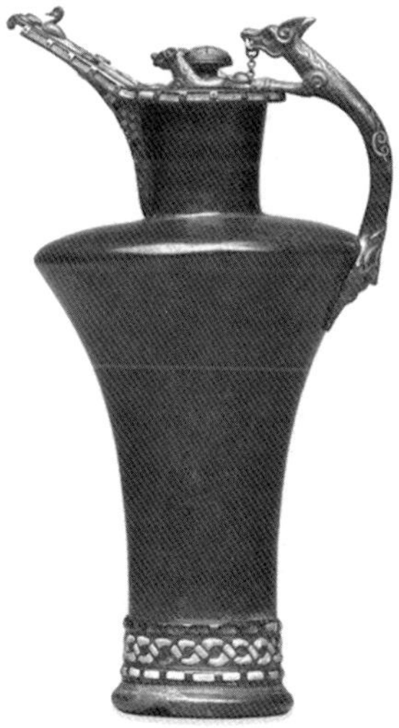

Figure 2. Bronze flagon from Basse Yutz, Moselle.

during the war, and could they have been brought there from Italy, or, as some said, from Romania? Major museums and collectors had been hoaxed in the recent past, and there was an understandable reluctance to purchase the artefacts. Accounts of their discovery were changed, so that the find spot was now declared to be a medieval abbey, but, as the metalwork passed from hand to hand, it sold for increasing sums of money. Eventually, two of the original finders who had provided misleading information about the discovery were prosecuted for theft, and all the artefacts were exported to London where they remain to this day.

If the location of the find remained in doubt—it was not re-established until 1929—so did its archaeological context, and it is because of this that the metalwork is difficult to interpret. At the time of the discovery there were rumours that other artefacts had been found—a belt buckle, and a torc or neck ring which may have been of iron—but, if so, they have never been traced. This leaves the original significance of the deposit in doubt. If the flagons and the *stamnoi* had been accompanied by personal ornaments then they might have been the contents of a grave: one of a number of rich burials recorded from this region. On the other hand, if they were the only artefacts from Basse-Yutz the site could perhaps be interpreted as a 'trader's hoard': a problematical category which calls for more critical examination. In the absence of any additional information, there is nothing to study but the objects themselves. Once the details of their context had been obscured, it was only natural to treat them as works of art.

The last example is the Gundestrup Cauldron which was discovered by farm workers in Jutland in 1891 (Kaul 1995). Although the find spot was carefully recorded, there were similar disputes over who should receive a reward, and again the question reached the law courts. Another feature which recalls the situation at Basse-Yutz is that parts of this elaborate silver vessel were missing. It was never established whether it had been complete when its remains were found and whether any fragments had been stolen (Figure 3).

One observation is particularly important. The vessel had been taken to pieces and the fragments had been deposited in a peat bog. It is the character of this find that poses problems. Not far away was the unusual fortified village of Borremose which was located in a similar environment. Pottery vessels may have been deposited as offerings in the enclosure ditch, and in the vicinity four bog bodies have been recorded, although they are older than either the cauldron or the settlement (Martens 1988). While it would be tempting to interpret the Gundestrup Cauldron as another votive deposit, it had two unusual features. It is clear that the pieces had been placed on the surface of the peat; they were not deposited in a wet environment, as was the case with

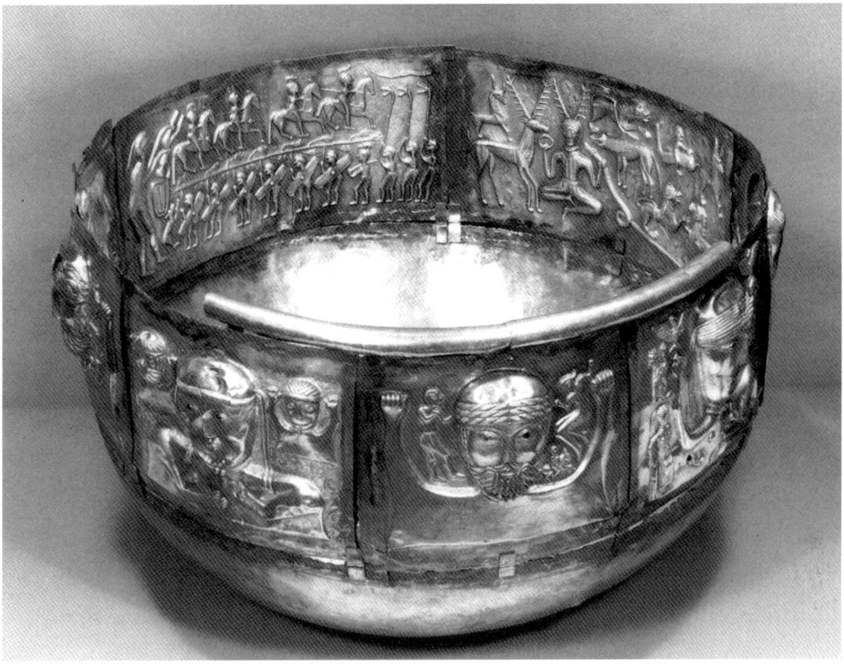

Figure 3. The Gundestrup Cauldron.

other objects during the Iron Age. Moreover, the cauldron had been dismantled and the decorated plates were carefully stacked inside its base. The metalwork could hardly have been less conspicuous, and for Bergquist and Taylor (1987) this suggests an attempt to conceal it. In this case something is known about the original context of this find, but the detailed evidence is so ambiguous that it is yet another object that has to be treated on its own terms.

There is more to say about the ways in which this find has been studied. According to Bergquist and Taylor, the Gundestrup Cauldron 'has the distinction of being the single most discussed artefact from European prehistory. It is the subject of five monographs and several hundred pages of periodical literature' (1987: 10). That total has risen since they wrote these words. If it is one of the most celebrated objects, it is also one of the least understood. Just as the reasons behind its deposit remain obscure, so do the questions of where it was made and how to interpret its distinctive imagery.

At different times the cauldron has been given a variety of dates extending over no fewer than seven hundred years, although now there seems to be some consensus that it should be attributed to the second century BC. It was not the only imported cauldron to be deposited in Denmark, as another example was found in a pit at Brå. The example from Gundestrup is particularly remarkable for the relief decoration on the sliver plates from which it is made. It occurs on both the interior and exterior of the vessel.

The interpretation of these images has posed many problems, and different authorities have been quite confident in assigning them to more widely distributed styles. For Klindt-Jensen (1961) the cauldron was an important addition to the corpus of Celtic art. He proposed that it should form the basis for a distinctive sub-style which would supplement those already defined by Jacobstahl (1944). Other authorities have argued that both the style and the technique of metalworking are more akin to Thracian traditions which were current in the Lower Danube, a region including parts of modern Bulgaria and Romania (Bergquist and Taylor 1987).

The details of the images raise further problems, for they have been claimed as distinctively Celtic by some writers and as distinctively Thracian by others; there is even a claim that some of the images originated in India (Taylor 1992). Bergquist and Taylor (1987) comment that none of the designs supposedly associated with Celts was absent from the corpus of Thracian art: a view which was supported by Kaul in 1995. In any case there were historically documented contacts between these different peoples. Even so, there are counterclaims that the cauldron was made in Gaul. If the designs really did refer to features of Celtic belief and iconography, it might be because it was commissioned by a member of a Celtic community but made by Thracian smiths according to their own artistic tradition. Yet another possibility is that the cauldron was taken back to Scandinavia by a war band, perhaps members of the Cimbri, who had fought in Eastern Europe; they may also have introduced the cauldron from Brå which was buried in Jutland together with part of an Attic lamp. These are not the only cases in which a problem of this kind arises as occasional items of Thracian metalwork have been found as far west as the Channel Island of Sark (Allen 1971).

The decorated plates that make up the Gundestrup Cauldron can be reunited in more than one way. They are not complete and it is by no means certain that the reconstruction made soon after their discovery was correct. Even so, there seems to be some agreement that the decorated panels are telling a story, or stories. What is extraordinary is that different researchers have been able to offer completely different versions of that narrative and to relate it to texts that have nothing in common with one another. Thus Olmstedt (1979), who considers that the cauldron was made in Gaul, identifies the images with the story told in the Irish epic Tain Bó Cuailnge (the Cattle Raid of Cooley). To do so he not only postulates an early date for a poem which contains elements that are usually thought to refer to the late first millennium AD, he also suggests that it had an unrecorded prototype in Gaul.

Another view is that the figures on the cauldron illustrate a cycle of Thracian tales, some of which were mentioned by Herodotus (Kaul, Mazarov, Best, and De Vries 1991).

In short, there is disagreement about almost every aspect of the Gundestrup Cauldron. It may have been hidden in the bog by people who had brought it to Denmark as loot, or it could have been intended as a votive offering. It may have been made either by Thracians or by Celts, and it may, or may not, be considered as Celtic art. In either case the argument is based largely on stylistic criteria. The stories that it illustrates may be associated with Thrace, with Gaul (or even with Ireland). In any case Denmark was outside the distributions of both Thracian and Celtic metalwork, and the circumstances in which the cauldron was brought to Northern Europe must be postulated on the basis of written sources. It is frustrating to study such ambiguous evidence, and the confidence with which individual scenes have been interpreted brings the credibility of prehistoric archaeology into question.

This situation arises because the cauldron is studied as a work of art, using techniques of visual analysis that would be as appropriate to Greek vases or Renaissance paintings. Since there is little to suggest why it was ever in Denmark, and still less to indicate why its fragments were deposited, it is hard to integrate its study with the main currents in Iron Age archaeology. Its apparent isolation has turned it into an artwork, and it is as an artwork that it is generally analysed. In that guise it provides one of the most common illustrations in popular accounts of Celtic art. That is unfortunate, for it is a style with which it has little in common.

Perhaps this is an extreme case, but are there no alternatives to such obscure procedures? This book has been written in the belief that more productive approaches do exist. Their potential is considered in Chapter 2.

2

Pattern and Purpose

NAMES AND DEFINITIONS

It seems as though archaeology acquired a category of prehistoric art through a series of accidents: the pattern of discovery in the nineteenth century; a growing appetite for 'primitive art' in the twentieth; and the expansion of the market in antiquities. Could it have been any different? A useful comparison is with research in social anthropology.

Chapter 1 discussed how archaeologists had met with problems in defining prehistoric 'art'. They were aware that it was very different from its modern counterpart, and much of the discussion focused on the contrasts between these genres and the extent to which they could be compared with one another. Social anthropologists have faced some of the same uncertainties, but they have also been concerned with questions of terminology. It is demeaning to describe something as 'primitive' art, yet the term 'tribal' art fares little better since the very notion of the tribe is a product of the colonial era. 'Ethnographic' art or 'indigenous art' are neutral terms, but they are not particularly explicit, while the notion of 'non-Western' art is equally unsatisfactory, for in practice it describes the visual culture of regions like Africa and the Pacific rather than the more complex products of areas like India, China and western Asia.

If it is difficult to find an appropriate adjective, it is still more challenging for anthropologists to offer a definition of art itself. In his influential book *The Anthropology of Art*, Robert Layton says this:

> There are two approaches to the definition of art which are applicable across cultural boundaries, even if neither seems to have quite universal application. One deals in terms of aesthetics, the other treats art as communication distinguished by a particularly apt use of images. (Layton 1991: 4)

A comparable definition is offered by Howard Morphy:

> Art objects are ones with aesthetic and/or semantic attributes (but in most cases both), that are used for representational or presentational purposes. (Morphy 1994: 655; cf. Morphy and Perkins 2005)

This contains two key notions, aesthetics and semantics, each of which can be considered in relation to prehistoric archaeology. It is unfortunate that both these concepts have proved to be controversial.

DEBATING AESTHETICS

1996 saw the publication of an unusual book, *Key Debates in Anthropology*, which recorded the proceedings of a series of annual meetings held at the University of Manchester (Ingold ed. 1996). As the title suggests, each was organized as a formal debate on a theme of general interest to anthropologists. It was structured around a specific motion, which was proposed and seconded by two well-known researchers and opposed by two other scholars of similar standing in the discipline. There followed a general discussion, the proceedings of which are recorded in the book, and, finally, a vote.

The novel format focused the discussion on the most important issues. It certainly happened in the 1993 debate which considered the proposition that 'aesthetics is a cross-cultural category'. This discussion is particularly relevant to the study of prehistoric art, as aesthetics is one of the elements in Morphy's definition of the 'art object'.

In fact Morphy was the first speaker at the meeting and proposed the motion for debate. His argument depends on the proposition that 'aesthetics is concerned with the human capacity to assign qualitative values to properties of the material world. We do not assert that the particular attributions made are universal... Aesthetics is concerned with the whole process of socialization of the senses with the evaluation of the properties of things' (Ingold ed. 1996: 258).

The values that people attach to such properties differ from one society to another, for it is the process that is the common element rather than the criteria employed. Morphy's argument refers to the wide variety of different attributes that have been highlighted in particular communities. They include the weight, texture, hardness and brightness of certain substances, and the qualities of the things made out of them. As Gosden has observed, 'each culture creates its own sensory environment, both physically through constructing a material world with its own sensory properties, and culturally through emphasizing and valuing certain types of sense impressions over others' (2001: 166). In non-Western societies aesthetic appreciation is not limited to questions of design and technology, as it has been in accounts of prehistoric art.

The motion was seconded by Jeremy Coote, who had already co-edited a volume of essays on *Anthropology, Art and Aesthetics* (Coote and Shelton eds.

1992). He argues that a basic notion of aesthetics is shared by quite different societies. The important point is that not all of them relate to any conception of art. The best illustration comes from a paper that he wrote in the 1992 volume. It employs a definition of aesthetics which is very similar to Morphy's: 'The anthropology of aesthetics... consists in the comparative study of valued perceptual experiences in different societies' (Coote 1992: 247). Whereas much of Morphy's fieldwork has taken place among native Australians who produce artworks for their own needs and for the commercial market, Coote worked with people in the Sudan who 'make no art objects and have no traditions of visual art' (1992: 245).

On the other hand, Coote argues, they possess a developed aesthetic sense which is based on the visual qualities of their cattle. There is a complex classification of the different colours of these animals, and care is devoted to grooming them and to maintaining the sheen on their hides. Animals which are considered to be exceptionally beautiful are a source of great prestige and are never used as breeding stock. The same attention is paid to the humps on the cattle and to the exact configuration of their horns. In fact Coote observes that their owners imitate the appearance of the cattle in their dances and even in their body decoration. Although children may make tiny models of these creatures, the same concerns do not find expression in anything that can be described as art.

In the Manchester debate the thesis put forward by Morphy and Coote was opposed by two other speakers, Joanna Overing and Peter Gow. For Overing the concept of aesthetics is closely associated with Western notions of art. She describes the 'Cult of the Art Object' which revolves around 'a sacred triad comprised of the individual artist, the art object, and the individual contemplator of the object'. By contrast, among the Piaroa of the Amazon the concepts of the artist, the art object and the 'aesthetically astute subject' do not exist. There are certain objects that people describe as beautiful, but most of them are everyday items like tools, and their beauty cannot be treated separately from the ways in which they are used. They do not occupy a distinct domain and are part of the everyday world. 'Objects and people are beautiful because of what they can do' (Ingold ed. 1996: 264).

Like Overing, Gow considers that the use of the term aesthetics is prejudiced by Western ideas about art. Moreover, he concludes that such ideas are based on judgement and comparison as a strategy in contemporary society. It is not the business of anthropologists to make value judgements of this kind and therefore it is wrong to export European aesthetic notions to the study of other societies.

Part of the disagreement was caused by problems of terminology. It is clear that many societies do not have any word for aesthetics, just as they lack a word for art itself. Nevertheless they may have an elaborate vocabulary for discussing the visual and tactile qualities of objects, animals, places and body decoration. For example, there are many different terms for the colours of Nuer cattle. While Morphy and Coote discuss the sensory impact of different media, from sand paintings to live animals, Overing is more concerned with what Western collectors think of as artworks. They are not present among the Piaroa, where concepts of beauty are associated with everyday objects and their use. The very idea of a beautiful artefact suggests that aesthetic judgements are made in that society; but they take a different form from those in contemporary Europe. Her argument does not contradict the wider definition of aesthetics put forward by the proposers of the motion.

Similarly, Gow's diagnosis of the perils of aesthetics is based on Bourdieu's analysis of the ways in which art is deployed as a source of cultural capital in contemporary society (Bourdieu 1991). That process depends on making critical judgements, but comparisons of this kind do not form any part of the case advanced by Morphy and Coote. The competing arguments put forward in the debate do not engage with one another because they are based on different premises. Although the Manchester meeting ended with a vote that rejected the notion of aesthetics, such a radical step was not justified by the arguments presented there. James Weiner, who convened this particular meeting, seems to have taken a similar view and says so in his introduction to the proceedings (Ingold ed. 1996: 251–3).

In any event the concept seems to have survived the critical onslaught, and five years after the text of the debate was published an entire issue of the journal *World Archaeology* was devoted to *Archaeology and Aesthetics* (Gosden ed. 2001). It considered such topics as the use of lustrous raw materials, the production of faience figurines, pottery decoration, body painting and the siting of monuments. Its contents have had a significant influence, and other studies have followed. One of the simplest and most convincing demonstrates the importance of colour in the creation of prehistoric artefacts and monuments (Jones and MacGregor eds. 2002). Another draws attention to the significance of distinctive minerals for prehistoric people (Boivin and Owoc eds. 2004).

THE QUESTION OF SEMANTICS

In Morphy's definition 'art objects are ones with aesthetic and/or semantic attributes' (1994: 65). Having considered the status of aesthetics, how should semantics be understood?

The dictionary definition of *semantics* is 'the branch of linguistics concerned with meaning'. The adjective *semantic* has two definitions, although they are quite similar. In one case it refers to features 'relating to meaning in language', and, in the other, to those 'relating to the connotations of words' (*Concise Oxford Dictionary*). It is obvious that any application to the visual arts must be metaphorical. To what extent do images act in a similar manner to speech? This is an issue that has been debated in both archaeology and anthropology and one where there has been an unusual convergence of interests.

The idea that material culture is employed in a similar manner to language goes back to the work of Lévi-Strauss whose ideas were influenced by research on the structure of language itself (Tilley 1990). Saussure argued that the relationship between words and the things they represent is entirely arbitrary: taken in isolation, a term like 'art' gives no clue to what it means. That must be established by its context in relation to other terms. At the same time, the use of language depends on the human capacity to bring together concepts that are linked and to distinguish them from others to which they are opposed. Thus language develops through a process of association and contrast.

Lévi-Strauss argued that this process reflects a fundamental property of the human mind. This is the way in which it analyses and orders experience. For that reason it is not confined to the construction and use of language and extends into other domains. The same idea lay behind the structural analysis of myth which pervades many of his writings, but it has also influenced his accounts of visual imagery. By considering how particular images are created and juxtaposed, anthropologists acquire vital clues to their meanings and the information that they are intended to convey. Of course researchers may have access to a further source of information, as some of those designs are made by known individuals and are deployed in contexts that can be observed. Thus the anthropologist can turn to local informants to learn about the interpretation of particular images. He or she can also infer something of their significance from the ways in which they are used. Again it is necessary to go beyond the conception of artworks as portable artefacts of the kind that can be displayed in museums, for the same ideas are just as applicable to the embellishment of buildings, body decoration and rock paintings.

Although Lévi-Strauss was less concerned with ethnographic art than he was with other subjects, his original insight inspired a whole series of studies of visual images in anthropology. The trend continued and even intensified as the influence of structuralism declined. Notable contributors to this kind of research have included Anthony Forge (1973), who wrote about indigenous art in Papua New Guinea; Nancy Munn (1973), whose study *Walbiri Iconography* did much to inspire work in this field; Robert Layton (1992), who has written on Australian rock art; and Alfred Gell (1993), who analysed the significance of tattooing in Polynesia.

Lévi-Strauss's work is less fashionable today, but it had a direct influence on the study of prehistoric art through the research of André Leroi-Gourhan. Leroi-Gourhan occupies a unique place in the history of the discipline as his publications span both archaeology and anthropology. Among social anthropologists he is best known for his investigations of technological systems, while prehistorians are influenced by his innovative approach to excavation. He brought his diverse interests together in studies of Palaeolithic cave paintings (Leroi-Gourhan 1965 and 1982). Although his conclusions are questioned, his approach remains important today.

Leroi-Gourhan treated the images in these caves in much the same way as Saussure treated words. He did not distinguish between the depictions of animals and humans, and the abstract signs that were disregarded in earlier accounts. Like Lévi-Strauss, he was seeking order in this diverse material, and was doing so by trying to establish which elements were commonly found together and which other components were kept apart. His main concern was with patterns of association and exclusion. These design elements occurred in different combinations and were found in different parts of the decorated caves.

On this basis Leroi-Gourhan (1965) put forward two interpretations. These caves were really sanctuaries in which considerable attention had been paid to the proper organization of space. Distinctive designs, or groups of designs, might be associated with separate areas (Figure 4). There was nothing haphazard about the placing of the images. At the same time, the painted and engraved motifs could be combined into groups which had different distributions from one another. Each included depictions of certain species of animals, combined with a specific range of apparently abstract motifs (Figure 5).

Leroi-Gourhan also sought to identify some of the non-figurative designs, and on that basis he divided them between one series which he characterized as male and a second group which he identified as female. Each group had different associations. For that reason he suggested that certain animal species were used to represent gender distinctions. He concluded that the decorated caves were places where, among other activities, rituals were conducted to increase the fertility of the human and animal populations.

In his later work Leroi-Gourhan expressed doubts about the validity of this interpretation, and it has not been followed by subsequent writers (Leroi-Gourhan 1982). It may have been unwise to look for a single scheme among images that spanned thousands of years, and today more attention is paid to the contents of individual caves. The real importance of his study is its methodology. Although his empirical observations have been challenged—the entrances to these caves have sometimes changed; his distinction between passages and chambers is not always convincing; some of the source material employed by Leroi-Gourhan has proved to be misleading (Ucko and

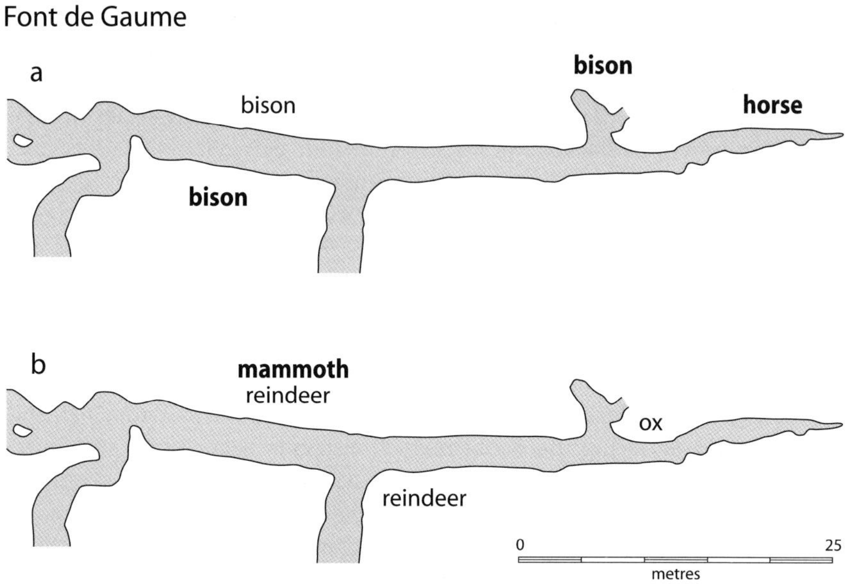

Figure 4. The distribution of Upper Palaeolithic paintings of animals in the French cave of Font de Gaume, showing the main groups according to species. The largest concentrations are indicated in bold.

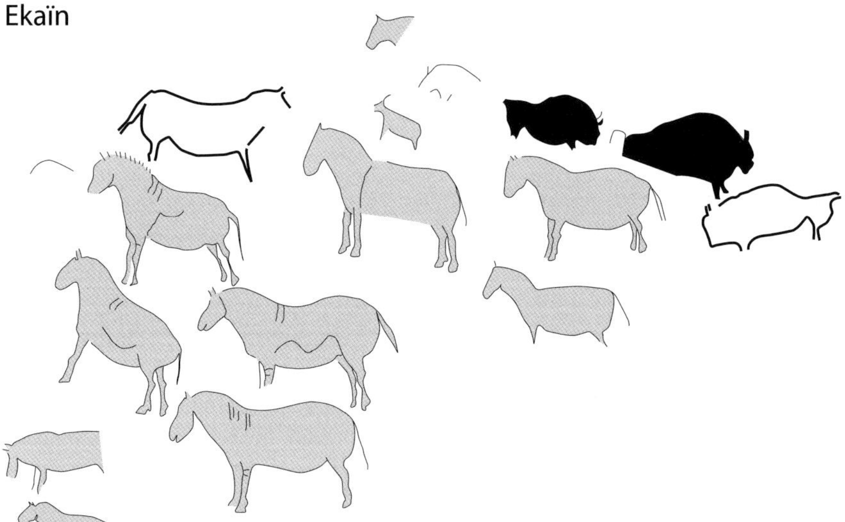

Figure 5. Upper Palaeolithic paintings at Ekain, illustrating the division between depictions of horses and those of bison.

Rosenfeld 1967)—it was a project which brought together the perspectives of prehistoric archaeology and structural anthropology and made no attempt to distinguish between these disciplines.

To a large extent the same has been true in studies of Australian rock art, but with the important difference that some of the decorated caves and rock shelters are still in use today. In many cases they feature paintings of animals which can be interpreted as ancestral beings. Their depiction in these places codifies local beliefs, and access is carefully controlled. Their interpretation depends on the testimony of informants. A good example of the use of ethnography is provided by the strange composite creature known as the Rainbow Serpent. It is associated with the Dreamtime—the period of the mythical creation—and archaeological evidence suggests that this distinctive image has been painted in Arnhem Land over a period of six thousand years (Taçon, Wilson, and Chippindale 1996). It is often associated with paintings of flying foxes and is believed to dwell in the sea or in deep waterholes. According to Mike Morwood, the serpent is 'associated with fertility and the creation of rain' (2002: 160).

In other cases it is through archaeology that the paintings and engravings are interpreted. For instance, in the highlands of Central Queensland it seems as if hand stencils were located in parts of the caves which would be visible from a distance, while other decorated panels focused on crevices, shelves and tunnels that were partly hidden. Those images seem to have been concealed because they were associated with unusual deposits:

> At Native Wells a cache of macropod bone and twigs was found immediately behind an abraded vulva motif... The lack of any other art nearby makes it clear that the vulva, a fertility symbol of universal significance, was deliberately placed next to the cache.... Central Queensland rock art, which emphasizes the vulva motif, is often associated with burials. (Morwood 2002: 225)

It may be possible to takes this interpretation even further. If the hidden depictions of vulvas were associated with the dead, were the prominent paintings of handprints a symbol of the living?

Both these cases use similar methods of analysis to the Palaeolithic example. The paintings of the Rainbow Serpent are associated with depictions of a flying fox, just as Leroi-Gourhan recognized associations between different species on the walls of French and Spanish caves. There are other points of comparison, for handprints and vulvas were represented in Europe as well as Australia. Just as Leroi-Gourhan had claimed that prehistoric drawings of wild animals were kept separate from those of herbivores, in Queensland the drawings of handprints were in different locations from those of vulvas. One group was placed where it could be seen from a distance, while the other was hidden. The motifs that had been concealed were associated with human remains. Because of that association Morwood could suggest a link between fertility and death that is not entirely different from Leroi-Gourhan's reading of the Palaeolithic evidence. Although the significance of the Rainbow Serpent is documented by ethnographic evidence, the other patterns have been identified by archaeological methods.

THE AGENCY OF ARTWORKS

Anthropological studies of aesthetic qualities and meanings had little value for Alfred Gell. At the end of his life he wrote a book, *Art and Agency*, in which he attempted to construct 'an anthropological theory of art' (Gell 1998). It was an ambitious project which in some respects he left incomplete. While his text is provocative and often witty, some sections are extremely abstruse. Although its thesis has been criticized (Tanner and Osborne 2007), the study has been influential. The basic argument is an elaboration of an earlier paper, together with *Wrapping in Images*, his account of tattooing in Polynesia published in 1993. Gell accepts the category of art without much question, perhaps because he was an accomplished artist himself, but he argues that a specifically anthropological approach to indigenous art should not be concerned with its meanings or aesthetics. Just as those who study religions must adopt a methodological atheism, the anthropologist needs to espouse a 'methodological philistinism'.

Is there a more productive approach than those described so far? Gell considers that:

> An anthropological theory of art is one which 'looks like' an anthropological theory... The aim of an anthropological theory is to make sense of behaviour in the context of social relations. Correspondingly, the objective of the anthropological theory of art is to account for the production and circulation of art objects as a function of this relational context. (Gell 1998: 10)

There is nothing to be gained from studying non-Western art using methods developed outside social anthropology:

> For the anthropology of art to be specifically anthropological, it has to proceed on the basis that, in relevant theoretical respects, art objects are the equivalent of persons, or more precisely, social agents. (Gell 1998: 7)

Thus his concern is with the agency of artworks. He is not interested in their qualities or symbolism—only in their effects. Rather than analyse what artworks mean, he considers *what they do.*

For present purposes, the most significant part of Gell's book builds on an article that he had published in 1992: 'The technology of enchantment and the enchantment of technology'. Its premise is disarmingly simple. Works of art possess the power to influence the conduct of those who come in contact with them. They are directed towards an audience whom they are intended to impress. Indeed, the word 'impress' is not strong enough, for artworks are mean to enchant the viewer. They do this because they have been made with unusual virtuosity and because the exercise of such skills possesses something of the qualities of magic.

Gell uses a bewildering variety of examples to illustrate this idea. One of the most convincing concerns a widely distributed phenomenon: the depictions of labyrinths which are found in many different societies. Another is peculiar to a single ethnographic context: the lavishly decorated prows of canoes in the Trobriand Islands.

Gell is not concerned with the historical origins of labyrinths or with the reasons why this form should appear in so many cultures. He is more concerned with the way in which it is used. In his opinion it is apotropaic; that is to say, it is used defensively in order to provide protection. Gell argues that patterns with a hidden logic to their design trap the viewer by their sheer complexity:

> One knows that there is a way through the maze; one may even know that the maze is created by the simple application of an iterative rule in connecting up lines and points... but one cannot, all the same, see one's way through the maze except very laboriously by tracing out its winding course. (Gell 1998: 88)

Gell suggests that it is for this reason that mazes are so often 'associated with the passage between the worlds of the living and the dead. Those worlds are close together.... yet far apart, separated by an impassable frontier' (Gell 1998: 90). The same principle applies to body decoration and even to the decoration of buildings; in every case these intricate patterns baffle potential adversaries and neutralize the threat they pose. Gell, ever the master of the unexpected metaphor, characterizes such designs as 'demonic fly-paper'. He even employs an archaeological example—one of the few in his book—suggesting that a labyrinth is depicted on the entrance to the Irish megalithic tomb of Newgrange: a monument which he characterizes as 'a twisting tunnel leading, presumably, to the world of the dead' (Gell 1998: 87). That is a little inaccurate, for the carved 'labyrinth' is actually a spiral, but the comparison illustrates the potential of his approach. A better archaeological example is provided by the Bronze Age house urns of Central Italy (Bartoloni, Bursanelli, D'Atri, and De Santis 1987). These are ceramic models of domestic buildings and are found in cemeteries. Like the passage grave at Newgrange (O'Kelly 1982), they contain deposits of cremated human bone. Sometimes their

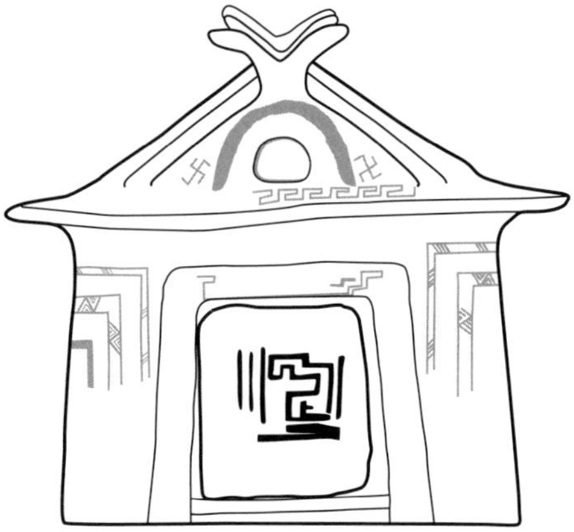

Figure 6. A Late Bronze Age house urn from Central Italy, emphasizing the complex decoration on the doorway.

doorways are decorated with complex abstract motifs which resemble those studied by Gell, but it is not clear whether similar designs had been associated with the dwellings of the living (Figure 6). This is apparently a case where they are linked directly with the passage between life and death.

In such cases art was employed to ward off danger. In other cases its role was to mesmerize the viewer. Gell's most celebrated example of this process is provided by the decorated canoes of the Trobriand Islands. They are used by participants in the cycle of competitive exchanges known as the *Kula*. In this system social standing depends on attracting as many valuables as possible, although they must be passed on to other participants through a series of fresh transactions. In this context it is imperative to overawe those offering such goods. Gell suggests that the lavish decoration on the visitors' canoes makes this easier to achieve. He describes it as 'a means of thought-control':

> Sometimes objects are explicitly intended to function as weapons in psychological warfare: as in the case of the canoe prow-board from the Trobriand Islands.... The intention behind [their] placing.... on Kula canoes is to cause the overseas Kula partners of the Trobrianders, watching the arrival of the Kula flotilla from the shore, to take leave of their senses and offer more valuable shells or necklaces to members of the expedition than they would otherwise be inclined to do. The boards are intended to dazzle the beholder. (Gell 1992: 44)

Why should the decoration have this effect? Gell suggests that this is not just a function of the designs, arresting though they undoubtedly are (Figure 7). Rather, they are formed with so much skill that their creators must be imbued with magical powers: an idea which is encouraged by the rituals that accompany

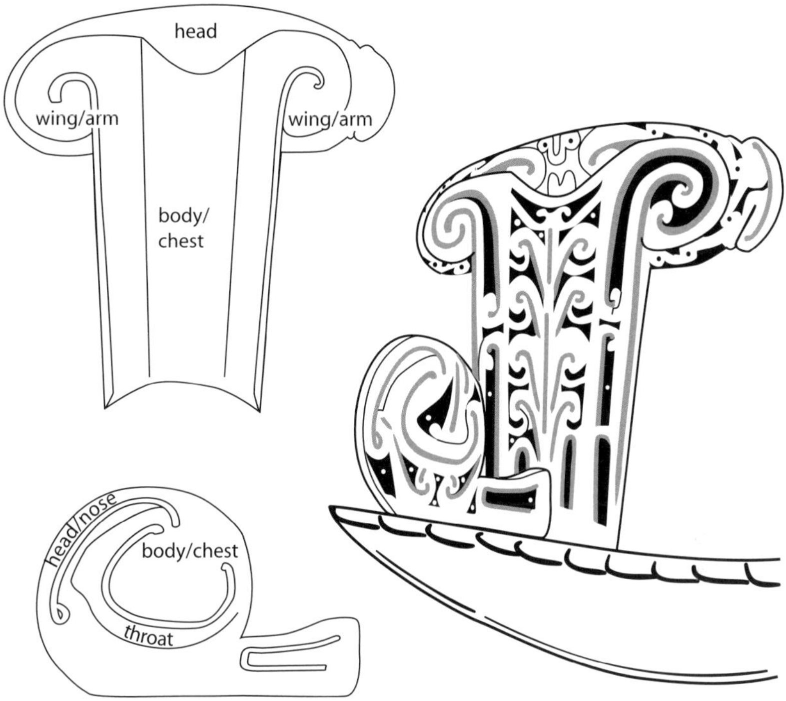

Figure 7. A Trobriand decorated canoe prow and its interpretation.

the making of canoes. His term the 'technology of enchantment' describes the effects of the decorated canoes on the people who encounter them. 'The enchantment of technology', on the other hand, describes the special powers that go into the production of these designs. Gell makes this point directly when he refers to the artist as an 'occult technician'.

This is a novel and intriguing argument, but it is incomplete because it makes no use of what is known about the meanings of the carved designs. Gell refers to them in passing, but does not employ them anywhere in his account. That is unfortunate, for they add weight to his argument. The decoration on the canoes has been studied by Sheila Campbell (2001), whose research provided one of the starting points for Gell's original analysis. The designs make visual references to a number of creatures, both real and mythical, whose characteristics are important to the people who use these vessels. Three kinds of birds are represented, the osprey, the egret and the bat, all of which have specific connotations. Among them are ideas of wisdom, knowledge, skill, success, intelligence, and danger. The mythical creatures, of which there are also three, have similar associations, as well as the less tangible qualities of elusiveness, attractiveness and fallibility. Some of these associations are related to observations of the real world—the bat is associated with the night; the osprey is very successful at taking fish—while others are projections of more abstract attributes. Even so, the associations of at least some of these images would not have been lost on the people who were visited by the boat crews. Interpretations of this kind would have added to the impact of the designs described by Gell.

Again it is helpful to compare this study with accounts of archaeological material. The Battersea Shield was briefly considered in Chapter 1. It belongs to a small group of lavishly decorated examples recovered from English rivers. They share certain features in common (Fitzpatrick 2007). Apart from the earliest example, they are decorated with intricate curvilinear imagery, together with pairs of enigmatic creatures which combine the attributes of animals and birds. It is these images that would have confronted an opponent, but normally they are small and difficult to identify. What would have attracted more attention was the virtuosity with which the surface of the shield had been embellished, the sheen of the metal itself, and an obvious predilection for the colour red which extends to other weapons of the same period (Giles 2008). In addition to the fine decoration that characterized the boss and spine of the shield, an example from the River Witham includes a large representation of a boar.

These artefacts are so finely made that they were probably intended for display rather than use in combat, but it is clear that they had circulated over a significant period of time. Their high quality, imagery, colour, and shining metal would all have had an impact on those who encountered them. Just as the use of red materials for decorating weapons may have referred to human blood (Giles 2008), Frey (1995), and Fitzpatrick (2007) both suggest that the birds or animals that feature in the decoration were connected with death.

In fact the images found on these shields may have played a dual role. If they were intended to unnerve an opponent, they also offered protection to their owners. This is clear from the earliest of the British finds, from Chertsey (Figure 8). Unusually, the outer face of this example is largely plain, but a pair of creatures identified as 'dragons' is located on either side of the grip. There are other cases in which the most elaborate decoration occurs on the outer face of the shield, but in this case 'when the warrior gripped the handle . . . he was placing his hand right behind the fantastic animals on the boss' (Fitzpatrick 2007: 344). Perhaps this was believed to keep him from harm.

Similar ideas are proposed by Tania Dickinson (2005) is a recent study of early Anglo-Saxon shields. Indeed, the title of her paper refers to 'symbols of

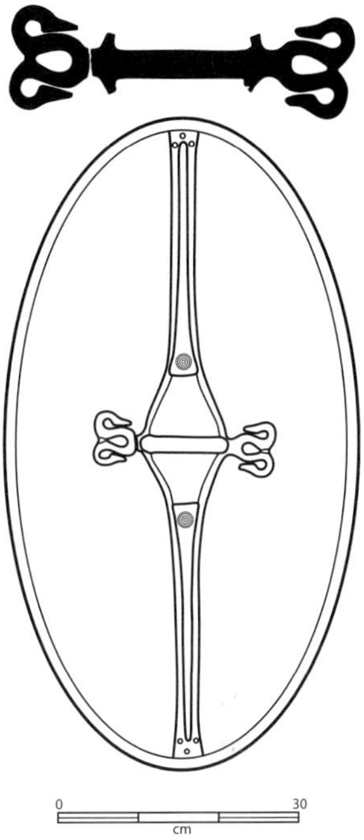

Figure 8. Paired dragons on the Iron Age shield from Chertsey, England.

protection'. Two parts of these weapons were embellished: the shield boss, and a series of small metal fittings, the details of which could only be identified at close quarters (Figure 9). The main images represent predatory birds, aquatic creatures and dragons, but in this case an additional source of information is available. This is provided by the earliest literary sources in Northern Europe. Dickison suggests that 'it is the protective capacity of Odin.... which lies at the centre of the iconographic web' (2005: 160).

The early Anglo-Saxon shields are associated with male burials. Such weapons seem to have been used in warfare, but it is unlikely that in this case the decoration was intended to unnerve an opponent. It was too small to be interpreted except at very close quarters. The contorted animal decoration has something in common with the labyrinths described by Gell, which, he suggests, confuse the hostile forces and render them powerless. Dickinson argues that the use of these visual devices symbolized the role of particular men as protectors of the community. Thus on a purely practical level the shield was a defensive weapon employed in fighting. On another level, its characteristic decoration acted as a protective device and involved a set of images that referred to supernatural forces.

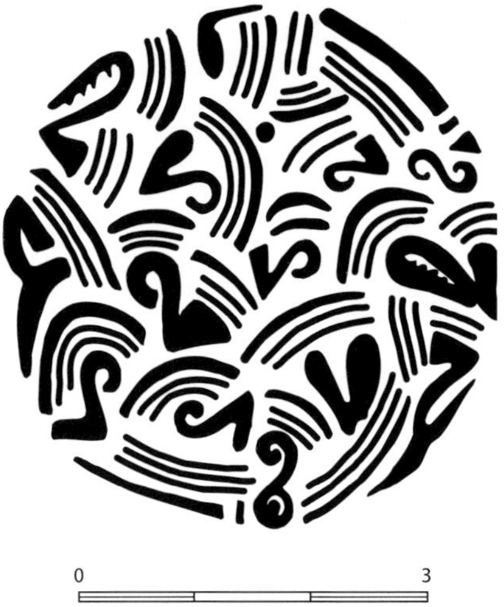

Figure 9. Decorated attachment on an Anglo-Saxon shield from Barrington, England.

The comparison with the Iron Age evidence is revealing. Both groups of decorated shields featured a range of distinctive designs, and the earlier examples were mostly directed towards a potential adversary. They also offered protection to the people who carried them, and in that respect they share certain features in common with their Anglo-Saxon counterparts. Gell's notion of 'enchantment' supports these interpretations, but in both periods they are strengthened by considering the meanings of the decoration.

To sum up, Gell's approach to the anthropology of art certainly provides a source of inspiration for research in archaeology, but it has its limitations. He is not concerned with aesthetics, nor does he show much interest in the semantics of non-Western art. Both these criticisms were made by contributors to a recent symposium dedicated to his ideas (Osborne and Tanner eds. 2007). If such works are meant to overawe the people who see them, surely it is important to know how they are interpreted. In rejecting previous approaches to the anthropology of art, Gell made excessive claims. He even seems to have rejected sources of information that could have strengthened his argument. His achievement was to develop a new way of looking at indigenous art, but there seems no reason to discard other approaches to this material.

Perhaps Gell took such an extreme position because of his liking for debate. In a posthumously published essay he discusses his predilection for 'seminar culture', which he characterizes as a kind of virtuoso intellectual performance designed as much to stimulate as to persuade. That is not unlike his characterization of ethnographic art. It is a medium that casts a spell over those who encounter it. Is it possible that *Art and Agency* was conceived with the same idea in mind? In Gell's own words:

> The seminar is a social occasion, a game, an exchange, an ordeal, an initiation . . . It more exciting for me to write a paper for presentation at a seminar than it is to write for an imaginary reader . . . I think of seminar culture as something more central to my true interests than anything else I have done. (Gell 1999: 2)

Perhaps it is the absence of live debate that makes the argument in *Art and Agency* appear over-stated.

A QUESTION OF CONTEXT

Gell's analysis concerns the effects of non-Western artworks rather than their aesthetic qualities. That is only possible because he is able to document the contexts in which they were used. It depends on participant observation, one of the most important methods used by social anthropologists. Archaeologists are denied this opportunity, even in historically documented periods, and prehistorians are especially impoverished. This is only too apparent from the various meanings of the word *context.*

One might suppose that the context of an artwork is the situation in which it was made and used, for in Gell's terms that is when it exerts its power over the viewer; it has a different kind of agency when it acquires a market value. 'Context' has another meaning in prehistoric archaeology. It describes the situation in which an object was discovered, and any other artefacts that were associated with it. Thus the archaeological context of the Battersea Shield was the River Thames, and the context of the Gundestrup Cauldron was the surface of a peat bog. By contrast, the original context of the Basse-Yutz flagons remains unknown, although two Etruscan stamnoi came from the same deposit. Similarly, the Battersea Shield was found with a large number of human skulls, but it has not been established that they entered the river together.

Artefacts may have circulated for a lengthy period between their creation and their deposition. Like the shields found in English rivers, the Basse-Yutz flagons were modified in the course of their history. Elaborate artefacts could have been moved over long distances during the course of their lives. That is why it was so difficult to work out where the flagons were made, and the same certainly applies to the controversies over the origin of the Gundestrup Cauldron, which had been dismantled at some stage before it was discarded in a bog.

These characteristics make it difficult to carry out the kind of analysis advocated by Gell, for there are only two opportunities to study such artefacts in their original contexts. The first concerns their ostensible functions: weapons may have been made for use in warfare as well as public displays; cauldrons and flagons were apparently used in feasting. In each case it is possible to infer something of the audiences who would have encountered them. The second possibility is provided by the contexts in which they were discovered by archaeologists. This may yield more secure information, but it necessarily refers to the final stage in the biography of these particular objects. Thus the Bass-Yutz flagons were probably buried with the dead, and that was certainly true of Anglo-Saxon shields. Similarly, the Battersea Shield and the Gundestrup Cauldron were most likely votive deposits. The problem is that the role of these artefacts is only apparent as their use came to an end.

Just occasionally there may be a more direct relationship between the images on a decorated artefact and the circumstances in which it entered the archaeological record. Despite their lengthy histories, the English Iron Age shields might have been made with their final deposition in mind. One reason for suggesting this is their unusual decoration. They feature pairs of fantastic creatures, which are closely related to prototypes in Continental Europe. There is also a contrast between them. The finds from the European mainland represent what have been described as 'dragons', but their English counterparts are subtly different: 'the fantastic animals on the metal-faced shields appear as birds' (Fitzpatrick 2007: 351). Those on a bronze disc found in the River Bann in Northern Ireland have even been identified as swans (Jope 2000: 272). Is it possible that this design was chosen because the finished object was to be deposited in water? If so, the same argument might explain one element in the decoration on the Battersea Shield. Ruth and Vincent Megaw suggest that it features a number of human heads (2001: 200). Is it entirely coincidental that the shield was found together with more than a hundred skulls?

In other cases visual imagery is associated with prehistoric monuments or with features of the ancient landscape. They differ from portable objects because their locations are fixed. Their roles may have changed over time and those images may have been modified or replaced, but their original contexts still survive. Characteristic examples include decorated tombs like Newgrange, cave paintings, or panels of 'rock art' in the open air. In such cases it may be possible to investigate the original settings of the designs because they remain *in situ*. This can be achieved using the methods of field archaeology. For that reason it seems paradoxical that such evidence has played a limited role in studies of prehistoric society. As mentioned in Chapter 1, the use of this kind of material has all too often been seen as a specialist field, cut off from the rest of the discipline. It is a missed opportunity.

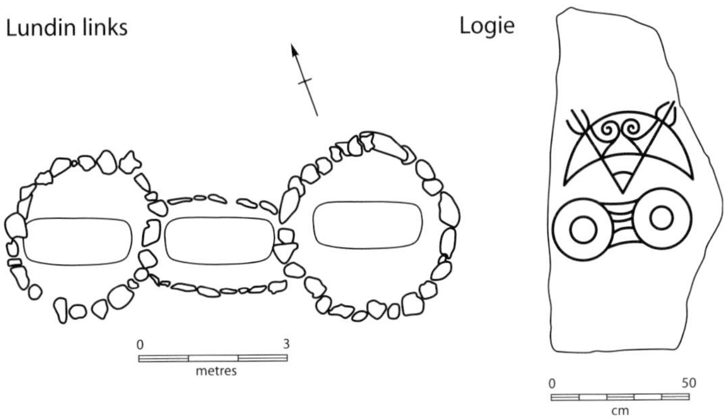

Figure 10. Outline plans of two Pictish cairns and associated graves at Lundin Links, Scotland, compared with a decorated stone of the same period from Logie. Both seem to feature the same design.

Although the painted and carved images may lack the mesmerizing quality of decorated metalwork or other artefacts, there are often close connections between them. The same visual images recur in modified forms in both genres. This process happens in many different contexts; some of the evidence is discussed in Chapters 3 to 8. Thus Late Neolithic ceramics in Britain share a few motifs with the walls of chambered tombs; the designs painted in Spanish rock shelters during the Copper Age are also found on decorated pottery; and the decorated metalwork of the South Scandinavian Bronze Age has features in common with rock carvings in Denmark, Sweden, and Norway. At times the range of possible comparisons is even wider and extends beyond the evidence of decorated artefacts. Nanouschka Myrberg (2006) has compared the labyrinths of early medieval Scandinavia with the organization of hill forts; these supposedly defensive enclosures have even been claimed as representations of dragons. Similarly, in Scotland the ground plans of two groups of cairns dating from the fifth or sixth century AD resemble the motifs carved on Pictish symbol stones (Figure 10). Comparable designs even feature in the metalwork of the same period. In this case a common thread links decorated objects made of bronze, carved rocks and even geogyphs (Williams 2007). The relationships between the images formed in these different media should shed some light on their contexts. In certain cases all three may have been used to commemorate the dead.

PRESENTATION AND REPRESENTATION

Archaeology suffers from certain limitations compared with social anthropology, but are they enough to preclude a more ambitious approach to ancient art? It is important to understand where archaeologists have most to offer and where they are at a disadvantage.

Morphy's account of the anthropology of art highlighted four separate elements. Two of these—aesthetics and semantics—have been discussed already. He also says that 'art objects are... used for representational or presentational purposes' (1994: 655).

Representation is a complex and controversial topic, but in this case one element is particularly important. That is the capacity of visual images to convey information. It is less significant whether the designs are described as figurative or abstract. Every society has its norms according to which pictures can be read, and what may be incomprehensible to an outsider may be understood by someone brought up within that tradition. The designs on a Trobriand canoe may represent ospreys, egrets, and bats, but only to those people who know how to recognize them. The relationship between an image and its audience is all-important here.

This has several implications. Distinct styles of visual imagery may be used concurrently to convey different kinds of information. In Aboriginal Australia simple geometric designs coexist with elaborate paintings of animals. It would be easy to assume that these paintings carried most significance, if only because of their scale and visual complexity. In fact it is the simple non-figurative images that are sometimes sacred (Layton 1991: 191). That is because they cannot be understood without special knowledge. Indeed, such basic motifs could mean so many different things that awareness of their significance can be controlled. In her monograph *Walbiri Iconography* Nancy Munn (1973) distinguishes between motifs with a 'discontinuous meaning range' and those whose meaning is continuous. For example, the first group includes simple outline drawings of humans, trees and snakes, while the second features even simpler designs that can only be understood according to the contexts in which they are used. Among other things, a straight line can stand for a path, a tree trunk, a spear, a backbone or a fire, while an unbroken ring can stand for a yam, a waterhole, or a circular path. In this case the design elements are not abstract in the sense that the link between the motif and what it stands for is arbitrary, but it is only possible to read them if one has been taught how to do so; and different people may possess different levels of skill in interpreting these images.

At the same time, even an apparently naturalistic image can have more than one level of significance. Thus the meanings of contemporary Australian rock art change according to the composition of the audience (Morphy 1991). There are different levels of knowledge which may be acquired over the course of a lifetime. A painting may have both an inner and an outer meaning, and they will vary according to the social identity of those who see it; in time some people may be initiated into the full significance of the imagery, some may never acquire more than a superficial understanding, while others may not be permitted to view it in any circumstances. Some of those distinctions are based on age and gender. In the same way, supposedly figurative images may also be understood metaphorically. A classic case is provided by the eland which figures prominently in the rock paintings of Southern Africa. An outsider would be able to identify the species of animal, but would not know that it was associated with the activities of the shaman and with making rain (Lewis-Williams 1987).

Too much emphasis can be placed on visual approaches to non-Western art. Again there is the question of aesthetics. Different raw materials may be selected for making particular kinds of artworks. The choice may be influenced by their colour, their brilliance or their tactile qualities, but it can also be influenced by the kinds of sounds that different materials produce. Thus, in Utah, rocks were selected for painting and carving because of their acoustic properties. The images were located in places where sound is amplified (Waller 2006). In California, rock art was associated with deposits which contained quartz—a mineral with unusual physical properties—and the same relationship has been observed in Portuguese prehistory (Whitley, Dorn, Simon, Rechtman, and Whitley 1999; Alves 2002). Even the colour of a natural outcrop might have been significant. In Spain there are instances where Neolithic or Copper Age paintings were attracted to outcrops of red stone (Diaz-Andreu 2002).

These features are also relevant to the question of presentation, but in this case it is easier to appreciate the implications of Morphy's definition of art. Presentation implies the bringing together of an artwork and an audience in a way that is closely related to the archaeological notion of context.

Here the main considerations are practical rather than theoretical. It is not possible for a prehistorian to decide who was allowed to visit certain places or to view certain images, nor is there any basis for working out who was forbidden access. On the other hand, the configuration of the places where artworks were deposited or displayed can provide clues to the character of the audience to whom such practices were addressed. Were certain images prominently displayed, and were others concealed from view in the way that certainly happened in the caves and rock shelters of Central Queensland? Were there differences of size among the different images? Someone who could recognize the outline of a boar on the Witham Shield might not have been able to identify the tiny birds' heads on the decorated surface. A significant number of people could examine the images on an Iron Age sculpture or a weapon, but that could not have happened when similar designs were made on coins. The Gundestrup Cauldron is only 69 centimetres in diameter. Even if it held the food for a sizeable gathering, how many people would have been in any position to trace the narratives illustrated by its decoration?

Would particular images have been inspected in a specific order? That is certainly the implication of Leroi-Gourhan's study of Palaeolithic painted caves, for certain design elements were created close to the entrance, some occupied the main chambers, while others were concealed in the deepest spaces of all (Leroi-Gourhan 1965). At the same time, these locations could have accommodated different numbers of viewers. It is impossible to say whether the paintings were inspected by people in single file or whether visitors entered these places as a group, but there is an obvious limit to the amount of space that was available. Was it necessary to consult certain designs individually? That is certainly suggested by the confined spaces in which some of them were painted. Still more important, was there a discernable relationship between the choice of designs that were used and the audiences who saw them?

Similar question apply to open-air sites like decorated rock shelters. Here it is not simply a matter of how many people could view the images on the same occasion; there is a more basic question of access. Some sites were readily accessible, close to settlements or paths, but others were hard to find and even more difficult to reach. They might be located on cliffs or mountaintops, and certain places could only be approached along narrow ledges. They would never have accommodated a large audience, but, still more important, the local topography meant that it would have been easy to restrict access to these locations.

Many problems remain. Perhaps the process of creating ancient artworks was more important than their subsequent history. It is by no means obvious how long they were intended to last, or whether the careers of those artefacts that were to end up in burials or votive deposits were predetermined from the outset. There is no way of telling whether all the images were addressed to a living audience, for some may have been directed solely to the dead or the supernatural. The presentation of prehistoric art still poses many problems, but most of the questions that have been asked here can be investigated by archaeological methods.

If art has agency in the way that Gell has argued, it can only exercise its power when it confronts an audience. If artworks are ways of communicating information—whether it is sacred or secular, practical or entirely arcane—they can only do so because people are in a position to interpret them. It is rare for archaeologists to infer the meanings of ancient images, but there are unusual instances in which this is possible, and they should not be deterred from doing so. Where the meanings of ancient artworks continue to elude, it should still be possible to investigate the contexts in which they were *meaningful.* That depends on using archaeology to shed light on the relationship between the image and its audience. It is an ambitious undertaking, but it provides a method for enlarging the study of prehistoric art.

Part II

Image and Audience in Megalithic Art

3

Notes from Underground

MEGALITHIC ART: A READER'S GUIDE

This chapter provides a brief overview of two related phenomena: megalithic tombs and megalithic art. Their relationship to one another will be considered in more detail in Chapters 4 and 5 (Figure 11).

Megalithic art is the conventional term for the wide variety of painted and pecked designs associated with stone-built tombs. It is a well-known feature of the prehistoric archaeology of Western Europe (Shee Twohig 1981). The main regions where it occurs are in Spain and Portugal, the west and north of France, and Ireland, although a few additional examples are known in Orkney, Wales, and central Germany. Although its distribution is supposed to follow the Atlantic coastline, recent fieldwork has established that it extends across large parts of the Iberian Peninsula (Figure 12; Bueno Ramirez and Balbín Behrmann 2003). Almost half the evidence of decorated tombs comes from monuments in the Boyne Valley, towards the northern limit of its distribution (Eogan 1999).

Those tombs take different forms and were not all built at the same time, although the great majority date from the Neolithic period. Similarly, the images associated with them are by no means uniform. They can be painted or carved, and areas of exposed stonework are enhanced by pecking. Most of the tombs were decorated when they were first built, but there is evidence that in some cases carvings were altered or replaced and painted surfaces were renewed (O'Sullivan 1986; Carrera Ramírez and Fábregas Valcarce 2006). In certain instances already-decorated stones were introduced when the monuments were first constructed. They might have been taken from older structures that had been demolished (Eogan 1998), or they could be sculptures that had stood in the open air. They were incorporated in chambered tombs either as fragments or in their original forms (Cassen 2000; Bueno Ramírez and Balbín Behrmann 2006a).

Some of the tombs were painted, while others appear to be decorated entirely with pecked or incised motifs. That may be deceptive. Marc Devignes (1996) has pointed out that the distribution of these designs extends across two very

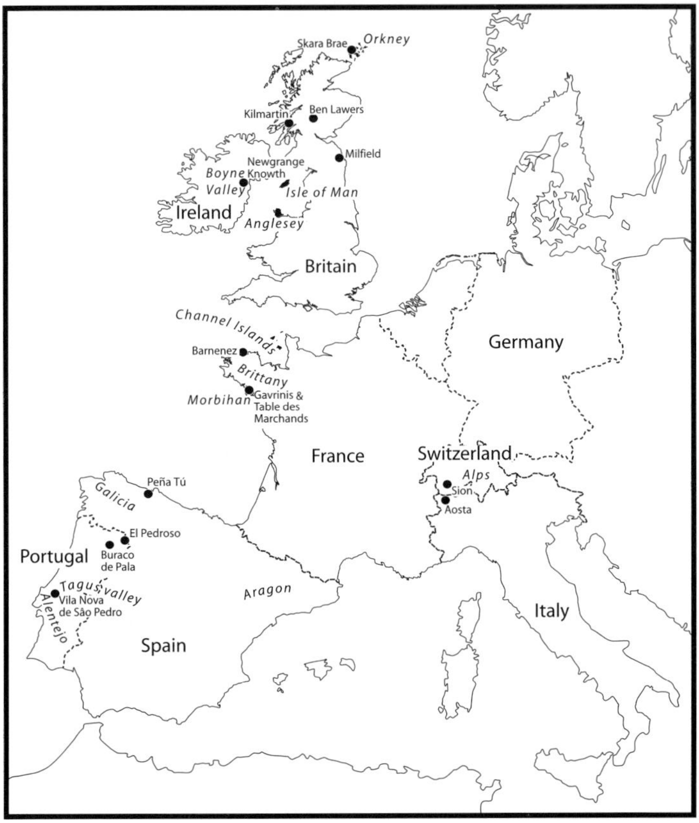

Figure 11. The sites and regions discussed in Part II.

different climatic zones. Paintings are found in areas that are drier and warmer; carvings occur in isolation where conditions are cooler and damper, although the evidence from north-west Spain does not conform to this pattern. It is perfectly possible that tombs were originally painted where no evidence survives today. In that case nothing may remain but the lines used to delimit areas of pigment. That argument has been proposed to explain the patterns scratched on the walls of Orkney chambered tombs (Bradley, Phillips, Richards, and Webb 2001), and there is similar evidence from southern Spain (Bueno Ramírez and Balbín Behrmann 2000a). There is so much variation that the only common element in 'megalithic art' may be the presence of the megalith itself.

This is a case in which a tradition of ancient art has been defined by the contexts in which it is found rather than its characteristic imagery, for the designs associated with these monuments are extremely diverse. The motifs

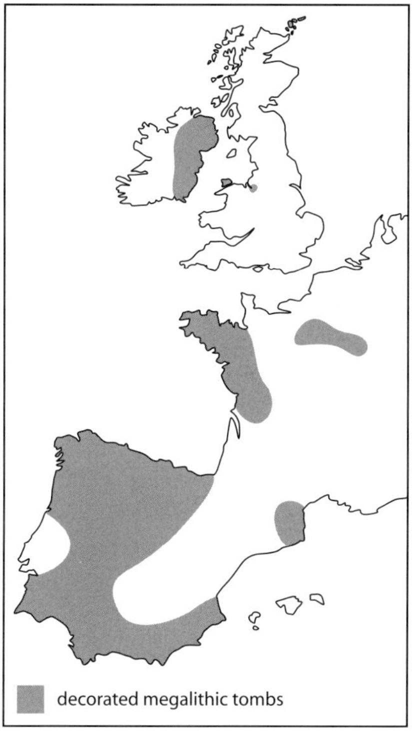

Figure 12. Outline distribution of megalithic art in Western Europe.

associated with Irish tombs are almost entirely non-figurative and any resemblance between individual images and the human form may have arisen through chance. By contrast, it has been argued that the designs found in the Iberian Peninsula were largely anthropomorphic. They might represent parts of the body, or even entire bodies. Both these principles are found in north-west France, but here the earlier tombs also contain depictions of artefacts and animals, as well as a range of apparently abstract designs. The later tombs in France introduce still further elements and include human figures carved in relief. In no sense can megalithic art be identified through its visual forms (Shee Twohig 1981; Bueno Ramírez, Balbín Behrmann, and Barroso Bermajo 2007).

FACES AND EYES

That has not always been accepted. It is one of the ironies of studying prehistoric art in Europe to find that the history of research owes so much to one productive scholar. Henri Breuil is best known for his research on Palaeolithic cave paintings (Breuil 1952), but he was also an authority on the post-glacial rock paintings of Spain and Portugal which he documented and discussed in several volumes (Breuil 1933–5). Given his intellectual energy, it is not surprising that he turned his attention to megalithic art.

Breuil favoured one all-encompassing explanation for each of these styles. Thus he interpreted Palaeolithic paintings in terms of hunting magic—that explained their obvious emphasis on animals. Megalithic art, on the other hand, was essentially anthropomorphic. Its successive manifestations could be understood as variations on the human form and, in particular, as representations of the face (Breuil 1934). O. G. S. Crawford took this even further, suggesting that the paintings and carvings depicted an 'Eye Goddess' who was portrayed over a wider area than the distribution of chambered tombs (Crawford 1957; Figure 13). These ideas were echoed in a still more extreme form by Marija Gimbutas (1991).

Such views have not found favour among more recent writers, and some images of the 'goddess' may not have been female after all (Fleming 1969). Breuil's suggestion of a long distance connection between Iberian and Irish tomb art seems increasingly tenuous, although it has supporters (Bueno

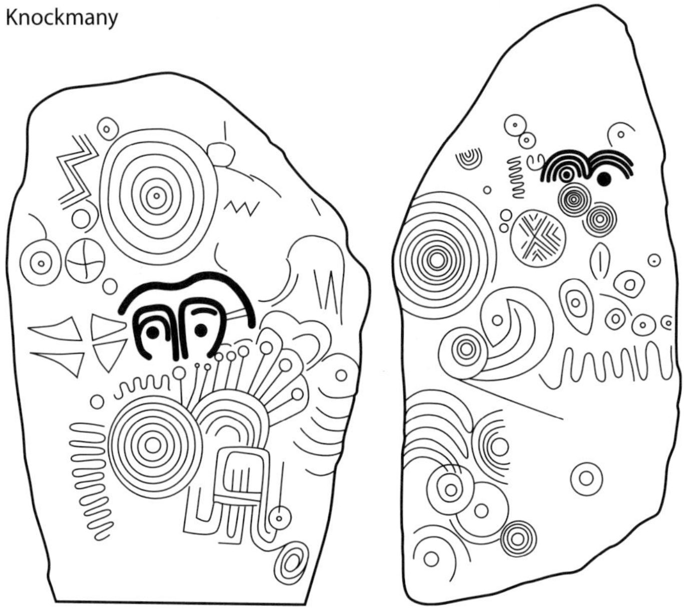

Figure 13. Carved stones from Knockmany, Ireland, interpreted as evidence for an 'eye goddess'. The motifs considered to represent the human face are emphasized.

Ramírez and Balbín Behrmann 2002). It is easy to appreciate why the idea was so attractive. Before the advent of radiocarbon dating, it was difficult to establish the sequence in which the tombs were built and only too tempting to treat the most reliably dated and architecturally sophisticated examples as prototypes for the others. Thus it was commonly supposed that chambered tombs originated in the Mediterranean and were adopted by communities in Western Europe as part of the same process as the development of farming. The adoption of cereals and domesticated animals presupposed the movement of people, so the diffusion of megalithic monuments was interpreted in similar terms. The links between different areas were emphasised by common religious beliefs, and, for Breuil and some of his contemporaries, they were expressed by a single style of art.

The work of Glyn Daniel epitomises this line of thought, although radiocarbon dating led him to modify his views in later life. Concluding his book *The Megalith Builders of Western Europe*, he said this:

> We have been concerned with one area and one time—western Europe between 2500 and 1000 BC. The main answer to [the megalithic] 'problem' is the spread of chamber tombs and collective burial from the east Mediterranean to the west, and the diffusion of the megalithic version of these tombs through western Europe.... In our.... discussion of what is meant by the spread of tombs it is possible to forget that behind these movements there are not only people, but human beings who were intrepid navigators. (Daniel 1958: 125)

MEGALITHIC ENQUIRIES

Problems developed once radiocarbon dates became available. The first is that the chronology of megalithic tombs was too conservative. Because scholars like Daniel postulated connections with the Minoan and Mycenaean worlds, the age of such monuments had been underestimated. He also stressed the role of burial caves in the Aegean, but they cannot have provided the prototypes for stone-built tombs which now appear to have originated in the fifth millennium BC rather than the third. In most regions it was during the third millennium that the latest tombs were constructed (Joussaume, Laporte, and Scarre eds. 2006; Bueno Ramírez, Balbín Behrmann, and Barroso Bermajo 2007).

The second problem arises from this observation. The oldest dates for megalithic tombs come from sites in Atlantic Europe rather than their supposed predecessors in the Mediterranean. It is no longer so clear quite when and where the first examples were built, but there can be no doubt that they were the creation of communities in Western Europe. Renfrew (1973) has suggested that the idea of building these structures might have been developed independently in a number of different regions, but this view has not been substantiated by detailed analysis.

That is because of a third problem raised by radiocarbon dating. It would be inaccurate to talk of a 'horizon' of tomb building along the Atlantic coastline, but it is certainly the case that the oldest monuments were built in the middle to late fifth millennium BC. This is apparent in Portugal, Spain and France. The building of these monuments intensified around 4000 BC when the earliest examples in the west of Ireland were constructed. It happened at about the same time as the first use of domesticates, but it is not clear that the two processes occurred simultaneously, for there are examples of early chambered tombs that were built on top of older Neolithic settlements.

The distribution of these monuments did not show the gradual expansion from south to north that the diffusionist framework required. If anything, it seems more likely that there were periods of fairly rapid change, punctuated by phases in which few new developments took place. Thus the first tombs in southern and western Iberia were probably contemporary with those in north-west France; the first Irish tombs represent a second phase; and those in Britain and Northern Europe probably illustrate a third (Joussaume, Laporte, and Scarre eds. 2006).

Another problem arises from the results of radiocarbon dating. In the absence of other evidence the ground plans of megalithic tombs had been studied in detail. The individual monuments had been sorted into types, and prehistorians had tried to work out the most logical ways in which their architecture might have developed, using similar principles to the analysis of portable artefacts. In a few cases they could test these schemes against stratigraphic evidence for the construction and modification of particular tombs. They could also study the objects associated with these sites. One fundamental distinction was between closed chambers which were inaccessible once they were covered by a mound or cairn, and other mortuary structures which could still be visited. The chamber might be reached by an entrance leading directly into the tomb, or in the case of *passage graves* it might be separated from the exterior by a kind of tunnel or corridor. It was generally agreed that the closed chambers were older than the other monuments.

Although this sequence can be identified at individual sites, it may not have the general application that was once supposed. Instead it is likely that a variety of very different structures existed at the same time as one another and that the main chronological developments were local ones. That is certainly the implication of a growing body of radiocarbon dates, particularly those from south-west Iberia, north-west France and southern Sweden where it is difficult to relate the accepted tomb typologies to a succession of chronological phases (Bueno Ramírez, Balbín Behrmann, and Barroso Bermajo 2007; Scarre 2002; Persson and Sjögren 1995). It runs counter to the traditional ways of analysing these monuments, and the full implications of the new dating evidence have still to be assimilated. At present it is in Brittany that the sheer variety of overlapping practices is most apparent (Scarre 2007a).

In contrast to the diffusionist scheme which would favour the gradual adoption of structural devices between neighbouring regions, some of the closest architectural links are between areas that were farther apart. The same applies to a few of the artefacts found in megalithic tombs, and to the paintings and carvings associated with these monuments.

There are structural similarities between the first passage graves in Britain and Ireland and examples in north-west France, but these tombs are without any decoration (Bradley 2007a: 49–50). There are other links between buildings associated with megalithic art. Thus the stepped exteriors of mounds and cairns in Orkney recall the forms of Breton monuments (Davidson and Henshall 1989), and George Eogan (1990) has drawn attention to equally striking similarities between the architecture of passage graves in Ireland and northern Portugal. In each case they are confined to the organization of the tombs and do not extent to the designs associated with them. Eogan has also claimed that there are artefacts of Iberian origin or inspiration in the chambered tombs of the Boyne Valley, and again the resemblance is strong enough to suggest a connection between those regions

Although Breuil saw similarities between anthropomorphic images in Ireland and Iberia, they have not convinced many subsequent writers. That is partly because of doubts about the identification of human features among the designs. On the other hand, there may be links between Irish megalithic art and the motifs associated with a selection of monuments in north-west France. Muiris O'Sullivan (1996) has argued that they developed in parallel in both areas, but, while the visual resemblance is undeniable, such images are relatively uncommon. Otherwise the best parallels for some of the motifs associated with Breton monuments are not with Ireland, which was readily accessible by sea, but with a series of structures in the Portuguese Alentejo (Calado 2002: 25–31). These are arrangements of standing stones which bear a certain resemblance to the megalithic enclosures of the Morbihan in southern Brittany, but in this case the potential connection is plausible because they are decorated in a similar style. Other claims for long distance links are much less credible and recall the ambitious typological schemes that were created before radiocarbon dates became available. The clearest example is a study by Göran Burenhult (2001) who identifies the same motifs in Ireland, south Scandinavia and the Neolithic temples of Malta.

It is the fact that there are so few explicit links between chambered tombs along the Atlantic seaboard that makes it difficult to propose a single interpretation of megalithic art. There is an obvious distinction between the non-figurative imagery found in Ireland and occasionally in France, and the representations of people, animals and artefacts in regions further to the south. There are also contrasts in the ways in which the same designs were used in different regions. The chambered tombs of Spain and Portugal provide an obvious example

Bueno Ramírez and Balbín Behrmann (2006a) have argued that many of the images in Iberian passage graves depict the human form. It is represented in a number of different media, from freestanding sculptures to paintings, and similar designs occur in miniature on decorated plaques and 'idols'. Although these images have much in common with one another, they can be organised in very different ways. Thus the tombs which have been studied in southern Spain feature a series of separate motifs distributed at specific points within the structure of the monument. Each is independent of the others. In northern Portugal, however, related images were sometimes painted as a continuous frieze which extended across the separate orthostats, with the principal designs at the rear of the chamber (Figure 14; Jorge 1997). The individual motifs share features in common between these regions, but even within the Iberian Peninsula they could be arranged according to local conventions. For

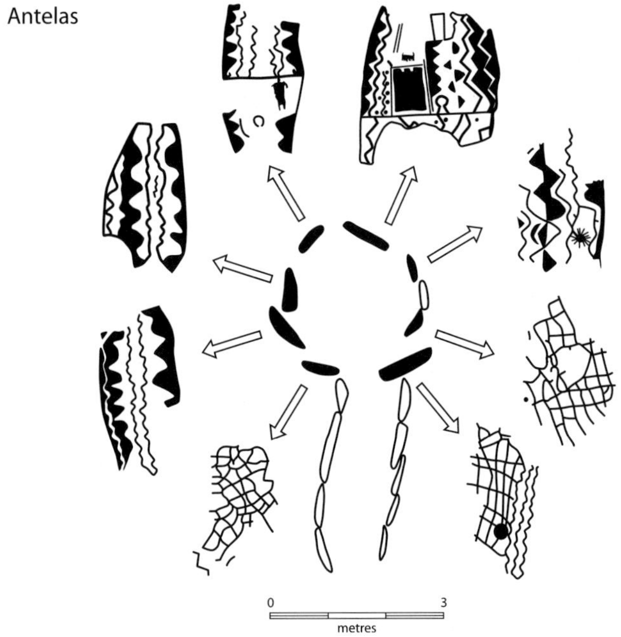

Figure 14. The organization of the painted designs inside the Portuguese passage grave of Antelas. The more complex decoration is furthest into the interior.

that reason it would be wrong to suggest that both groups of monuments were decorated in the same *style*.

ACCESSIBLE ARCHITECTURE

Before discussing these images in detail it is worth saying more about the buildings in which they occur.

The architecture of most megalithic tombs depends on a few simple principles. These structures take three distinct forms in relation to the local topography. Burial chambers might be erected on the ground surface and left exposed without any covering monument. They include what may have been the earliest examples in Wales and Ireland (Bradley 2007a: 49–50). Alternatively, they could be buried by mounds which marked their position in the wider landscape. That is the most common situation, but there are also examples where the same kind of structure was excavated into the subsoil so that the site was hidden from view. In this case a single architectural form was rendered in two different media. In some places the tomb was built of stone; in others, it was dug out of the bedrock (Tarrete 1996; Villes 1997).

If tombs could be hidden or displayed, they could also be accessible or inaccessible. Most structures were provided with entrances and sometimes with passages leading to a chamber, or chambers, but others lacked these features entirely. There were also cases in which access was controlled by manoeuvring a blocking stone to close the entrance, or even by the construction of temporary walling. As a result, the architecture of the tombs emphasized the distinction between those who were allowed inside them and those who were not admitted.

The first students of megalithic architecture recognized another distinction. Just as *passage graves* were tombs in which the chamber was approached down a kind of tunnel, the *gallery graves*, which developed during a subsequent phase, were monuments whose interior was readily accessible from outside. In practice these categories overlap, but the distinction remains important. In northern France these kinds of architecture were employed in succession (L'Helgouach 1996; Boujot, Cassen, and Vaquero Lastres 1998; Le Quellec 2006) and the same seems to be true in Ireland, but in Orkney the usual sequence is reversed and the monuments most closely related to gallery graves predate the classic passage graves (Davidson and Henshall 1989). In the Iberian Peninsula passage graves had an exceptionally long history, but were constructed in different ways at different times; it was the latest and most elaborate tombs with corbelled chambers that had been compared with monuments in the Aegean. They date from the third millennium BC (Bueno Ramírez, Balbín Behrmann, and Barroso Bermajo 2007). The term gallery grave itself has gone out of favour, but the classification of chambered tombs remains important in working out how these buildings were used.

There is one way in which both kinds of structures are related to megalithic art. Although the decoration of the stone-built tombs may have taken many forms, it is a feature of those examples with entrances and/or passages; it hardly features in the monuments with closed chambers (Figure 15). The decorated tombs were those that people could visit over a significant period of time, and that may be one reason why certain of the carvings were altered and some of the images were repainted. It does not mean that the designs were necessarily addressed to a living audience, but it certainly raises that possibility. Nearly all the decorated tombs were directed towards the south or east, meaning that the entrance could have been illuminated by the sun (Hoskins 2001). The same observation applies to most traditions of undecorated monuments. The only exceptions to the general trend were towards the limits of the chronological and geographical distribution of these structures. Thus several groups of passage graves in the Mediterranean faced west rather than east, and so did some of the latest megalithic monuments in Scotland and Ireland (Bradley 2007a: 173–4).

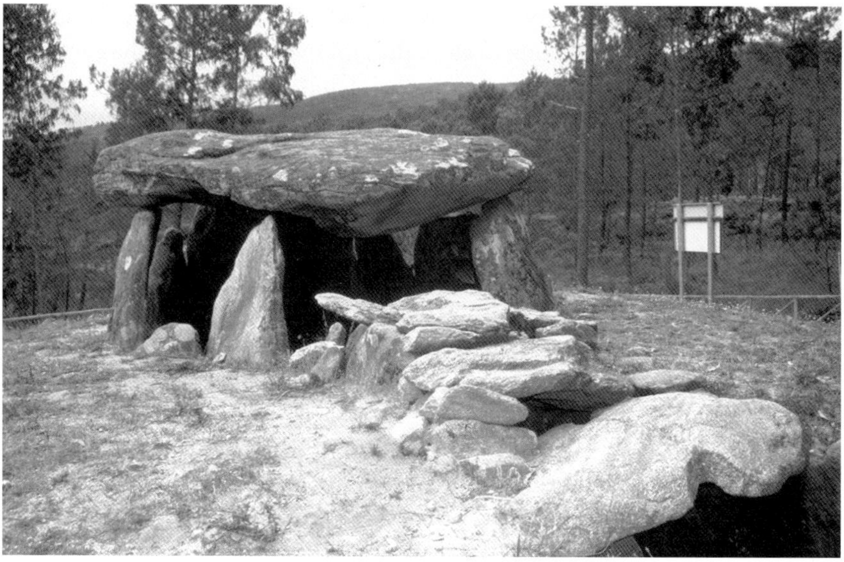

Figure 15. The Portuguese passage grave of Anta de Cerqueira.

There are two ways of thinking about the orientations of these buildings. As visitors to these monuments, contemporary archaeologists usually consider how people would have viewed the designs inside them. They emphasize the passage of sunlight *into the tomb*, but it is easy to forget that for most of the time the light would be fairly weak and would not travel far along the passage. It may be just as important to consider the view *from the chamber itself*. The only source of illumination was through the entrance which could have been some distance away. If that view was obstructed, the centre of the building would have been in darkness and any burials inside it would have been cut off from the outside world (Figure 16). That has important implications for the relationship between the dead and the living.

These simple principles were obviously exploited in the course of the archaeological sequence. Towards the northern limit of the distribution of passage graves, a number of outstanding examples were aligned on the sun at the solstices. That may also have happened at the equinoxes, although this is more controversial. These alignments are mainly a feature of Irish passage graves, but they have also been identified in Orkney, Anglesey, the Channel Islands, and Brittany. Where the tombs are well preserved, direct observation has shown that the rays of the sun reach into the central chamber (Ruggles 1999: chapter 8). That is especially important as all these structures had been decorated.

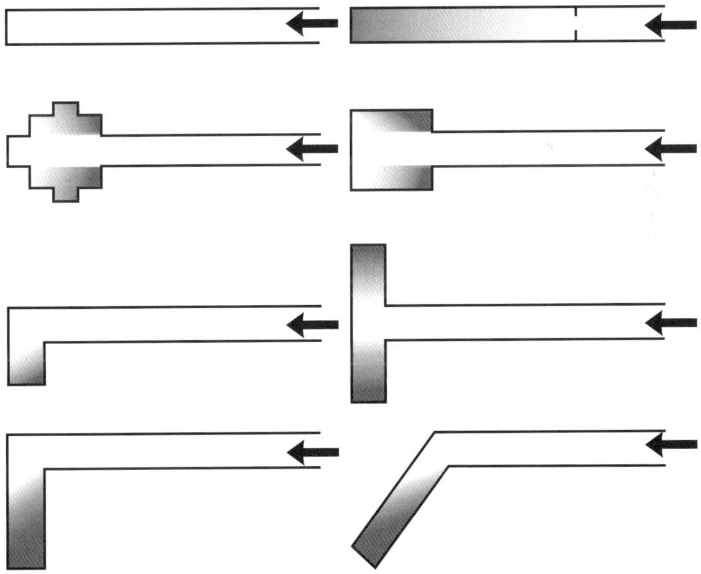

Figure 16. The flow of light inside chambered tombs, showing the areas illuminated by sunlight and those remaining in shadow.

There were other ways of controlling the movement of light into the interior of a chambered tomb. The entrance or the passage might be constricted by a stone slab breached by what is sometimes described as a 'porthole'. This could have acted rather like a lens and would have focused the flow of light from the exterior. At the same time that passage could change direction and might not lead straight to the chamber. In that case the movement of light would be obstructed and large areas would remain in darkness. That is most obvious with the angled passage graves of Brittany. The same is true of other monuments in the same region, for sometimes an elongated chamber runs at right angles to the entrance passage (L'Helgouach 1965: chapters 10 and 11). In each case they were built after passage graves of the classic form.

How were these architectural devices related to the decoration of the tombs? In certain cases it seems likely that sunlight travelled far enough along the entrance passage to illuminate the decoration in the chamber. That may be why the most striking images in the passage graves of northern Portugal were painted on the backstone opposite the entrance to the monument (Jorge 1997). The same was also true of the most lavishly decorated tombs in Ireland. Among the images that were emphasized in this way were those at threshold between the passage and the chamber. The light also picked out some of the carved stone basins in the heart of the Irish tombs (Brennan 1983).

Just as certain surfaces would be lit by the sun, others would have remained in darkness (Figure 17). Although some designs might have been identified as light was reflected off the chamber wall, they could only be examined in detail with the help of artificial illumination. If a naked flame was used, the

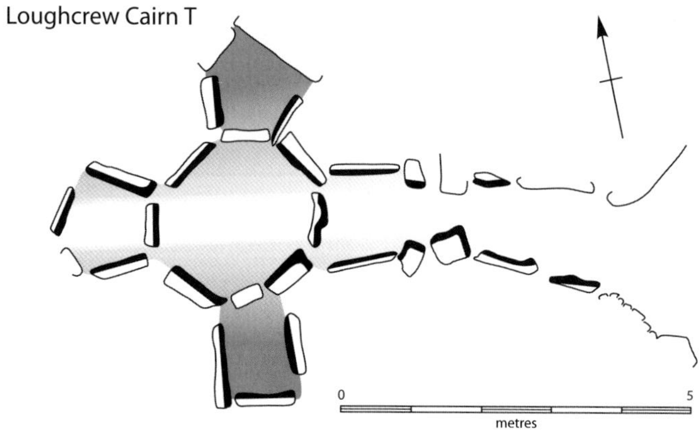

Figure 17. The flow of light inside Cairn T at Loughcrew, Ireland. The decorated surfaces are indicated in black, and the shaded areas are those which could not illuminated directly by the sun.

designs on the walls would appear to be in motion (Nash 2007). Particular paintings or carvings might have been placed well away from the axis of the entrance, on the hidden sides of individual stones, or even in recesses set back from the principal chamber. Moreover, the passage of the human body in or out of the tomb would have interrupted the flow of light, impeding visibility and casting shadows. The very structure of these tombs must have meant that movement was constrained. People had to pass through the monuments in a particular order, and it is clear that few of these places could have accommodated many visitors. As was the case in Palaeolithic painted caves, the very structure of these monuments must have meant that the images on their walls were seen in sequence (J. Thomas 1992).

In those monuments where the passage does not lead directly to the chamber the movement of light from the entrance is curtailed, and large areas remain in darkness. This can give rise to dramatic effects. For instance, in Brittany the decoration associated with such monuments features what appear to be strange anthropomorphic creatures. They are depicted in both the passage and the chamber, but a more important distinction is between the carvings in the area that would have been illuminated from outside and those located in the remainder of the monument. The 'hidden' designs are especially dramatic because they can be larger than the others (Figure 18).

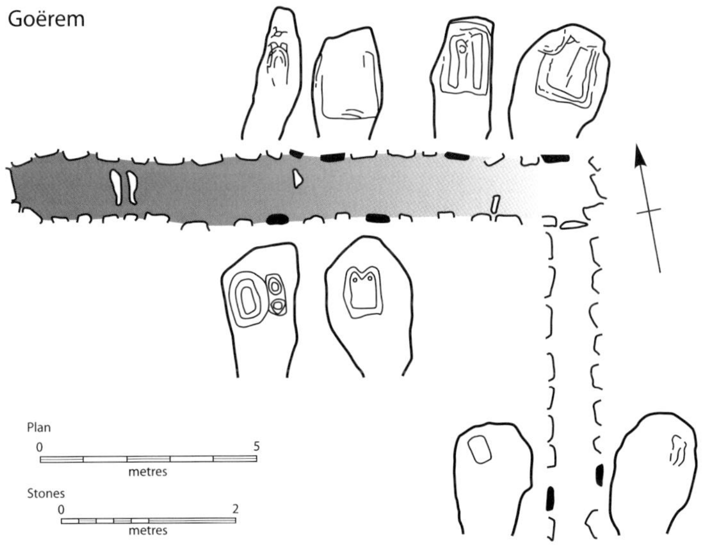

Figure 18. The chambered tomb at Goërem, Brittany, distinguishing between the areas that would have received some light from outside and those that would have remained in darkness. The carved designs are larger in the latter area.

The opposite situation can be identified in the megalithic tombs that lack an entrance passage, in particular, French *allées couvertes*. These structures are generally divided into two parts: an elongated rectangular chamber which housed the remains of the dead, and a small antechamber which is sometimes separated from it by a porthole slab or a narrow entrance. In this case it is the antechamber that is most often decorated; although some images do occur elsewhere, they are generally smaller than the others (Shee Twohig 1981). The main designs are clearly anthropomorphic and consist of schematic representations of the female form, often a pair of breasts linked by a necklace (Figure 19). They would be readily identifiable at the entrance to the tomb and could well have been seen by people who were not allowed inside the principal chamber. Other images were depicted on these sites, not all of which can be identified, but carvings of hafted axes are certainly found at the

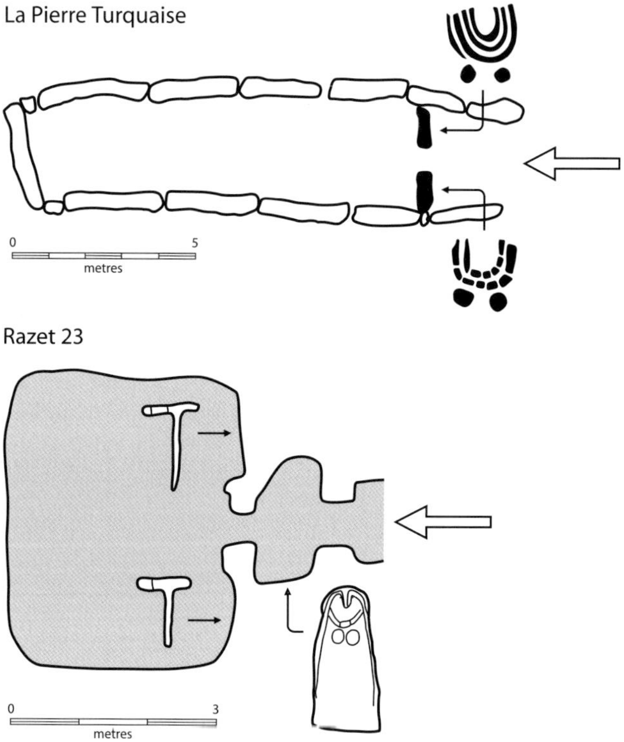

Figure 19. Two French tombs featuring female imagery. The arrows indicate the source of light from the exterior. La Pierre Turquaise was built at ground level, and Razet 23 was excavated into the subsoil. In each case the main designs are close to the entrance.

entrance and in the deeper spaces of the interior. *Allées couvertes* were normally conspicuous field monuments, but the same kind of structure was also created below ground (Tarrete 1996; Villes 1997). In this case the organization of the images was more rigidly controlled but conformed to the same conventions. The main difference is that they would have received less natural illumination. The contrast is not unlike that between conventional passage graves and angled passage graves.

THE MIND IN THE TOMB

Henri Breuil's notion of a prehistoric religion has gone out of favour, but there is another interpretation which considers the wide distribution of megalithic tombs together with the images found inside them. This is the thesis advanced by David Lewis-Williams and David Pearce (2005) in their book *Inside the Neolithic Mind.*

Their approach builds on Lewis-William's earlier study of Palaeolithic art, *The Mind in the Cave* (Lewis-Williams 2002). In each case the reference to the mind is all important, for central to both these studies is the significance of altered states of consciousness. They can be brought about by many agencies, from rhythmic dancing to the taking of drugs, and from fatigue to sensory deprivation. In every case the important point is that these processes affect the nervous system in a similar way. That is because all human beings share the same neuropsychology. Certain sensations are recorded in very different cultures, including the illusion of flight, a sense of falling or descent, and, most important of all, the experience of travelling through a tunnel or vortex. The latter is also associated with near-death experiences.

These sensations are reported in many different societies because they are created in the nervous system. To some extent they can be reproduced under laboratory conditions. Although they may be provided with a scientific explanation, for the people who undergo these experiences they have a profound significance. They are subject to different interpretations, but one of the commonest ways of accounting for them is in terms of a three-tier cosmology, in which the familiar world is only one of a series of superimposed planes. There is also an upper world, which is evidenced by the sensation of flight, and there is a lower world into which people descend (Chippindale, Smith, and Taçon 2000). Often there are special places where it is possible to make the transition. They include mountains which reach into the sky, and caves that lead to the underworld. In fact caves are especially important for they recreate the effect of a vortex. The best-known accounts of these phenomena concern the experiences of shamans, whose role it is to travel between the different levels of the cosmos. That is as true of the shamans of the Arctic, where the term originates, as it is of other people—not necessarily religious specialists—who describe similar journeys (N. Price 2001).

It is significant that Lewis-Williams had first studied Palaeolithic art. The caves in which many of the images are found have much in common with the features perceived in altered states of consciousness. As well as bodily hallucinations, the subject experiences intense visual effects which are also generated by the nervous system. Again they are shared from one culture to another as they originate inside the brain. They are sometimes described as *entoptic* phenomena. The forms that are commonly observed are called *phosphenes* (Lewis-Williams and Dowson 1988).

Lewis-Williams and Dowson have sought to define these shapes and the ways in which they were changed. There was a transformation in the character of these visual effects as the subject entered deeper states of trance. Thus they might begin as simple geometric patterns, but ultimately they could be interpreted as realistic images. That would account for the combination of abstract signs and painted animals that figure in Palaeolithic art. Such images would vary from one society to another because people were reflecting their own concerns when they construed these visions.

Many aspects of this interpretation have been controversial. The phosphenes are simple geometric forms and not everyone is convinced of their significance. Might they have been depicted by chance? Was Palaeolithic art such a unitary phenomenon that it can be explained by one hypothesis? Did different methods of inducing altered states of consciousness result in different kinds of visions (Dronfield 1995a)? There is uncertainty whether shamanism should be described as a cross-cultural phenomenon, or whether the term applies only to the region in which it took its name (Kehoe 2000). It is not surprising that Lewis-Williams's and Pearce's account of Neolithic beliefs has been equally contentious (Le Quellec 2006).

As the dust jacket says, *Inside the Neolithic Mind* 'continues the . . . story of *The Mind in the Cave*'. The book is in two parts, prefaced by an introductory section which discusses the relationship between human consciousness and ancient cosmology. The first detailed case study concerns the Neolithic of Anatolia and Western Asia and is primarily an account of settlements and shrines like Çatalhöyuk and Göbekli Tepe. The second is an analysis of megalithic tombs.

Lewis-Williams and Pearce state their hypotheses at the outset:

> The west European monuments reflected and at the same time constituted, with greater or lesser elaboration, a culturally specific expression of the neurologically generated tiered cosmos. (Figure 20)

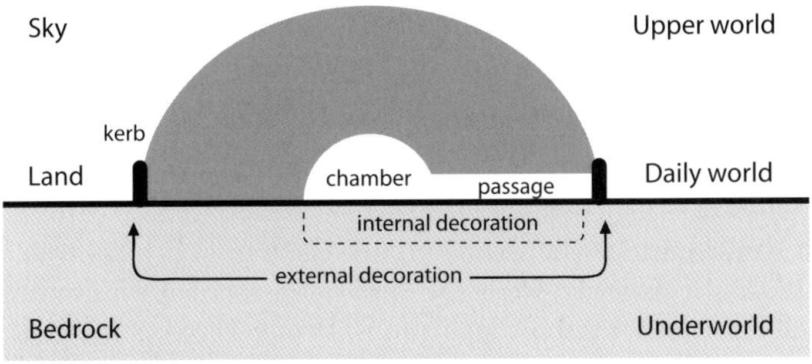

Figure 20. A Neolithic passage grave interpreted in terms of the three-tier cosmology.

That cosmos was mediated by a complex system of symbols through which people represented and engaged with it.

The neurologically wired concept of flight and passage through a vortex help us to understand the ways in which the massive stone monuments of the west functioned in their social and mythical contexts.

The ways in which the monuments were laid out reflected and controlled social distinctions that were, in turn, related to neurologically wired concepts. (Lewis-Williams and Pearce 2005: 171)

It is interesting that some of these ideas were first propounded in a study of decorated caves, for it was long believed that caves and underground burial chambers provided the source of inspiration for the earliest megalithic tombs (Daniel 1958). That view is no longer tenable, for the two phenomena rarely occur at the same time or in the same areas. Either they are found in different regions, or the cave burials are later in date than the first megaliths (Soler Díaz 2002). Even so, the comparison is provocative and still remains important.

THE TOMB IN THE MIND

Lewis-Williams and Pearce provide an interpretation that should apply to all megalithic tombs. Can the argument be sustained?

The first point to make is that their case is based on passage graves in Wales, Ireland, and Brittany. They do not draw on the evidence from South-West Europe, nor does their analysis consider other kinds of chambered tombs. That is unfortunate, for it is obvious that among the oldest of these monuments are structures with closed chambers. This raises questions concerning the special significance of the tunnel leading between the exterior and the interior. The cairn and the burial chamber might represent the upper and lower tiers of the cosmos, but the vortex that features so prominently in Lewis-Williams's and Pearce's account was not present at every site.

On the other hand, the pecked designs found in Irish passage graves do conform to their scheme. Jeremy Dronfield (1995b) has compared the motifs in chambered tombs with three control samples taken from other art styles. One came from societies whose members are known to have entered altered states of consciousness. The second sample came from peoples who did not engage in similar practices, while the third was associated with communities for which the evidence is more ambiguous. Dronfield recognised that certain images were only present in the first of these categories and distinguished them from the motifs found in the other traditions (Figure 21). On that basis he provided a more exact definition of the phosphenes discussed by Lewis-Williams and other writers. He also distinguished them from less specialized forms. The repertoire associated with altered states of consciousness matched the designs in the Irish tombs, while the other art styles did not. One particularly telling comparison was between the spirals associated with the entrance passage at Newgrange and the vortex described in ethnographic and clinical accounts (Dronfield 1996). This is particularly intriguing as the motifs towards the base of the entrance stone appear incomplete, as if they were thought to continue beneath the monument itself (Figure 22; Shee Twohig 2000).

The Irish evidence certainly supports the interpretation favoured by Lewis-Williams and Pearce, but even here there is a problem. Since Dronfield's research was carried out, renewed investigation of the principal tomb at Knowth has shown that the pecked motifs that he had studied were not the earliest designs there. They were superimposed on a network of finely incised lines which delimited a series of panels composed mainly of triangles and lozenges (Eogan 1997). They are quite different from the images considered in his study. They do not include any circles or spirals; nor do they show the

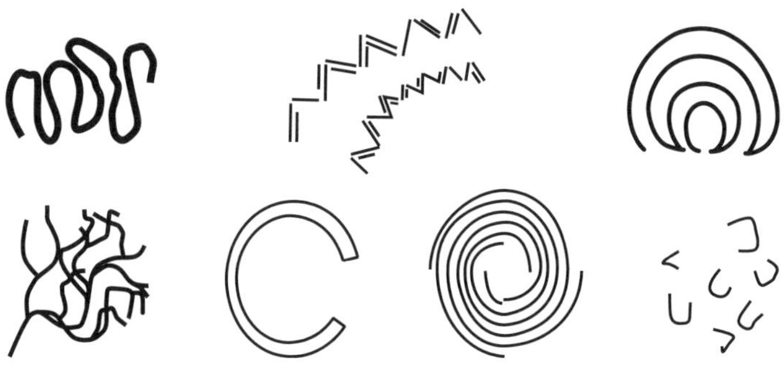

Figure 21. Phosphenes apparently associated with megalithic art.

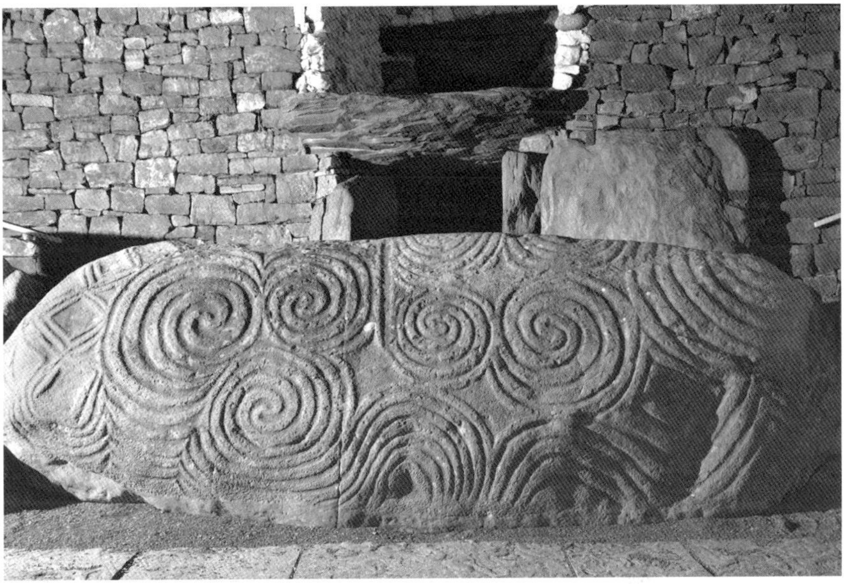

Figure 22. The entrance stone at Newgrange, Ireland.

same emphasis on phosphenes. If the megalithic art of the Boyne Valley did refer to altered states of consciousness—and the case is certainly suggestive—this association may not have been present when the tombs were first constructed. In the circumstances it is a moot point whether the architecture of these monuments refers to a three tier cosmology.

If the strongest arguments in favour of the hypotheses put forward by Lewis-Williams and Pearce are provided by megalithic art, their account is limited to Ireland, Wales, and Brittany, and only the tombs of the Boyne Valley are considered in any detail. The images in north-west France include fewer motifs that can be interpreted as entoptic imagery, and in Portugal and Spain they are by no means common. The phosphenes identified by Dronfield may have been a local phenomenon.

It is worth recalling some of the widely shared characteristics of passage graves. Their chambers would have been cold and inaccessible, and for much of the time they would also have been dark. The interiors of these structures must have been lit by lamps or torches which would create the illusion that the walls were in constant motion. Like caves, they would induce a feeling of sensory deprivation, especially if people were to remain there at night or for significant lengths of time. The entrance passage was often low and narrow and was difficult to traverse. Negotiating this space would have added to the drama of visiting the tomb, and so would the presence of human remains inside the monuments. In these circumstances the people who visited the dead might have been unusually suggestible.

Passage graves have a further characteristic which has become apparent in recent years. The monuments have unusual acoustics (Watson 2001; Watson and Keating 2000). Activities in a long narrow passage and high stone chamber produce distinctive sound effects. The pitch of the human voice seems to be raised or lowered in different parts of the building, and the chamber has a striking resonance. Such effects disconcert the visitor and even create auditory hallucinations. Rhythmic chanting or drumming would have been even more dramatic, for at certain frequencies people could have entered altered states of consciousness. Of course such practices are entirely hypothetical, but the physical basis of such experiences is well documented (Cook, Pajot, and Leuchter 2008), and the same is true of the behaviour of sound inside this kind of structure.

The last two examples emphasize characteristics of the chambered tombs that are all too rarely described. They are often secluded, dark and cold, and they have unusual acoustics. All these features might have encouraged the kinds of experience that Lewis-Williams inferred for Palaeolithic caves. That comparison is particularly important, for those caves were natural features of the local geology. However they might have been interpreted in the past, they contain archaeological evidence because they were *selected* for use by prehistoric people. There is no reason to suppose that megalithic tombs were modelled on burial caves, and in any case these structures were *designed* and built by human labour. Indeed, they were frequently constructed on a monumental scale.

It is most unlikely that passage graves were built in order to contrive particular acoustic effects. That would require a knowledge of theoretical physics. It seems much more likely that certain unusual phenomena were experienced by people entering these buildings (Watson 2006). Once that had happened, there is no reason why these features should not have been treated as one of the characteristics of the tombs. In the same way, the secluded chambers of the passage graves might have created the ideal conditions for entering altered states of consciousness, but it is perhaps too subtle to suggest that they were built for that purpose. In turn it would imply that the designs inside the Irish tombs referred to the experiences of the living when they visited these places.

The discovery that passage graves had unusual properties could account for some of the problems raised by Lewis-Williams's and Pearce's account. It could explain why entoptic imagery is not associated with all, or even most, of the decorated monuments. Because it was never integral to the concept of a megalithic tomb, it seems to have been mainly a feature of one region, and when it occurs elsewhere it need not have taken exactly the same form. That is because it could have developed independently in several parts of Europe. A similar argument would account for the distinctive sequence in the main monument at Knowth, where the earliest decoration has a different character from the phosphenes identified by Dronfield. *Such designs were a secondary development* and were not created until the tombs had already been in use for some time. Still more important, this approach would explain why passage graves could coexist with monuments containing closed chambers where the idea of a tunnel or vortex would not have any relevance. Megalithic art may have been employed in a variety of different ways, and only locally need it have referred to altered states of consciousness.

DISCUSSION: THE ART GALLERIES OF THE DEAD

So far this account has drawn attention to a set of contrasting relationships between particular kinds of images and specific kinds of monuments. They can also be used to shed light on the relationship between those images and their audience.

It is easy to lose sight of such connections. There are huge numbers of megalithic tombs, and it is obvious that more have been destroyed. On the other hand, the proportion of decorated monuments is increasing as additional examples are identified by fieldwork. Radiocarbon dating suggests that the history of these structures spanned nearly two thousand years. Although many points remain obscure, some general patterns can be identified.

The first of these is so obvious that it often passes without comment. Megalithic art, of whatever variety, is a feature of tombs that could have been visited by the living. It is not a characteristic of closed chambers, and for that reason it seems unlikely that it was directed exclusively to the dead. That is not to say that the designs were intended solely for the living as they are often located in close proximity to human remains. Rather, they might have been addressed to both kinds of audience.

There is also a striking relationship between the character of the designs and their placing inside the monuments. That is particularly true of the small selection of non-figurative motifs that have been identified as phosphenes. They have an uneven distribution, with most examples towards the northern limit of the distribution of megalithic art and significantly fewer to the south. Even so, they are virtually restricted to those monuments where the burial chamber was distanced from the outside world. They are associated with passage graves, often those with long tunnels leading into the interior, and are hardly found in more accessible monuments. Not only were these specialized designs placed in secluded locations, they had to be accessed by a passage. It recalls the vortex that plays such a prominent role in Lewis-Williams's and Pearce's interpretation.

These designs—and other, less distinctive abstract motifs—were sometimes placed in prominent positions where they might be illuminated by sunlight at particular times of the day, or on particular days in the year. More often they were concealed and occupied the parts of the chamber that would remain in shadow. Indeed, the contrasts between the forms illuminated by the sun and those that remained hidden might have been an important element in the organization of the tombs.

This introduces another important issue. Although most passage graves were aligned on the sun, only a few examples emphasised the turning points of the year. On such occasions a beam of intense light travels along the passage to illuminate the burial chamber. That relationship has been interpreted in terms of fertility and renewal. The effect seems to be most common in the monuments with carved designs. It is often supposed that solstitial and equinoctial alignments are a specifically Irish phenomenon, but they have also been observed in Orkney, north Wales, the Channel Islands, and Brittany (Ruggles 1999: chapter 8). All the monuments had been decorated.

There is evidence for anthropomorphic images in other chambered tombs in France, Portugal, and Spain. They will be considered in greater detail in Chapter 4, but one point is worth making at this stage. Such images could be more or less naturalistic, so that sometimes it is hard to identify the human form; in other cases it is unmistakeable. Certain of these depictions were extremely schematic and might even be embellished with abstract designs.

Again there is a direct relationship between the character of these paintings and carvings and the contexts in which they were seen. The more schematic the anthropomorphic paintings and carvings, the more likely they are to be found in secluded locations. They are a special feature of the passage graves. Some of these images were on the backstone, facing the entrance passage, but others may have been placed at the threshold of the chamber. Unless they formed part of a continuous frieze, they tend to occur in isolation, and it would have been necessary to view them by artificial light in order to pick out their characteristic features. That is how they have been recognized in recent years, for they can only be identified by careful observation. Of course the process would have been simpler if some of the incised and carved designs were originally painted, but such evidence rarely occurs even where pigment should be preserved. Perhaps it was intended that these representations should be hard to locate and difficult to interpret. That is certainly true in Iberia where entire bodies were represented. It was also the case in France, where some of the images had originally stood in the open air and had been reduced to fragments before they were built into the tombs. Again this process will be considered in the following chapter.

Such schematic and fragmented images are often found in association with non-figurative designs. They contrast with the more naturalistic images which are a striking feature of French *allées couvertes* and their subterranean counterparts (Tarrete 1996; Villes 1997). Although they can be accompanied by motifs which have been hard to identify, there seems little doubt that some of them represent actual objects. The anthropomorphic images are prominently displayed and are associated with the entrances of the tombs where they could have been seen by many people. In this case they do not appear to be found with abstract signs, although they can be accompanied by drawings of personal ornaments. Most were readily accessible. They must have posed fewer problems of interpretation than the more schematic figures employed during earlier phases.

The siting of anthropomorphic images close to the entrances of *allées couvertes* introduces another issue. They would have been visible to a significant number of people and were not directly associated with the dead. They would only have confronted the corpse as it was introduced to the tomb. Some of the largest and most impressive passage graves in Ireland take this process even further, for at quite a late stage in their development they were provided with decorated kerbs (Eogan 1998). Not only were the entrances embellished with abstract designs, the decoration continued around the perimeter of the monuments. It seems likely that it was addressed to a larger audience than those who could enter the tomb.

Although there are certain contrasts between the images in these two groups, it may be more important to emphasize a difference of technique, as it has implications for how the designs were to be viewed. At three points around the decorated kerb at Newgrange there are elaborately carved kerbstones. The images are moulded to the contours of the rock. They are prominent and confidently executed and are easy to recognize from a distance (O'Kelly 1982; O'Sullivan 1986). For that reason they might have been addressed to a larger audience than their equivalents in the chamber. One of these formal designs is at the entrance to the tomb and another is directly opposite it at the back of the mound. Still more striking effects can be seen at the neighbouring site of Knowth, where the decorated kerbstones are longer towards both entrances of the largest tomb (O'Sullivan 2006). Here the visual impact of some of the more prominent designs is enhanced because they are flanked by kerbstones which had been left undecorated; in other cases the composition is framed by stones with simpler designs. George Eogan (1996) has identified six such 'panels' in the kerb of the large passage grave at

Knowth, five of them on the east side of the monument, where they would have been illuminated by the morning sun.

Inside Newgrange and Knowth there are some stones with equally elaborate decoration, and on the latter site one group of rectilinear designs is restricted to the inner section of both the passages and the chambers (Eogan 1986). At Newgrange, however, other motifs are more difficult to recognize because of their positions inside the monument or because they were not carved to the same depths as their counterparts in the kerb. Certain of the designs are clearly superimposed on one another and others are partly hidden by the structure of the monument, perhaps because they were reused from an older building. There are cases in which particular images were wholly or partly obliterated and replaced by areas of pecking (Eogan and Aboud 1990). The overall effect appears fluid, even chaotic, especially when the interior is illuminated by the midwinter sunrise (Cochrane 2005 and 2006). Something similar may have happened at the east tomb at Knowth during the spring equinox (Brennan 1983), but many of these designs would be hidden from view in the darker parts of the chamber and would need lighting if they were to be seen at all. At Newgrange the decoration of the kerbstones shows a similar level of disorder, but at Knowth the situation is subtly different, and here there are hints of a more orderly arrangement in the outer kerb.

The contrasts between the exterior and interior are most obvious in the west tomb at Knowth. It may have been directed towards the sun at the autumn equinox, but in this case the passage changes direction by approximately twenty degrees. The light of the setting sun would never have reached the chamber, which must have remained in darkness. The contrast between these tombs is emphasized by the distributions of the carved motifs. In the eastern tomb, which seems to be associated with the light of the rising sun, they are found throughout the passage and the chamber. In the western tomb, which may have been orientated on the sunset, there was a stone basin where the passage changed direction, but many of the designs were in an area that lacked illumination (Brennan 1983: 102–8). Here they could only be found by searching for them using lamps or torches.

INTO THE INTERIOR

The best way of summarizing the main themes of this chapter is by comparing the experience of entering three different kinds of tomb. Each is found in a separate country.

The passage graves of northern Portugal had a relatively simple structure (Jorge 1997). They lacked a monumental kerb, and a well-preserved entrance passage led to a central chamber. Both were often embellished with paintings. There was a clear structure to the decorated surfaces which were sometimes conceived as a continuous frieze, with the most complex design facing the entrance, where it would have received what little light percolated into the monument. It was also the rear wall of the chamber where the decoration was most likely to evoke the human form. Sometimes it was associated with drawings of animals or the sun. The images on the side walls were often less ornate and did not always extend far along the entrance passage. Some of them would need careful lighting for their vivid colours to have much impact. Anyone entering these buildings would have been aware that the paintings became larger and more elaborate with distance from the outside world.

In many respects that was a different experience from entering a passage grave in the Boyne Valley (Eogan 1986). Here two separate groups of carvings may have been addressed to two distinct audiences: large gatherings of people who may have moved around the decorated kerb as individual images were highlighted by the sun at different times of day; and a smaller number who could have entered the tomb itself. Inside the monument the decorated surfaces were organized with less formality (Figure 23). Some were

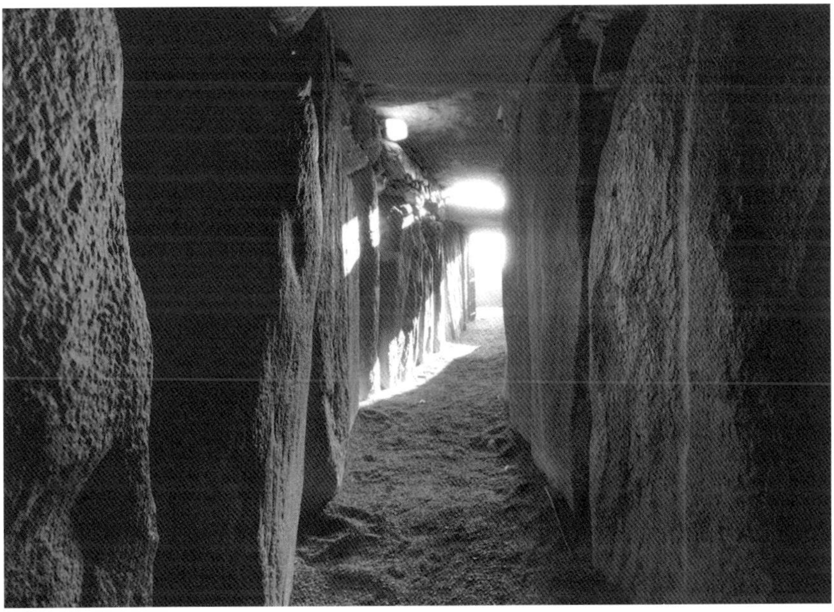

Figure 23. Interior view of the entrance passage at Newgrange at the midwinter sunrise.

concealed, or had been partly defaced as one design was superimposed on another. The carvings were completely non-figurative, and certain of them perhaps referred to altered states of consciousness. Those inside Newgrange were seen to best advantage when the chamber and passage were flooded with light at the midwinter sunrise. This dramatic effect would have been lost on anyone outside the monument.

Perhaps there was a similar distinction between those permitted inside the main chambers of French *allées couvertes* and the people who could not proceed beyond the entrance, but in this case the imagery was entirely different, and so was its distribution within the monument (Shee Twohig 1981: 70–86). The most striking features were the naturalistic sculptures associated with the antechamber, rather than the more enigmatic designs found in the interior. The two groups of images were often separated by a narrow entrance or even by a 'porthole' through which it would be difficult for many individuals to pass. Moreover some of these chambers were buried below a mound while others were underground. Again the images were addressed to two different audiences, who must have played quite separate roles in the commemoration of the dead.

Of course there were even more variations on these simple principles, but enough has been said to establish an important point. The relationship between the paintings and carvings and the monuments where they occur was by no means arbitrary. It is not a radical step to suggest that the same applies to the relationship between megalithic art and the people who encountered it in the past. This point is considered in greater detail in Chapters 4 and 5.

4

The Lives of Statues

THE MINIATURE AND THE MONUMENTAL

It is curious that some of the smallest three-dimensional images in prehistoric Europe should have been treated in the same ways as the largest ones. It is still more striking that such practices occurred at opposite ends of the Continent (Scarre 2007b). With only a few exceptions, small models of human bodies are associated with Neolithic and Copper Age sites in Eastern Europe, while monumental sculptures occur mainly in the west.

Their contexts are very different, too. The finds from regions like the Balkans come mainly from settlements, although they can be associated with human remains. Those in Western Europe share the same distribution as chambered tombs, and fragments of such statues were sometimes incorporated in the fabric of these buildings. In this case there is little to associate the sculptures with domestic sites. Rarely has any attention been paid to the striking parallels between the treatment of such monumental images and the ways in which small figurines were employed, yet there are advantages in comparing these phenomena with one another, for an analysis of this kind might shed light on why such similarities occur.

The ideal starting point is a study by the Rumanian archaeologist Dragos Gheorgiu (2001) which considers 'the cult of ancestors' in south-east Europe during the fifth millennium BC. He is concerned with the Cucuteni-Tripolye culture, in which two distinctive phenomena have been identified, although they also appear in the archaeology of neighbouring groups (Bailey 2005). Human remains are frequently associated with settlements. They do not represent entire bodies and only rarely do they occur in cemeteries. Among the other finds from the living sites are numerous ceramic figurines, the great majority of which have been deliberately broken. Only in the latest phase of the Cucuteni-Tripolye group did the situation change, and in a few instances entire skeletons are found together with complete figurines. The striking similarity between the treatment of the dead and that of these small images suggests that both processes were related to one another.

Gheorgiu's argument is strengthened by his analysis of the figurines associated with domestic sites. Their appearance was quite distinctive, and so was their treatment when their period of use came to an end. The bodies represented seem to be mostly those of women, although some examples certainly had male attributes. They were shown swathed in what are best described as bandages which extended from the neck down to the feet. They were tightly bound around the legs in the way that would prevent a living person from moving. He suggests that they represented the bindings on a corpse. Only the head was left exposed, and it lacked facial features (Figure 24).

Very few of these figurines are found intact, and detailed analysis of those in Eastern Europe suggests that not only were they broken in antiquity, different

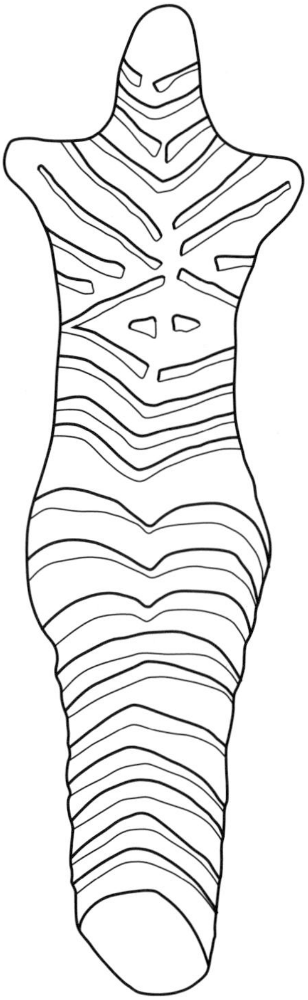

Figure 24. Ceramic figurine of the Cucuteni-Tripolye Culture, showing the bindings on the body.

fragments must have circulated within a wider community (Chapman and Gaydarska 2007: chapter 4). Most important of all, in the Cucuteni-Tripolye group the breaking of these images seems to have reflected the treatment of the dead, whose bodies may have been subdivided in a similar fashion. In particular, the decapitation of many of the clay figurines recalls the practice of removing the skulls from human skeletons and depositing them separately from the other parts of the body. Both the fragmentary artefacts and the disarticulated bones were often buried in pits inside the settlement.

That cycle is certainly distinctive and was followed to varying extents by other societies in this region of Europe. It focused on the places where people lived. The process itself left little trace behind, although the superimposition of successive buildings led to the formation of a mound (Bailey 2000).

Contrast this with the sequence in north-west France over the same period of time. Here stone images were displayed in the open air (Boujot and Cassen 1998; Lecerf 1999). They were more akin to statues and could assume monumental proportions. Some were arranged in formal settings or alignments, others were erected just outside burial mounds, and one example was apparently situated beside a Neolithic house, although it is not clear whether the two structures were contemporary with one another (Cassen, Audren, Hinguant, Lannuzel, and Marchand 1998). Perhaps the standing stone marked the dwelling of someone who had died.

In many ways they were very different from the Eastern European figurines. They are extremely schematic, so that it is a matter for debate how many examples portray the human form. The best argument is that their profile narrows towards the top as if to indicate shoulders and a head. Moreover, the earlier examples are not depicted with any kind of costume. Instead these *menhirs* are usually embellished either with non-figurative decoration or with drawings of artefacts or animals that would have been familiar in daily life. Some of them resemble huge upright axe heads. Other designs may have had a more specific interpretation, and two of the commonest motifs have been identified as whales (Cassen and Vaquero Lastres 2003). Serge Cassen (1999 and 2000) has also argued that the earlier sculptures were specifically associated with masculinity and include phallic imagery. Again that recalls the Eastern European evidence, for some of the clay figurines share this characteristic and may even portray bodies that in contemporary terms would be considered both male and female. Cassen also argues that at a later stage in the Neolithic sequence in north-west France female images assumed a greater significance. This was when some of the older statues were demolished.

Other scholars have favoured a different interpretation, although they are still attracted by the idea that the levelling of the menhirs resulted from iconoclasm (L'Helgouach 1996). Similarly, their destruction and reuse as building material has been interpreted in ideological terms (Whittle 2000). The statues, with their occasional references to archery and the sea, are thought to refer to the lives of local hunter gatherers who were acculturated through their earliest contacts with farmers. The destruction of these sculptures and their reuse in building tombs is associated with a new economy and, most probably, with an immigrant population. Thus the conflict between indigenous people and incomers is reflected by the history of these images.

Gheorgiu's work suggests another interpretation, for in his study the breaking of the figurines was part of the funeral ritual and even took a similar form to the treatment of the corpse. There was no sudden rupture, no confrontation between opposing systems of belief. In fact the reuse of statues in graves and mortuary monuments happens surprisingly often in the prehistory of Western and Southern Europe: so often, in fact, that it cannot always be interpreted in these terms (Bradley 2002: 36–41). If it occurs at the beginning of the Neolithic sequence in France, it also happens at the same time in the Iberian Peninsula; and it is found in the Copper Age in the foothills of the Alps and during the Early Bronze Age in Portugal and the Caucasus. It may be more informative to consider a common explanation. Some of the main elements are considered here; others will be discussed in Chapter 5.

The first point to make is that the Breton statues were not merely destroyed; their remains were sometimes distributed between different monuments (Figure 25). The most famous instance is the presence of parts of the same menhir at Gavrinis and Table des Marchand (Cassen 2000). Little is known about the treatment of the dead in this region because bones rarely survive, but what little information is available suggests that, in common with other areas, Northern France saw the circulation of human remains. Either they were arranged in formal patterns inside the monuments after the bodies had lost their flesh, or selected bones may have been treated like portable artefacts and moved from place to place (Patton 1993: 91–8). That is not unlike the fate of the broken menhirs. It is often supposed that by mixing human remains, or even transporting them from one site to another, individual identities were dissolved and the dead were treated as ancestors. Is it possible that some of the statues were thought of in a similar way?

That involves making a series of assumptions. The first of these is probably justified. The statues do seem to be related to the commemoration of the dead. There is evidence that standing stones and even alignments of menhirs were erected in the vicinity of burial mounds. Some of these mounds had closed chambers underneath them and could not be visited by the living after the structure had been built. It was only when the sites were turned into passage graves, or when passage graves were created in the vicinity, that the

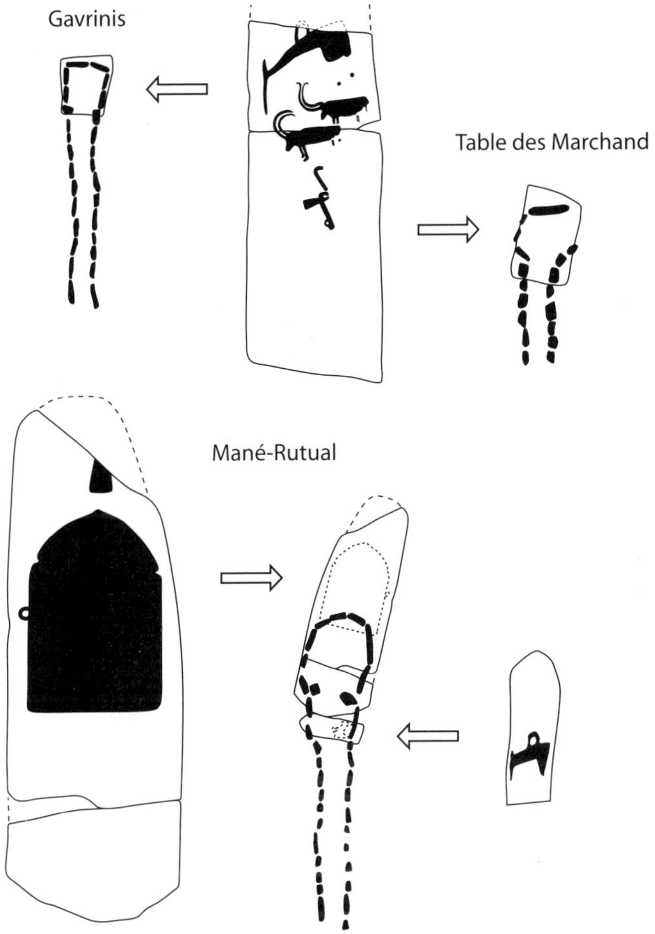

Figure 25. The reuse of decorated menhirs in Breton chambered tombs. The diagram illustrates the use of broken menhirs as capstones. The joining fragments from Gavrinis and Table des Marchand originally formed parts of the same monument.

statues were taken down and incorporated in new monuments (Boujot and Cassen 1998; Cassen 1999 and 2000). There is little evidence to suggest how long that process lasted.

A second assumption is that these statues represented specific people. That is not essential to the argument. It may be inappropriate to make a firm distinction between memorials to particular individuals, and statues that represented other powerful beings. That may be one reason why these images were embellished with such a variety of abstract and figurative images and even why a number of them may have been understood as more generalized symbols of masculine sexuality.

A third assumption is that the choice of already-used stone was made for social reasons and was not intended simply for economy of effort. That is surely shown by the fact that individual pieces had been moved over a significant distance, and that fragments of the same menhir or stone alignment were built into different tombs. In any case it would surely have been easier to quarry suitable stone from the friable granite bedrock (Mens 2008) than to engage in the less dependable procedure of moving the statues and breaking them into pieces of the appropriate size. So much effort would have been required that it seems unlikely that it was done for practical reasons.

The last assumption is that the transformation of the statues was carefully structured. This has sometimes been denied, but the arguments for rejecting the idea are unsatisfactory. It is true that the fragments, especially those with carved decoration, were not laid out with much formality. Some would have been difficult to identify, and others may have been inaccessible. A number of examples were employed as capstones. It could have been done deliberately, for by this means statues that had originally been addressed to a substantial audience were effectively hidden—and hidden in locations where few people would have had the opportunity to encounter them. When the carved stones moved from the public to the private domain, they took on a more specialized role. When they had stood outside the burial mounds they were distanced from the dead; but in their new configuration they *enclosed* them (Figure 26).

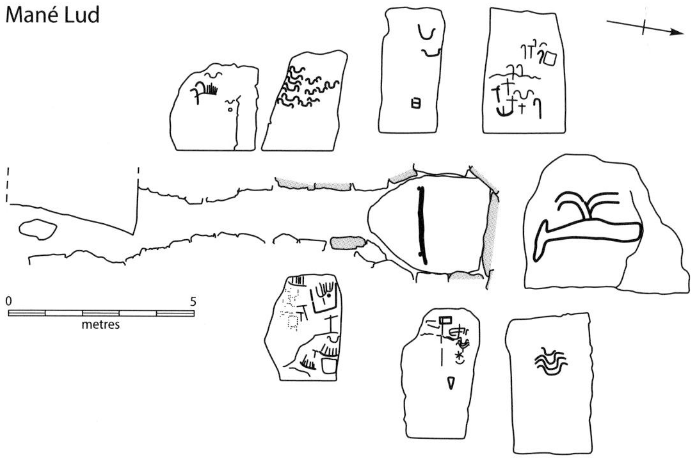

Figure 26. Decorated orthostats plus a capstone in the passage grave at Mané Lud, Brittany.

Although this runs counter to Cassen's argument that the destruction of so many statues was the result of ideological change, there is much in favour of his view that in northern France female images assumed a growing importance over time. Even if his claims for an early phase of masculine imagery are difficult to evaluate, it is certainly true that sculptures of women—usually represented by pairs of breasts—are associated with some of the later chambered tombs; other examples have been identified in the open air (Shee Twohig 1981: 70–89 and 128–30). One reason why this change is so apparent is that these images are more naturalistic than the earlier ones. For that reason they involve fewer problems of interpretation. As Chapter 3 has shown, they were often located in the antechambers of megalithic monuments. There they could be seen by many people. Indeed, it would have been necessary to pass them in order to bury the dead.

That observation raises certain problems, for they are among the images that have most often been identified as depictions of a Mother Goddess: a view which has gone out of favour in mainstream archaeology. There is another way of thinking about this sequence. Cassen interprets some of the earliest images in terms of male sexuality, but they could also symbolize fertility. Similarly, the female imagery might refer not only to reproduction but also to nourishing the young. That is even more apparent where sunlight reached the burial chamber at the turning points of the year, for it suggests a close relationship between the fortunes of the dead and the passage of the seasons on which life itself depends.

A useful perspective on this relationship is suggested by Maurice Bloch and Jonathan Parry (1982) in their edited book *Death and the Regeneration of Life*. This shows that the same interplay between funeral rites, fertility and sexuality is found in many different societies: societies which do not seem to have any contacts with one another. Bloch and Parry suggest that this is because those communities share a similar conception of the relationship between the dead and the living. In such cases human fertility is regarded as a finite resource, so that the death of one person releases the fertility required for another to be born. In this scheme life is characterized as a 'limited good'. Fertility, however, is a wider concept:

> We should make it clear that we do not use the term 'fertility' in any restricted or technical way, but in the dictionary sense of 'fecundity' or 'productiveness'. If death is often associated with a renewal of fertility, that which is renewed may either be the fecundity of people, or of animals and crops, or of all three. In most cases what would seem to be revitalized in funerary practice is that resource which is *culturally conceived* to be most essential to the reproduction of the social order. (emphasis in the original; Bloch and Parry 1982: 7)

The qualification is most important, for it suggests one reason why some of the French menhirs which Cassen (2000) interprets as symbols of male sexuality could be embellished with drawings of livestock or sea creatures, or with depictions of artefacts like axes, bows and arrows that played a role in the subsistence economy. All can be read as references to the same principle of fecundity. The work of Bloch and Parry suggests why such images should be associated with the dead.

THE PERMANENT AND THE PORTABLE

Similar problems arise in other parts of the distribution of megalithic art. As Chapter 3 has shown, it is also a feature of the Iberian Peninsula, but here the evidence is rather different. While the decorated tombs were certainly related to statues in the open air, there are other, equally important relationships to consider.

It is misleading to treat the decorated tombs of Spain and Portugal as a single category, as the style of the images varies from one region to another, and so do the conventions according to which they were deployed, but at present it is not clear how far these designs changed over time. Even so, there are points of similarity with the French sites that ought to be considered.

It is certainly true that freestanding statues have been identified in Portugal and Spain. Indeed, the small group in the Portuguese Alentejo resembles Breton examples in its characteristic decoration, which sometimes features designs that have been interpreted as crooks and snakes. Another possible connection is that they can form distinctive settings that have been compared with the megalithic enclosures of north-west France (Calado 2002 and 2006). There the similarity ends, for Iberia provides rather less evidence for their destruction, although some were reused in the fabric of chambered tombs. The decorated stones inside the Iberian passage graves are generally regarded as entire statues, however sketchy the carvings associated with them. Far from being concealed within the fabric of the monument like those in Brittany, they occupied the same positions from one site to another (Bueno Ramírez and Balbín Behrmann 2003; Bueno Ramírez, Balbín Behrmann, and Barroso Bermajo 2005a). Sometimes their distribution complemented that of painted panels and deposits of stone artefacts (Figure 27)

In this case there is another element that calls for comment. A few of the northern French monuments contain free-standing menhirs which are found within the chambers of passage graves like Barnenez (Giot 1987), but this is unusual. It seems to have happened rather more often in the Iberian tombs,

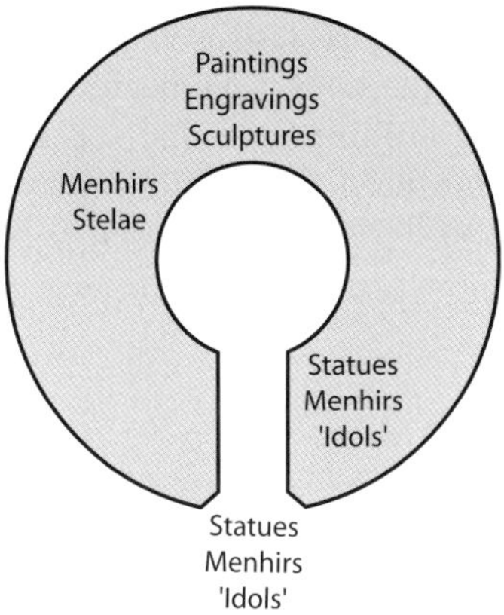

Figure 27. The organization of decorated elements in Iberian passage graves.

and this distinctive pattern raises a series of questions. These stones are of various sizes, but could the largest examples have been manoeuvred into position if the structure had already been built? If not, it seems more likely that the passage and burial chamber were constructed around these upright pillars and effectively enclosed them. Might the menhirs have been the earliest features at these sites? If so, the contrast with the French evidence becomes even stronger, for in one case statues were levelled and their remains were *concealed* in the structure of later tombs. In the Iberian Peninsula it is arguable that those very monuments were meant *to display* the decorated stones. They were often left intact when they were built into chambered tombs, and occasionally the entire building may have been raised around them.

Again this could have happened as part of a longer cycle of activity. Although the decorated tombs of the Iberian Peninsula are usually described as passage graves, in many case the passage has to be identified by excavation. That contrasts sharply with the structural evidence from northern France and Ireland and is mainly true of the earlier tombs in the western part of the Iberian Peninsula; in the later, more massive examples this feature is better preserved. One possibility is that certain of the earlier monuments were less carefully built than their successors, with the result that parts of them have collapsed, but that hardly accounts for the survival of the chamber when the remains of the passage have disappeared. Another is that the passage was never intended to have a lengthy history, or that in some cases it was demolished: an idea first suggested by Chris Scarre (pers. comm.). It seems a more satisfactory interpretation of the excavated evidence, but, if so, it sheds new light on how these structures were employed. The collapse of the entrance passage—for whatever reason—would have meant that after an interval of uncertain duration the dead were cut off from the living and the decoration in the central chambers was no longer accessible (Figure 28). Where the demolition of anthropomorphic statues had been the decisive event in the history of northern French sites, the demolition or closure of

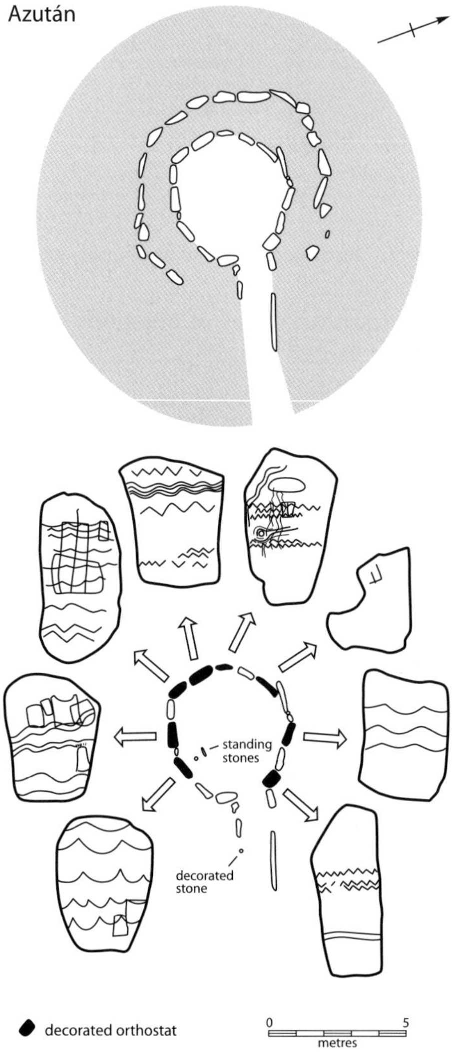

Figure 28. Outline plan of the excavated tomb at Azutan, Spain showing the poor survival of its entrance passage. The lower diagram illustrates the decorated orthostats. The designs seem to be more complex towards the rear of the chamber.

these entrance passages was the final stage in the use of Iberian monuments. Again it may have marked the point at which the dead were separated from the living.

THE LITTLE PEOPLE

In the west of Iberia there is another feature to consider. This was one of the few parts of Western Europe in which figurines played a significant part in mortuary ritual. In this case they take the form of a small stone artefact with a groove towards the top to suggest a neck (Fábregas Valcarce and Vilaseco Vázquez 2006; Bueno Ramírez and Balbín Behrmann 2006b). They are associated with passage tombs and can be set upright in the entrances of these monuments. They are inconspicuous and most examples are only a few centimetres high (Figure 29). On the other hand, their characteristic profile has much in common with that of freestanding menhirs along the Atlantic coastline of Europe. It also resembles the profile of the anthropomorphic sculptures identified inside the monuments of Portugal and Spain. Here the composition of the intended audience might be particularly important. Were these small objects offerings made by people who were unable to enter the chamber, or could the idols have been deposited to commemorate visits to the dead? Had the artefacts first circulated among the living, and were they intended to recall specific people? If so, what accounts for the difference between the monumental effigies hidden inside the monuments and the miniature 'idols' displayed in front of them?

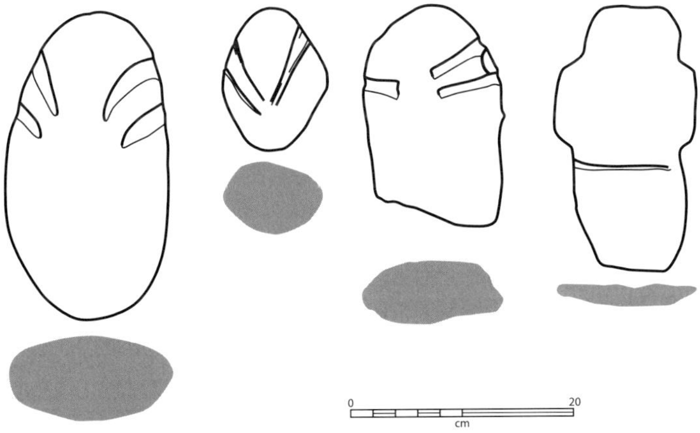

Figure 29. Stone idols from Galician megalithic tombs.

These artefacts are less well known than the decorated idols found further to the south, which are often described as 'schist plaques' (Figure 30). The term is unsatisfactory, for many are made of slate and occasionally of sandstone. They are associated with the late use of megalithic tombs in this region. Katina Lillios (2002 and 2003) has catalogued the accessible finds, of which there are more than a thousand (http://research2.its.uiowa.edu/iberian/index.php). According to her figures, only 1 per cent of the plaques are found in settlements, and nearly all the others were certainly or probably deposited with burials. 76 per cent come from megalithic tombs, although it is important to be aware that many of these monuments might have been reused after their original construction; 8 per cent were found with burials in underground chambers; and another 13 per cent came from the graves inside caves or rock shelters. The stone plaques are relevant to this discussion not only because they are found with the dead, but also because their characteristic decoration has been compared with the paintings on the walls of chambered tombs.

A few examples feature drawings of eyes. More commonly, the upper part of the plaque bears a single hole, suggesting that they might have been suspended from a cord and employed as ornaments. A number of writers

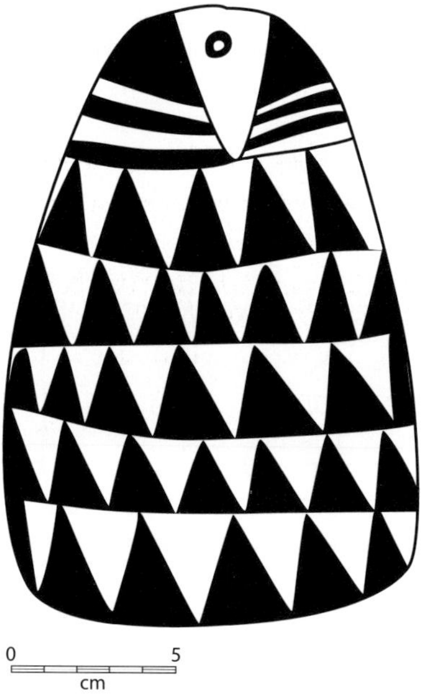

Figure 30. The design structure on a decorated 'schist plaque' from southern Portugal.

have observed that the characteristic designs resemble a woven fabric and may portray a kind of costume. If so, they could have resembled the appearance of the living. A striking feature noted by Lillios is that the lower parts of these designs are arranged in a series of horizontal bands. That is very important, for the painted designs inside a few of the tombs follow a similar convention; if the plaques represented people wearing a distinctive costume, the decorated orthostats must have done so too. That would suggest that they were full-size images of particular individuals, and in some cases the shapes of the uprights do resemble those of these artefacts. On the other hand, at other tombs bands of decoration in the same style extend from the top to the bottom of individual stones. They have rather less in common with the engraved plaques, although the similarities between these media are still so striking that some kind of cross reference was obviously intended. The designs on the plaques had been created in one operation and had not developed incrementally; the same may well be true of the decoration in the tombs.

Few of the plaques have been found in settlements, but it seems clear that it was where they were made. Some may have been produced for a specific funeral, and in these cases the perforation seems to have been freshly created. There are other examples where the perforation is worn, suggesting that they had been used for a significant period of time before their deposition. Moreover, 37 of the plaques in Lillios's catalogue—a small but significant 3 per cent of the total—showed signs of more than one period of use. Perhaps the plaques or their associated decoration had been modified before they were buried. Again this suggests that some of these artefacts may have circulated for an appreciable period of time before they accompanied the dead to the tomb. During that interval they could have been displayed among the living.

The last decorated plaques belong to the Bell Beaker phase and even share certain decorative devices with that style of pottery. It means that they were still being made and deposited during a period when metal became important in the Iberian Peninsula. That chronological point is significant for there may have been a final phase in the sequence of anthropomorphic images in this region of Europe.

THE STONE ARMOURY

That interpretation has been suggested by Bueno Ramírez, Balbín Behrmann, and Barroso Bermajo (2005b) who have drawn attention to a distinctive series of stone carvings which depict human figures together with weapons, normally daggers and halberds, although there are also drawings of bows. They occur in several different media, from free-standing menhirs to outline drawings on rock outcrops, and are distributed across most parts of the Iberian Peninsula, although they are never common (Figure 31). They represent the kinds of metalwork that are found in the graves of the Copper Age and the Early Bronze Age, and in Northern Spain it even seems possible that the location of one such carving in the rock shelter at Peña Tú was related to an important source of metal (De Blas Cortina 2003). These images are later in date than the megalithic tombs in the same regions, but they do seem to reflect a continuing desire to position images of powerful beings at particular places in the landscape. It may be that they are the ultimate successors of those in the passage graves: a suggestion which is especially plausible as some of those monuments were reused at about the time when the figures of warriors were made. If that is true, it suggests that long after the images of the dead had been sealed inside stone-built tombs there was a new phase of displaying stone sculptures in the open air. The audience for these images remained the same for a long time. Only in the Early Bronze Age of southern Portugal were any of the statues taken down and buried with the dead (Chenorkian 1998: 335–6). In other cases they remained where they had been made.

On one level it may be right to say that the first statues showing metal weapons represented a developed stage in a long history of anthropomorphic images in the Iberian Peninsula. On another level, this argument may be too geographically specific. Just as Bell Beakers and copper metallurgy were widespread features in the prehistory of Southern Europe, the same is true

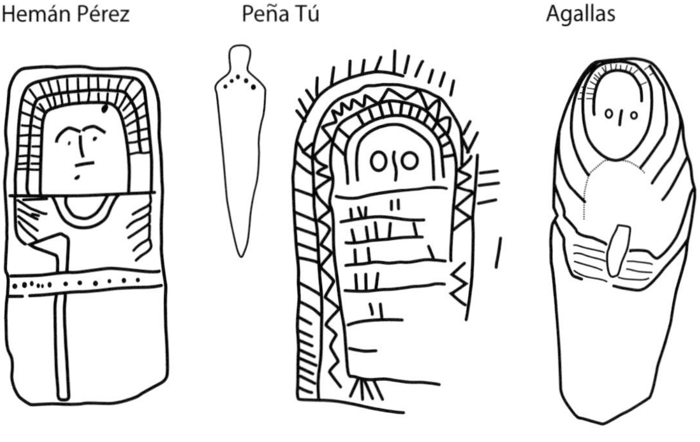

Figure 31. Depictions of human figures with weapons from the Iberian Peninsula.

of what have become known as *statue menhirs*. Other important groups occur in the south of France, northern Italy, and Switzerland (Chenorkian 1998; Keates 2000).

How are they related to 'megalithic art'? The normal view would be to see them as something different. It is usual to compare them with the carvings on natural outcrops. The distinctive repertoire of weapons and jewellery depicted on the statues is usually compared with the contents of prehistoric burials. On the other hand, there are cases in which statue menhirs are directly related to megalithic tombs in Italy and Switzerland. If the oldest decorated menhirs in north-west France are associated with the first chambered tombs, it is logical to extend the category of decorated tomb to include some of the latest examples. The well-preserved mortuary monuments at Sion in Switzerland were built between 2700 BC and 2400 BC and are very similar to those at Aosta in northern Italy. This account follows the recent reinterpretation of these sites by Richard Harrison and Volker Heyd (2007).

The carvings associated with the last megalithic tombs in this region have an unusually wide range of associations and often portray artefacts that are found in graves. They are relevant because their presence in the landscape may have set a precedent for new developments. During the third millennium BC there were changes in the character of the rock carvings. Although they can be traced through the types of artefacts that feature in the drawings, their contexts were equally diverse. That has implications for their interpretation and for the character of the audiences who encountered them.

The work of Geoffroy De Saulieu (2004) is of special importance. Rather than treating the individual design elements as if they were portable artefacts, he has studied their wider settings. Although chronological considerations remain important, the main differences that he identifies are based on context. He makes an important distinction between *'art ostentatoire'* (or *'art monumental'*), and what he calls *'art discret'.* The two series ran in parallel throughout most of the archaeological sequence, although 'art discret' might have developed first and was certainly important during the Copper Age, between about 2900 and the middle of the third millennium BC. For part of that period it ran in parallel with 'art ostentatoire', but the latter became the dominant medium for visual images for the next two or three hundred years. From 2200 BC, the start of the Early Bronze Age, 'art discret' became important again and 'art ostentatoire' disappeared.

De Saulieu's analysis is particularly significant since it considers image and audience together. His scheme does take account of the contents of these two traditions, but it is based primarily on where the images were made. Thus 'art ostentatoire' is associated with vertical surfaces and is prominently displayed. Some of these designs are associated with monuments: decorated menhirs,

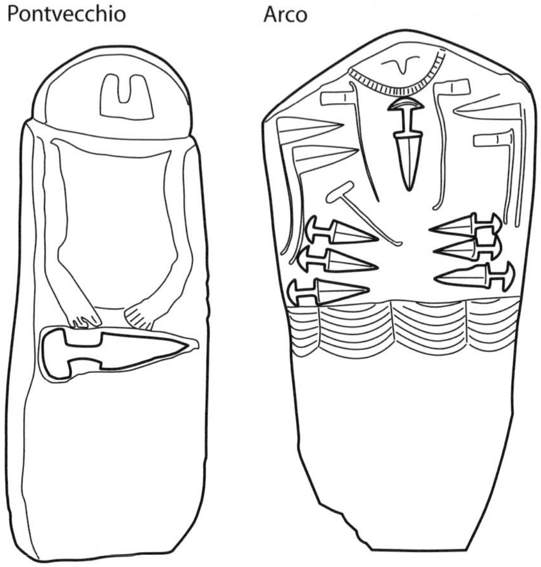

Figure 32. Statue menhirs in the southern Alps.

stone alignments, large cists, and chambered tombs (Figure 32). Others are ostentatious because they were carved on conspicuous outcrops. In either case they would have been easy to find and were probably addressed to a significant number of people. 'Art discret', on the other hand, is not so easily discovered, for it tends to occupy horizontal surfaces, often in mountainous country, and is not associated with menhirs.

There are striking contrasts between both series of rock carvings: contrasts which have important implications for the ways in which they were used. The statue menhirs were sometimes destroyed, and in other cases examples of 'art ostentatoire' were adapted and re-carved, so that the images themselves were changed. It seems as if these designs were revised according to political circumstances. The panels that have been described as 'art discret' developed along very different lines. Here fresh drawings might well be added to existing panels, but what was already there was respected, and there is little sign of superimposition or damage. In this case the elaboration of the decorated surface would have traced the histories of the people responsible for its creation.

De Saulieu identifies important differences between the images in these groups. Although they do share certain motifs—in particular drawings of weapons and what have been interpreted as sun symbols—the designs on vertical surfaces include elements that are not found in other contexts. The human figures portrayed in these 'public' carvings—both men and women—are shown with elements of their costume and wear a variety of ornaments. Daggers, halberds and axes also feature in this group, and in many instances the weapons are attached to the body. Carvings of the human figure are sometimes accompanied by depictions of the sun. Similarly, 'art ostentatoire' features wild animals and hunting. These animals are usually shown with horns or antlers and are predominantly ibex and deer. The motifs that were created in the other medium show domesticates instead. There are no drawings of personal ornaments and, although there are numerous weapons, they look more like accumulations of trophies. They can be separate from any human figures.

It seems as if one group of images was grounded in domestic life, while the other showed more concern with the activities of a small section of society. They may have celebrated a restricted elite, and so the carvings were modified as the social order changed. It may be no coincidence that these public images assumed greater importance during the Bell Beaker phase, when long distance networks became increasingly important in ancient Europe. Individual burials also appear at this time. The weapons and ornaments that feature on statue menhirs might be the equivalent of the offerings placed in the grave.

THE INSTABILITY OF ICONS

The last megalithic tombs are particularly relevant here. Two sites have been extensively excavated and it is not clear whether there had been many more. The monuments consisted of massive stone cists located at the broad end of a low triangular platform or cairn. The cists were probably covered over, but may have been readily accessible. The best known examples are two neighbouring monuments on the Petit Chasseur site at Sion, but a very similar structure has been investigated as part of a monument complex at Aosta (Figure 33; Mezzena 1998).

Each of these carvings was directly associated with statue menhirs of the kind that De Saulieu describes as 'art monumental'. The monument complex at Aosta was unusually long lived. It consisted of an alignment of massive wooden posts supplemented by a row of standing stones, with another line of menhirs offset from it at right angles. There was a triangular monument like that at Sion. A few of the statues were altered while they remained in position, and stylistic evidence suggests that the designs were created in two phases. They feature the usual depictions of ornaments and weapons. They were associated

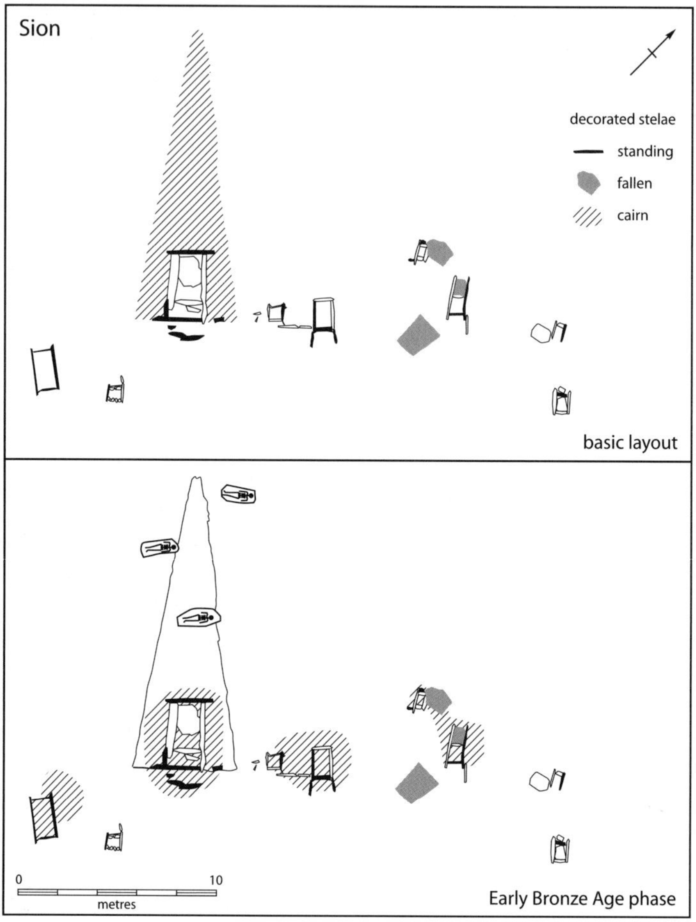

Figure 33. The excavated sequence at Sion, Switzerland, showing the changing relationship between decorated menhirs, a megalithic tomb, and other monuments.

with small stone platforms, one of which covered a deposit of human bones. Towards the end of the sequence those statues were felled and their heads were damaged or removed. Some of the fallen menhirs lay on the ground but others were taken away, although their bases were left in position. The broken pieces were used to construct a series of monuments which included some small platforms. In a final phase the site saw the construction of a series of massive cists, two of which abutted the older megalithic monument.

At Sion events took a similar turn. The megalithic tombs formed part of an alignment of monuments that faced the sun on exactly the same axis as those at Aosta. It also included a series of statues which showed so much variation that Harrison and Heyd (2007) conclude that they probably represented particular individuals who were buried on the site. They describe this row of sculptures as a 'wall of ancestors' and argue that they were arranged in line to codify a genealogy.

The file of sculptures defined a public space in front of the principal tombs. Estimates vary of the numbers of people buried there, but both the monuments at Sion may have housed the remains of nearly a hundred individuals. On either side of the entrance to one of these monuments there had been a statue menhir, so that, like the female images in French *allées couvertes,* these sculptures flanked the approach to the dead. Further statues were erected throughout the lifespan of these tombs. While the earlier examples are dated to the Late Neolithic period, the second group belongs to the first part of the Bell Beaker phase.

Around 2400 BC the site at Sion was transformed and, as happened at Aosta, the statues were levelled and partly destroyed. The megalithic tombs which had been the focal points of both these complexes were emptied and their contents rearranged. Now they became the burial places of a smaller number of people, and a sequence of monumental cists was constructed. They incorporated the remains of the older stelae. This process extended for about two hundred years, by which time collective burials had been replaced by those of individuals.

The situation is quite different from that discussed in the first part of this chapter. The statues at Sion were clearly anthropomorphic and might have been erected as public statements concerning the authority of certain people. Harrison and Heyd (2007) are probably right to identify them as ancestors. It is obvious that the sculptures already had a significant history of reworking and alteration, but now it seems as if they lost their significance altogether as the original burials were removed from the chambered tombs and new ones took their place. When that happened, some of the carved stones were levelled and their remains were incorporated in monumental cists. In contrast to Neolithic practice in Western Europe, the process was completely haphazard. In this case the images were no longer treated with any respect.

THE PARADOX OF PYGMALION

In Classical legend the sculptor Pygmalion fell in love with his statue of Galatea and asked the goddess Aphrodite to bring her to life. Alfred Gell's book *Art and Agency* addresses a similar problem (Gell 1998: chapter 7). Why are idols treated like living beings, how are they animated, and how can they influence human conduct?

These are important issues, but to a large extent Gell's discussion depends on ethnographic or historical sources and is not of much assistance in considering archaeological material. On the other hand, it provides a reminder, if reminder is needed, that in many societies statues are not merely *depictions* of people, they are living creatures. They are animated, not inert. Their well-being must be protected, and their vitality has to be sustained. It is unfortunate that these processes may not be reflected in the archaeological record. It is necessary to approach the question obliquely.

Gell's discussion is about the nature of idols, and his main concern is with the agency which they share with other works of art. Although his argument is among the most abstract in his book, it makes one point that might be particularly helpful in an archaeological analysis. He tells the reader that not all idols are figurative. There are many that do not resemble any living form, and yet they have similar properties and exercise similar powers. That is surely significant for an account which features menhirs which have undergone minimal modification. In such cases any resemblance to the human form might be entirely fortuitous. Gell's argument raises the possibility that unmodified stones might have possessed the same properties.

In the light of that observation any component of a stone-built tomb could have been treated as a living being. In principle so could any menhir. The point is especially significant in areas that are without 'megalithic art'. Here there is another possibility to consider. Were certain rocks endowed with special powers because of their shapes, colours, textures or mineral inclusions? This certainly seems to have been the case in Northern Europe where the orthostats employed in the construction of megalithic tombs appear to have been put on display (Scarre 2004a, b). Their shapes were certainly distinctive, and their individuality was enhanced because the uprights were separated from one another by panels of walling. At times the effect was enhanced by the use of coloured stone. Something similar may have happened on the west coast of Sweden where the raw material for building chambered tombs was immediately to hand, but in this case the shapes of the rocks seem to have been less important than their colouring and the mineral veins exposed in the surface of the stone. They included natural arcs, zigzags, and even spirals that are not unlike the designs created by painting and carving in other parts of Europe (Bradley and Phillips 2008). It would be wrong to make too much of this distinction, as similar considerations seem to have influenced the selection and deployment of raw materials even in areas that are well known for their decorated passage graves. That is particularly true of sites in north-west France where similar patterns extend not only to chambered tombs, but also to alignments of menhirs (Scarre 2004a, b). For that reason the prehistorian's conception of a 'megalithic art' is perhaps too narrow. It might be more productive to consider the treatment of different kinds of rocks on the same terms, so that orthostats which were chosen for their appearance are studied in exactly the same ways as those few that were painted or carved.

There is another lesson to be drawn from Gell's analysis. It may not be possible to discover the processes by which idols were animated in prehistoric times, but his account illustrates the close relationship between such images and the audiences who encountered them. Statues had to be looked after like human beings. It was an active process, for they were not created simply as subjects for contemplation. Gell talks about the ways in which images are visited, embellished, and even fed. Were their prehistoric counterparts the focus for offerings, like the artefacts placed in a grave?

It is also necessary to investigate the biographies of these stones. Here archaeology comes into its own. It may be without the kinds of evidence on which Gell's account is based, but it can pursue other objectives. Perhaps it should be studying the relationships *between the statues themselves*. They are sometimes found in groups, often in circular settings or alignments. Were they erected simultaneously, or was this a cumulative process. As new examples were raised, were others taken down? There is some evidence from the southern Alps to suggest that both these processes were important, and several of the statues at Aosta were set in the same foundation trench (Mezzena 1998). Were certain images created in relation to others because they represented the links between different people, in the past or even in the present? Could the files of statues have recorded a genealogy? That has been suggested at Sion. Were older images replaced or even obliterated as the descent line changed, or did this happen when the dead were transformed into ancestors in the way that has been suggested for north-west France? These are difficult questions, but they cannot be approached in the first place unless such issues are investigated in the field (Lyon Crawford 2007). The chronological and spatial relationships between the carvings are just as important as those between the burials in a cemetery, and in future they deserve to be studied in the same amount of detail.

The title of this chapter refers to 'the lives of statues'. It is certainly important to consider who would have seen these images and how they might have reacted to them, but it is no less revealing to investigate how the histories of the sculptures changed and the unexpected ways in which they were treated over time. It is a challenge that archaeologists are well equipped to meet.

5

In Open Country

MEGALITHIC ART AND THE WIDER WORLD

The conventional term 'megalithic art' raises many problems. Some have been addressed in Chapters 3 and 4, and more of them will be considered here. These difficulties arise for three main reasons. Despite the claims of early scholars, it lacks a single style of imagery and is defined almost entirely by the contexts in which it is found. At the same time, the decorated panels can be entirely abstract and might have made quite different references from naturalistic designs. Even in areas where the same motifs were shared between separate tombs, they could be organized in very different ways. It is not a promising starting point for research.

Further problems have arisen since this tradition was first defined. The decorated tombs are architecturally and chronologically diverse, and it seems possible that the selection of raw materials for building them was especially important. Indeed, it is hard to make a categorical distinction between those monuments which created a striking impression through the colours, shapes and surface appearance of the building stones and those in which an equally striking visual effect was achieved by paintings and carvings.

Another reason for questioning the existence of a discrete category of megalithic art is the way in which its repertoire overlaps with images found in the open air. This provided the subject matter of Chapter 4, which studied the complicated relationship between statues and designs within the tombs. If complete or fragmentary menhirs were incorporated in these structures, are they to be described as 'megalithic art'? How far can the category extend before it loses any meaning?

This chapter examines the wider relations of tomb decoration at an even larger scale. It considers the relationship between the motifs associated with megaliths and the decoration on portable artefacts. It comments on the possible links between the designs inside passage graves and those in domestic buildings, and it studies the connections between the images associated with monuments and those in natural places like cliffs, caves, outcrops, and rock shelters. How were these sites used, and who were the audiences for the paintings and carvings that were made there?

IMAGES, ARTEFACTS, AND HOUSES

One of the most obvious connections between tomb decoration and the design of portable artefacts is illustrated by the engraved plaques discussed in Chapter 4. Although their appearance is extremely distinctive, they can be compared with other objects dating from the Copper Age (Lillios 2002). Their characteristic decoration extends to a series of decorated crooks which share similar associations, while a few of the plaques have eyes which recall the *occuli* found in southern Spain (García Atíenzar 2006).

Occuli show other links (García Atíenzar 2006). They take a variety of different forms and are present in chambered tombs and walled settlements, but do not appear in megalithic art. Instead they feature in the paintings found in caves and rock shelters, some of which are located outside the distribution of funerary monuments. The same motif also occurs together with drawings of deer and the sun on the pottery known as *symbolkeramik* (Figure 34; Martín and Camalich 1982; Domingo, Roldán, Ferrero, and García 2007) and also on the clay plaques from the Copper Age fortified site of Vila Nova de São Pedro, in Portugal (Figure 35; Paço 1940). The cross references between these different media have rarely been discussed, but they would have been important to the people allowed inside the tombs. Were they

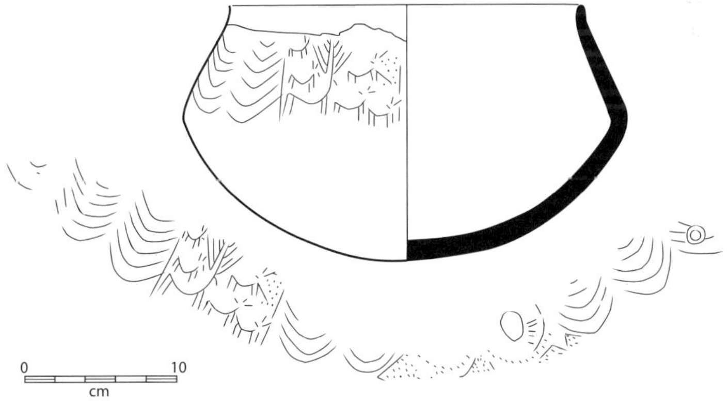

Figure 34. *Symbolkeramik* from southern Spain, featuring animals and other designs shared with Iberian Schematic Art.

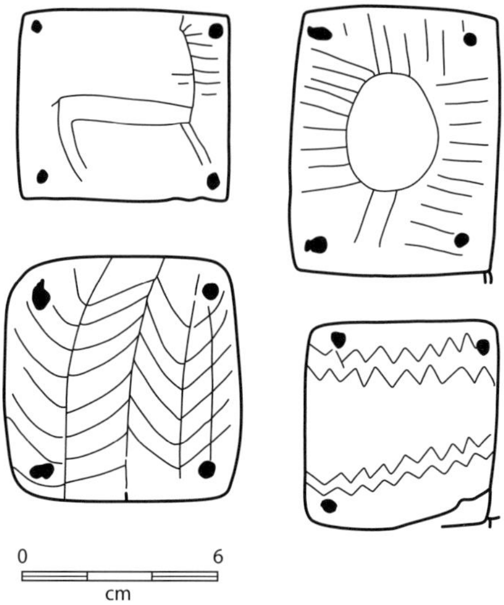

Figure 35. Decorated plaques from the fortified settlement of Vila Nova de São Pedro, Portugal featuring similar designs to Iberian Schematic Art.

associated with particular individuals, or with particular activities? Did their presence at enclosed sites lend them a special status? What made them such appropriate offerings for the dead?

Like its Iberian counterpart, Breton megalithic art recalls pottery decoration. Some of the most striking images associated with the tombs—and with the freestanding sculptures whose remains were built into these structures—were the crook, already described, and a pair of animal horns described by the term *bucrania.* Both were depicted on ceramic vessels, and horns were also represented by stone artefacts (Cassen and L'Helgouach 1992; Le Roux 1992). Both designs have a wide distribution, in the tombs and beyond. In this case they transgress three different media: portable sculptures, tomb decoration, and ceramics.

A similar set of connections is evident in Orkney where some of the earlier tombs were flanked by drystone walling constructed in a distinctive herring-bone pattern. The same design is found on the decorated pottery (*Unstan bowls*) associated with these sites (Davidson and Henshall 1989: 30–1). In the following period when passage graves were built, local ceramics changed and a new tradition was adopted. The earlier vessels in this style (*Grooved Ware*) were decorated with incised motifs very like those inside the local tombs (Bradley, Phillips, Richards, and Webb 2001). They also occur on a series of stone plaques and other artefacts which have been found at a small number of sites across Britain (Figure 36). The later ceramics in Orkney include

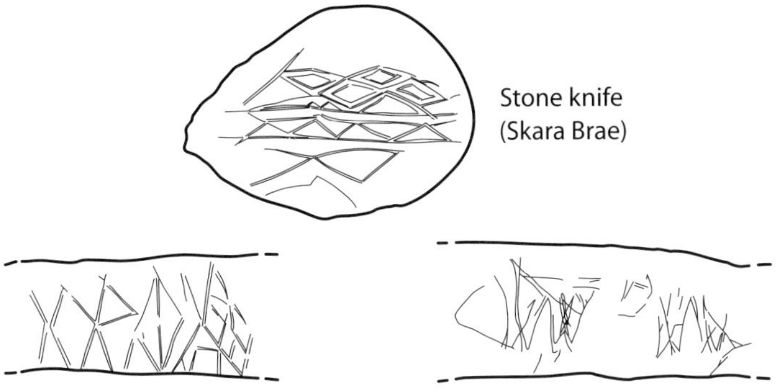

Figure 36. Linear designs associated with Neolithic houses, artefacts, and tombs in Orkney.

more plastic decoration, and again this is reflected by the designs in passage graves. There are striking links between these different media. The most characteristic motif among the later monuments in Orkney is usually described as a 'horned spiral'. It has also been identified on portable artefacts, ceramics and open-air rock carvings (Bradley 1997a: fig. 7.3). Other vessels in this style feature a distinctive rosette which they share with Irish passage graves. As happens in the monuments of north-west France, there is a significant overlap between decorated pottery and megalithic art.

Even where formal decoration is not found in megalithic tombs, it may be present in other media. The passage graves of Denmark and Sweden illustrate this point. They lack any paintings, and the only carved decoration consists of cup marks on the exposed upper surface of the capstone. Kaul (1997) has identified a number of small stone plaques which carry incised decoration executed in a similar style to Western European megaliths, but most of them are associated with other kinds of monuments. Numerous decorated vessels were deposited outside Scandinavian passage graves. They probably accumulated during feasts to commemorate the dead, but in this case ceramics seem to have provided a focus for visual elaboration rather than the architecture itself. The finest vessels of the Funnel Beaker Culture may have been the 'megalithic art' of Northern Europe.

The same style of pottery is associated with settlements. This is not the only link between the visual images associated with death and those connected with the living. Laporte and Tinevez (2004) have reconsidered the traditional argument that megalithic tombs were designed as houses of the dead. Not only were they the places where human bodies came to rest, their architecture was based on the forms of domestic buildings. This is a familiar argument in the case of long barrows and long mounds, but these authors break new ground in drawing attention to a series of circular dwellings along the Atlantic coastline which may have provided a source of inspiration for passage graves. Does the evidence of megalithic art add anything to this equation?

Again there is some evidence from Neolithic Orkney, where a series of domestic buildings has been excavated. They feature in the article by Laporte and Thivenez. Following earlier writers, they argue that the earlier megaliths, which have elongated chambers subdivided by slabs, resemble the plans of the dwellings of the same period. The idea seems convincing, but neither group of buildings has any decoration. They also claim that the later tombs of Maeshowe type show the same organization of space as the Neolithic structures at Skara Brae and other sites. The link with tomb architecture is strengthened by a recent discovery. Ever since the work of Gordon Childe at Skara Brae it has been recognized that the houses on the site, and some of the passages communicating between them, were decorated with linear motifs (Figure 36). Other examples have been identified at the settlements of Pool, Barnhouse, and Ness of Brodgar (Shee Twohig 1997; Shepherd 2000; Nick Card pers. comm.). Not long ago a survey of the later passage graves of Orkney identified strikingly similar designs in all the accessible and well preserved monuments. The same motifs were used to embellish both the houses and the tombs. The connection is even more compelling as these designs mark important thresholds in the architecture of both kinds of building (Bradley, Phillips, Richards, and Webb 2001).

TOMB ART AND OPEN-AIR ROCK ART

It is sometimes suggested that the decoration associated with megalithic tombs belongs to wider traditions of rock art which are also represented in the open air. It is an argument that has received some support in Portugal and Spain (Bueno Ramírez and Behrmann Balbín 2006c), and one which has also been advanced to explain the distinctive imagery found in Britain and Ireland (Bradley 1997). Before discussing those possible connections in detail, it is necessary to consider the distributions of these different styles.

The first point to make is that megalithic art does not coexist with open-air rock art in every region. On a local level their distributions may not coincide, as is probably the case in Orkney. There are larger areas over which the images found in the decorated tombs lack any counterparts in the wider landscape.

In north-west France, for example, cup marks are the commonest motifs on natural outcrops, but they are rare inside the chambered tombs (Le Quellec 2006). There is little to show whether these two traditions of stone carving had much in common, or even whether they were contemporary with one another. If the distribution of megalithic art overlaps with that of rock art in Britain, Ireland, Portugal, and Spain, the French evidence shows that such a connection is by no means universal.

Secondly, there are regions of Europe in which megalithic tombs—and, in particular, passage graves—were apparently undecorated. That certainly applies to Southern Scandinavia where the only carved motifs were the cup marks on the capstone. This is interesting, as there is little evidence for a tradition of open-air petroglyphs during the period in which these structures were built. Attempts to recognize motifs shared with Irish passage tombs have not attracted much support, as the Northern European images seem to date from the Bronze Age (Soggnes 1995). In a widely quoted article by Eva and Per Fett (1979) those few designs have been taken out of context and form parts of larger panels.

A third kind of relationship is more revealing. There is little doubt that some of the images associated with Iberian passage tombs resemble those painted and carved in the wider landscape. It even seems possible that the oldest pre-dated the building of the monuments. Such evidence must be treated with caution, for in some cases the chronological evidence is meagre. Even so, it is clear that in the south of Spain images were being painted in caves and rock shelters from the very beginning of the Neolithic period. That is because they also feature in the decoration on the earliest pottery. Radiocarbon dates suggest that the widely distributed tradition of Iberian *Schematic Art* was represented on ceramics up to 500 years before it first appeared in tombs (Martínez García 2006). Moreover, it continued to be made in natural places for some time after the building of passage graves had lapsed. Again ceramic chronology provides a vital clue, for a few of the most characteristic elements in this tradition were used to decorate Bell Beakers (Delibes de Castro and Guerra Doce 2004).

Iberian Schematic Art is widely distributed, and, like its counterpart inside the tombs, it could be executed as paintings or carvings, and sometimes in both media. Like megalithic art, the survival of pigment is influenced by the local climate so that painted images seem to be more common in the south of the Iberian Peninsula and carvings in the north (Martínez García 2006; Gómez Barrera 2006). On the other hand, its distribution is much wider than that of decorated tombs. It is more abundant then megalithic art along the north coast of Spain and is a particular feature of those parts of the south-east in which chambered tombs were never built. In fact its distribution extends to caves and rock shelters on the Mediterranean coast of France (Hameau 2003). Despite the presence of similar motifs at passage graves and in the wider landscape, their distributions were not the same.

That is equally apparent from the archaeology of north-west Iberia where a distinctive series of petroglyphs comprise the 'Galician' style of rock carvings (Peña Santos and Rey García 1999; Santos Estévez 2005). It is not well dated, but its currency seems to have overlapped with the history of Schematic Art, and probably with the later use of megalithic tombs. This style is distributed across an area in which Schematic Art is virtually absent and has little in common with the designs inside the passage graves. While the megalithic art in this region can be compared with the decoration of tombs in northern Portugal, its only link with other media is with a few cist slabs which may be later in date (Alves in press). Like the statue menhirs discussed in Chapter 4, they were probably contemporary with the earliest metalwork in the region.

It seems as though there are only two parts of Europe in which it is possible to compare the repertoire of megalithic art with the paintings or carvings created in the wider landscape. Towards the northern limit of its distribution there are potential connections between the passage grave art of Britain and Ireland and the rock carvings that have been studied during recent years. To the south, there may be similar links between some of the key elements in Iberian megalithic art and the repertoire of Schematic Art. No such studies are possible in northern or western France where open-air petroglyphs are rare and poorly dated, while in Galicia and parts of northern Portugal there is little overlap between the decoration found in passage graves and the carved rocks of the same region. At present it is not clear whether this is has chronological implications, but the fact that Galician rock art and Schematic Art have complementary distributions suggests that their histories overlapped (Alves in press).

On one level these relationships undermine any notion of a distinct style—or styles—of megalithic art. In certain cases it is obvious that the images on tomb walls coexisted with menhirs depicting the human form. Other designs were closely related to those in different locations, but that says very little about the contexts in which they were used. Here some important clues come from comparing the designs found inside the monuments with those distributed across the wider landscape. The following discussion begins with Iberian Schematic Art, which is partly figurative, before turning to the abstract rock art of Ireland and Britain.

OPEN-AIR ART AND MEGALITHIC ART: THE IBERIAN PENINSULA

Schematic Art is difficult to characterize (Hernández Perez 2006; Martínez García 2006). That is hardly surprising since it had such an extensive distribution across space and time. It seems most unlikely that its repertoire remained stable between the Early Neolithic period and the Copper Age, but at present there are few fixed points on which to base any detailed analysis. It is ironic that the best way of studying its evolution may be though comparison with the designs in megalithic tombs. They can also be compared with decorated pottery (Figure 37).

Its repertoire is varied, although the research of Pilar Acosta (1968) shows that some design elements were more widely distributed than others. As the name suggests, the motifs are rather stylized, but among the commoner elements are human beings (often men), animals (frequently deer), handprints, occuli, and drawings of the sun. They are accompanied by a variety of non-figurative designs (Figure 37). The motifs were of several sizes; sometimes they are conspicuous, but more often they are difficult to find. Their distribution is correspondingly varied. The painted and carved sites can occur in groups, but some seem to be genuinely isolated. They are found in many different settings. The decorated surfaces were on river banks, outcrops, cliffs or ledges and were frequently located inside caves and rock shelters (Figure 38). Sometimes the stone was selected because of its colour, or even because it contained distinctive mineral inclusions (Diaz-Andreu 2002; Alves 2002). Many of the sites overlooked large tracts of lower ground, but not all the paintings and carvings were readily accessible (Figure 39). This is rarely discussed in published accounts which tend to place more emphasis on the designs than the local topography. That is particularly true of Henri Breuil's studies of Schematic Art (Breuil 1933–5). Nevertheless it is revealing that so many of his photographs contain a ladder.

Only a small proportion of these sites preserve archaeological deposits, and those that have been excavated are very varied. They often include finds of pottery and stone tools, although the later examples can also contain metalwork and human remains. Only in rare instances were their contents much different from the open settlements of the same period. A few decorated caves, like Buraco de Pala in northern Portugal (Sanches 1997) or El Pedroso across the border in Spain (Bradley, Fábregas Valcarce, Alves, and Vilaseco Vázquez 2005), were extremely prolific, but others contain few, if any artefacts.

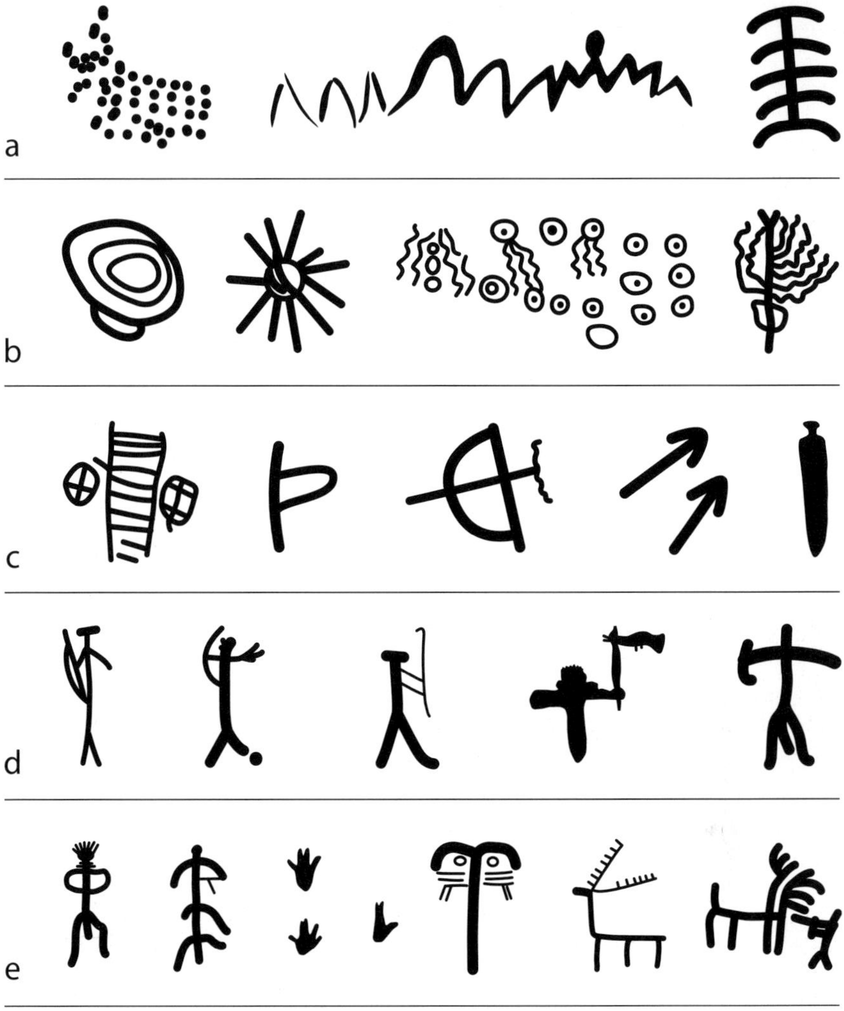

Figure 37. The repertoire of Iberian Schematic art. (a and b): apparently non-figurative motifs; (c): vehicles and weapons; (d and e): human figures, some with weapons or tools; handprints, occuli, and deer.

For that reason it may be easier to characterize these sites by considering the relationship between their locations and the images that were created there. One of the most informative studies is Sara Fairén's account of decorated sites in Valencia. During the Neolithic period there were three styles of rock art in this area—Levantine Art, Macroschematic Art, and Schematic Art—but it is clear that they were used concurrently. Images in these different traditions

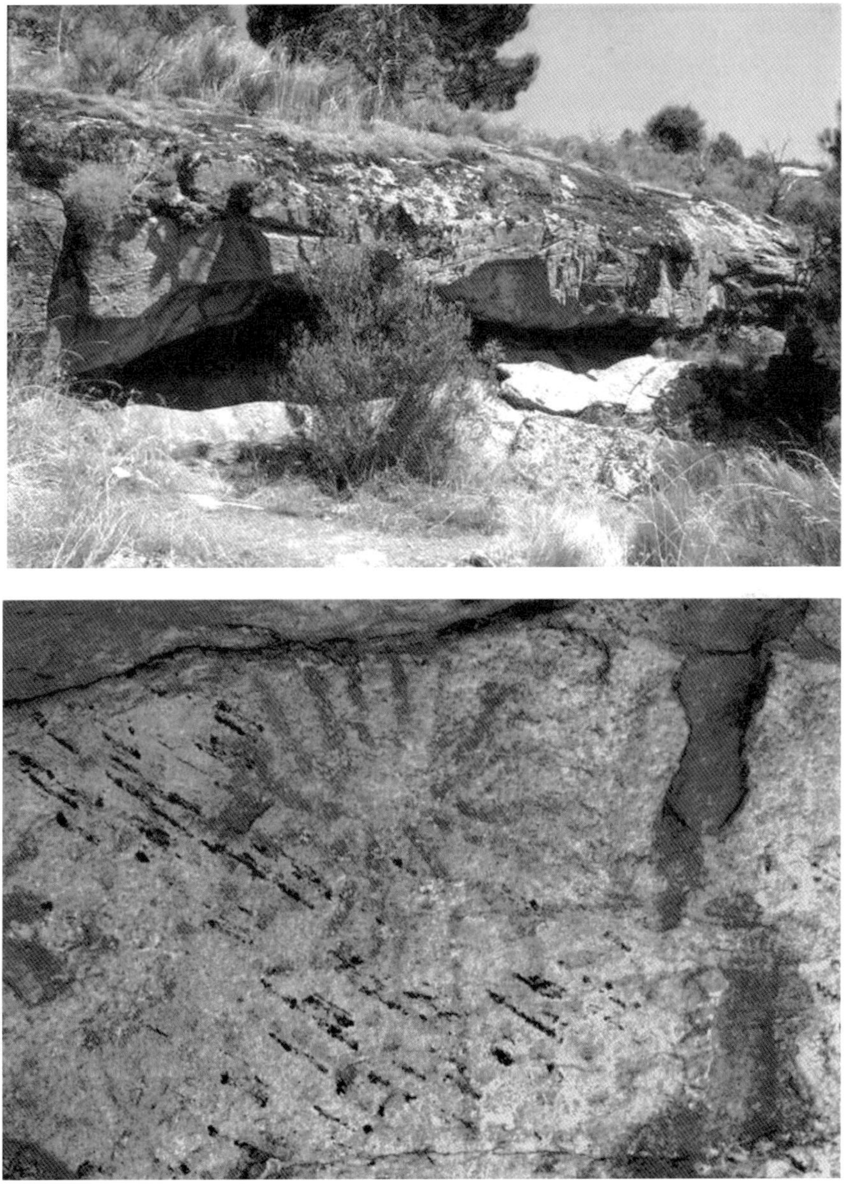

Figure 38. The decorated cave of Pala Pinta, Portugal, with a detail of a painted panel.

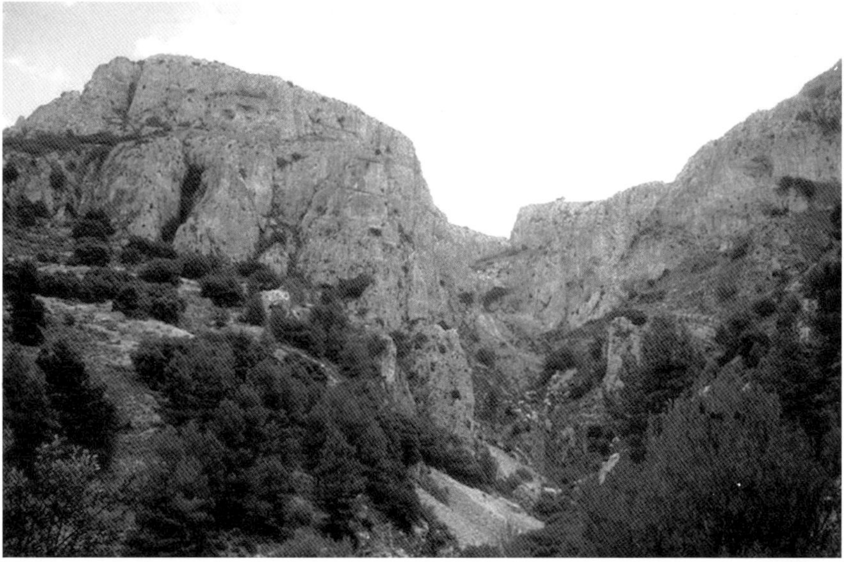

Figure 39. The location of the decorated cave with Schematic Art at Morro Carrascal, Spain.

were frequently superimposed, but the order in which they were made varied from one site to another. Fairén has classified the shelters in which the paintings are found and has considered both their size and their accessibility. Her analysis was based on a Geographic Information System. It demonstrated that while all these styles were associated with similar kinds of places, Schematic Art occurs in the most diverse locations (Fairén Jiménez 2006). Its distribution extends to sites that were particularly small and inaccessible. Schematic Art was the longest lived of the three traditions and the only one to be associated with human burials. Unlike the other styles, it was related to the images inside megalithic tombs.

Research in north-west Spain came to a similar conclusion (Bradley and Fábregas Valcarce 1998). Again it was based on comparisons between different styles of rock art, but in this case their distributions hardly overlapped. Again one was Schematic Art, while the other tradition was Galician rock art. Ramón Fábregas and the writer visited a number of sites with paintings and carvings extending along a transect leading between the areas in which each of these two groups is found. The project took in sites on either side of the modern frontier between Portugal and Spain.

The comparison was revealing. Galician petroglyphs were generally located on inconspicuous outcrops within the main part of the settled landscape.

They were often beside paths or close to natural basins which retain some moisture at the height of summer. The images were generally created on flat or gently sloping surfaces. There were more prominent rocks nearby which could have been carved instead, but that rarely happened. It was only towards the outer edge of the distribution of these designs that such conventions were relaxed, and here more use was made of larger outcrops. The images might be carved on steeper surfaces, and some of the designs incorporated elements shared with Schematic Art.

Within the distribution of Schematic Art the situation changed again. The decorated rocks were in more conspicuous positions and were further from the optimum areas for human settlement, although most of them commanded extensive views. The main rock paintings were in caves and rock shelters, or on narrow ledges in mountainous country. Sometimes they may have overlooked paths, but they were not always located beside them, and it would have required a special journey to visit these places. It would have been easier to have selected more accessible surfaces for painting and carving. Some of the main panels were in places which were difficult to find, and at times it was not obvious how to reach them. Moreover, the space in front of the images could not have accommodated many people, nor could large groups have travelled there. It seemed as if access to some of the decorated rocks might have been restricted.

In fact the sites studied in the course of this project showed considerable diversity. Some of the more accessible panels were actually among the simpler ones, while there was more ornate decoration and a greater variety of images in locations which could not have contained large numbers of people. Even the range of pigments was greater there, suggesting that the contents of the paintings changed according to their positions in the landscape.

Another important study took place on the Spanish Portuguese border in the valley of the River Tagus (Bueno Ramirez, Balbín Behrmann, and Barroso Bermajo 2004; Bueno Ramírez, Barroso Bermajo, Balbín Behrmann, and Carrera Ramírez 2006). This considered all the surviving components of the earlier prehistoric landscape, but for present purposes its most significant elements were rock carvings, paintings, and decorated tombs. Freestanding menhirs were also recorded in the survey.

The tombs were situated on the flanks of the valley in similar positions to the settlements. The locations of occupation sites were also indicated by a series of cup-marked rocks. On the highest ground there were painted rock shelters and caves which featured a considerable number of human figures. By contrast, the main series of carvings was beside the river where the motifs were generally on red stone. They contained a mixture of naturalistic and abstract images, the most prominent of which were on vertical surfaces and featured human figures. The petroglyphs also included hunting scenes and drawings of the sun. The decorated panels were usually near to places where it would be possible to cross the water.

Thus it is clear that there were important variations within Schematic Art. It is equally apparent from a new study of rock paintings in Aragon conducted by Philippe Hameau and Albert Painaud (2006), who have examined a series of caves and shelters. All these sites faced south and again they commanded extensive views, but the painted surfaces seem to have been selected because of the unusual colour of the bedrock. The majority were distributed in a compact group at the confluence of two rivers, but the local topography meant that it would have been necessary to pass certain of these places in order to reach the others. The more accessible shelters were also the larger ones but were not intensely decorated. Despite their size, they contained few painted motifs. The more distant sites, on the other hand, were less extensive and yet they had been embellished on a lavish scale. The paintings were more elaborate and more varied, yet less space was available there, and fewer people would have been able to see them. The conclusions reached by Hameau and Painaud reflect those of Fairén's study. They are also consistent with the results of fieldwork carried out on the border of Portugal and Spain.

How should these observations be interpreted, and what light can they shed on the roles of megalithic art? It is obvious that the paintings and carvings that comprise Schematic Art were not accessible to everyone. Although some examples were beside major rivers, others were distanced from the settled area, even though a few of the images were shared with artefacts that circulated in the domestic sphere. The decorated surfaces were unlikely to be encountered by chance. Few were readily accessible and some effort would have been required in order to view them. At times that may have involved a special journey out of the familiar lowlands into more mountainous country, where the colours and textures of the decorated rocks were perhaps as important as their settings in the landscape. The topography of some of the sites also shows that the audiences for these images were rather small. It would be impossible for any number of people to have visited them at the same time. Some of the caves and shelters could not accommodate large gatherings and had to be approached along narrow paths. In both social and practical terms they were dangerous locations. It is not clear whether the same applies to the rock carvings beside major rivers like the Tagus or the Guadiana, and the question needs further research. It may be that petroglyphs had a different significance from rock paintings. Alternatively, such rivers may have marked important boundaries.

It seems as if there was a continuum among the sites associated with Schematic Art. Not all of them were so difficult to find, but there are cases in which it was the smaller or more remote examples that carried the greatest significance. They could contain fewer people than the others, and yet they might be embellished with the most complex images. If those images were intended as a source of information, the most powerful messages must have been directed to the more restricted audiences. Indeed, they were occasionally reserved for those who had made the greatest effort to receive them. It is not clear how most of these places were used, but there are certain clues. A site like El Pedroso seems to have witnessed the preparation and consumption of food (Bradley, Fábregas Valcarce, Alves, and Vilaseco Vázquez 2005) A few caves in earlier prehistoric Iberia have produced the remains of hallucinogenic plants (Guerra Doce 2002 and 2003), and many more are associated with burials. Their use as cemeteries postdates the general currency of megalithic tombs (Soler Díaz 2002).

Further clues are provided by the subject matter of the paintings and carvings. The figurative elements seem to emphasize the importance of men and, in particular, their role as hunters. Weapons are shown occasionally, and, in common with Galician rock art, the images place a special emphasis on stags. It is true that the sites are ideally located for watching the movement of game, but they are often too isolated to have been used as hunting stands. The sun also features in many of the scenes, and that may explain why the images studied by Hameau and Painaud (2006) face towards the south. It meant that they might be illuminated during the course of the day, but it also ensured that these places were not as cold and damp as might otherwise have been the case.

The abstract elements are still more difficult to interpret, but certain of them share features in common with the entoptic imagery discussed by Lewis-Williams and Dowson (1988). In fact both groups of motifs often shade into one another, so that there is no clear-cut distinction between the naturalistic and abstract elements in these panels. That is important, for not all these designs would have been comprehensible to strangers. Their significance would need to be explained, and that information could be offered or withheld. The decorated surfaces may have played a part in many different transactions, including initiation ceremonies or other rites of passage. The obvious emphasis on masculinity suggests a comparison with the vision quest undergone by young men before they became full members of society (Whitley, Dorn, Simon, Rechtman, and Whitley 1999).

One way of thinking about this evidence is to suppose that admission to the sites was not readily available. It may have been restricted not only by the siting of the images but also by their subject matter. To see them might involve an arduous journey, and it is clear that in two different senses the most complex images were often inaccessible. They could be created in places that were difficult to find, and they seem to have been directed to the smallest audiences.

These observations can shed some light on the character of the decorated tombs in the Iberian Peninsula. It used to be supposed that passage graves were conceived as artificial caves, but there are problems with this argument. Cave burials are commonly found outside the distribution of these monuments, and the majority are later in date (Soler Díaz 2002). While the passage graves were embellished in a style that recalls the treatment of natural places, it is not clear whether both kinds of sites were used in mortuary ritual. The presence of similar artefacts in each of these contexts cannot shed light on the question as they are also known from settlements.

Where the comparison is much more helpful is in considering the audience for the images. Like so many of the places featuring Schematic rock art, the interiors of chambered tombs were remote and inaccessible. They could also be cold and dark, and could never have admitted many people. The links between the images displayed in these different contexts suggest that their roles were similar to one another; the major difference is that those who built the tombs were more concerned with the dead and the past, while a plausible interpretation of some of the decorated caves and rock shelters is that they were directed towards the living and the future roles of particular individuals. It seems likely that they were created and inspected by a restricted section of society. The emphasis on male figures, male animals, and hunting scenes might suggest that they were used for initiation. What Spanish archaeologists call 'tumbas de corredor' are known in English as 'passage graves'. That term is unconsciously revealing, for it seems as if both styles of 'art' played a role in the rites of passage. Perhaps one group of sites recorded the entry of certain individuals into the wider community, while the other signified their demise and the beginning of a new role as ancestors.

OPEN-AIR ART AND MEGALITHIC ART: IRELAND AND BRITAIN

This is the other region of Europe in which it is possible to compare the decoration of megalithic tombs with images in the natural landscape. In this case there are no paintings, although it does seem possible that the incised motifs on the walls of Orkney passage graves once defined areas of pigment (Bradley, Phillips, Richards, and Webb 2001). With that exception, all the images were carved. As mentioned earlier, they were also abstract (Figure 40).

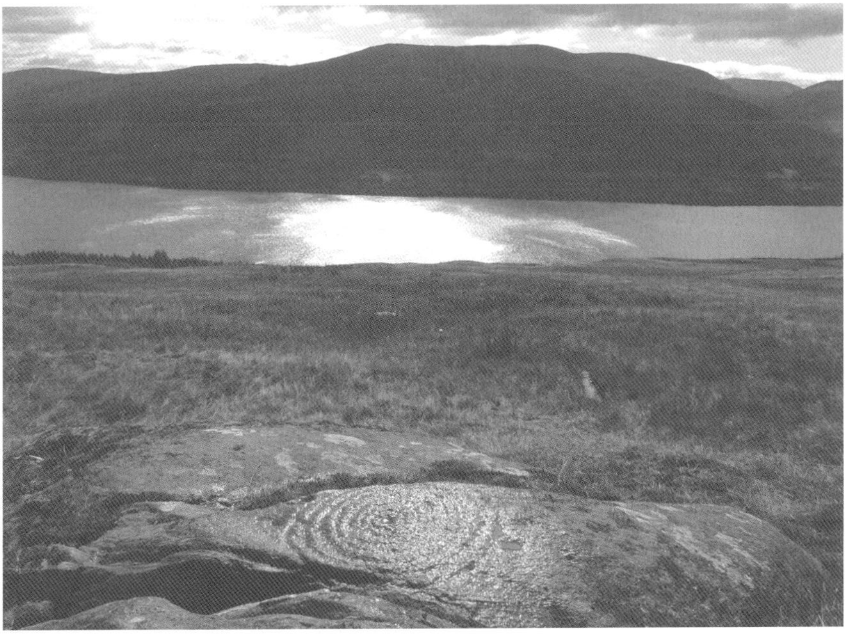

Figure 40. Carved decoration on Ben Lawers, Scotland.

Most of the megalithic art discussed in this section is found in a limited number of Irish tombs, although there are a few additional examples in Britain. Open-air rock art, on the other hand, is much more widely distributed and is mainly a feature of Ireland, Scotland, and northern England (Bradley 1997a: chapter 5; Beckensall 1999 and 2006). It is by no means clear whether these groups of images should be regarded as two separate styles. Although they share a few comparatively rare motifs (Johnston 1993), it is hard to understand why this small region of Europe should have seen the independent development of two traditions of stone carving, both of which are non-figurative and both of which employ curvilinear designs. Moreover, their chronologies may be poorly understood, but most authorities are satisfied that they overlap. Much has been written about which tradition developed first and exactly when that happened. At the moment it remains unknown(Bradley 1997a: chapter 4; Waddington 2007).

The problem is a simple one. The decoration inside passage tombs can be dated by its association with these buildings and with the artefacts found there. The evidence suggests that Irish megalithic art developed in the mid to late fourth millennium BC and continued in use until the early third millennium.

At present the only direct dating evidence from Britain comes from Orkney, but it is consistent with that scheme. Open-air rock art, on the other hand, was certainly long lived. Fragments of carved stone are known in association with Early Bronze Age burials, but most of them seem to be reused and may have been quarried from already-decorated outcrops: a practice for which there is good field evidence. On the other hand, the fact that certain motifs rather than others were selected for this purpose suggests that they retained their significance over a considerable period of time. It is still more striking that the images that were employed in secondary contexts were often those with affinities in megalithic art (Bradley 1997a: chapter 9).

The origin of open-air rock art is harder to determine, and here there have been differences of opinion. Most writers now agree that it developed during the Neolithic period, rather than the Bronze Age as had once been supposed, but a precise date is difficult to define (Waddington 2007). The links between rock carvings and pottery decoration would suggest a date around 3000 BC, while its overlap with Irish megalithic art might favour an earlier beginning. So would its occasional associations with diagnostic artefacts and monuments, although none is entirely satisfactory. For the purposes of this account it is enough to suggest that both groups of carvings ran in parallel, although open-air rock art clearly continued to be made over a longer period.

Unlike the Schematic Art of the Iberian Peninsula, British and Irish rock art is generally accessible and is often found in upland areas with Neolithic settlements and monuments. It is most common on level surfaces and made use of outcrops and boulders. It was seldom created on especially conspicuous rocks, although some occur nearby (Bradley 1997a: chapters 5 and 6). Most of the designs faced the sun. They are almost entirely curvilinear and can be arranged along a continuum from cup marks to circular enclosures with those motifs at their centre. The circular designs are often breached by a radial line and comprise between one and eight concentric rings. Where there were multiple circles, the motifs tend to be linked together in a more complex pattern, but simpler designs are much more frequent. In this case the cups are enclosed by a modest number of rings, and often by none at all. There are few cases in which such designs were superimposed on one another, making chronological studies even more problematical.

The carved rocks often show a broad gradation according to the topography, the local pattern of settlement or the presence of ceremonial centres (Bradley 1997a: chapters 6 and 7). The pattern changes from one region to another, but there are cases in which the simple designs dominated by cup marks are associated with lower ground than the other images. In the same way, the more ornate carvings featuring multiple rings tend to be found towards the edges of the settled land, often overlooking the surrounding area. The same contrast can be influenced by the presence of major monuments, such as stone circles or the earthwork enclosures known as *henges*. The visual complexity of the rock carvings increases in the vicinity of such sites and is reduced with distance away from them. The most elaborate designs overlook the routes leading towards ceremonial centres, like those at Kilmartin in the west of Scotland or the Milfield Basin in north-east England. On the other hand, the individual designs are far from uniform, and these tendencies describe only the extremes in a wider range of variation. Thus cup-marked rocks can be found alongside more complex carvings on the higher ground. They also occur amidst the main monuments of the same period.

It is not clear how the carved rocks were used, but recent research shows that they were not entirely isolated. Work at two sites in Scotland suggests that the choice of motifs on individual sites may also have been influenced by the characteristics of the rocks on which they were made. At Kilmartin the designs were mostly on surfaces that had been modified by natural agencies; they included natural cracks and channels, as well as veins of quartz (Jones 2005). On Ben Lawers in the southern Highlands, the carved designs enhanced the natural topography of the outcrops, so that a domed rock was surmounted by a series of concentric rings, while the edges of a natural basin in the surface of another stone provided the focus for a different set of images. In turn those designs were closely related to the positions of deposits of worked and broken quartz. Fieldwork conducted by the writer and Aaron Watson in 2007 showed that they were placed around the base of the rock that had been enclosed by rings (Figure 40), some of them on a platform which had been built for the purpose, while the hollow in the surface of the neighbouring outcrop was the focus for a similar group of artefacts (Figure 41). Fewer had been placed at the foot of the stone. There have not been many excavations on such sites, but recent fieldwork near Kilmartin has produced comparable results (Jones 2007a).

The best evidence for the chronology of megalithic art comes from Irish sites. It is not clear when the tradition began, but that is partly because the earliest passage tombs seem to have been in the west of Ireland where the bedrock erodes so severely that carved designs are unlikely to survive. There is more information from the Boyne Valley, where many of the images were superimposed. Muiris O'Sullivan (1986) has identified two successive ways of working the stone. An earlier 'depictive' style involved drawing motifs directly on the surface of the rock, while the later 'plastic' style was characterized by deeper three-dimensional images which formed more complex compositions moulded around the contours of the stone. More recently George Eogan (1997) has identified a series of overlays inside the main tomb at Knowth.

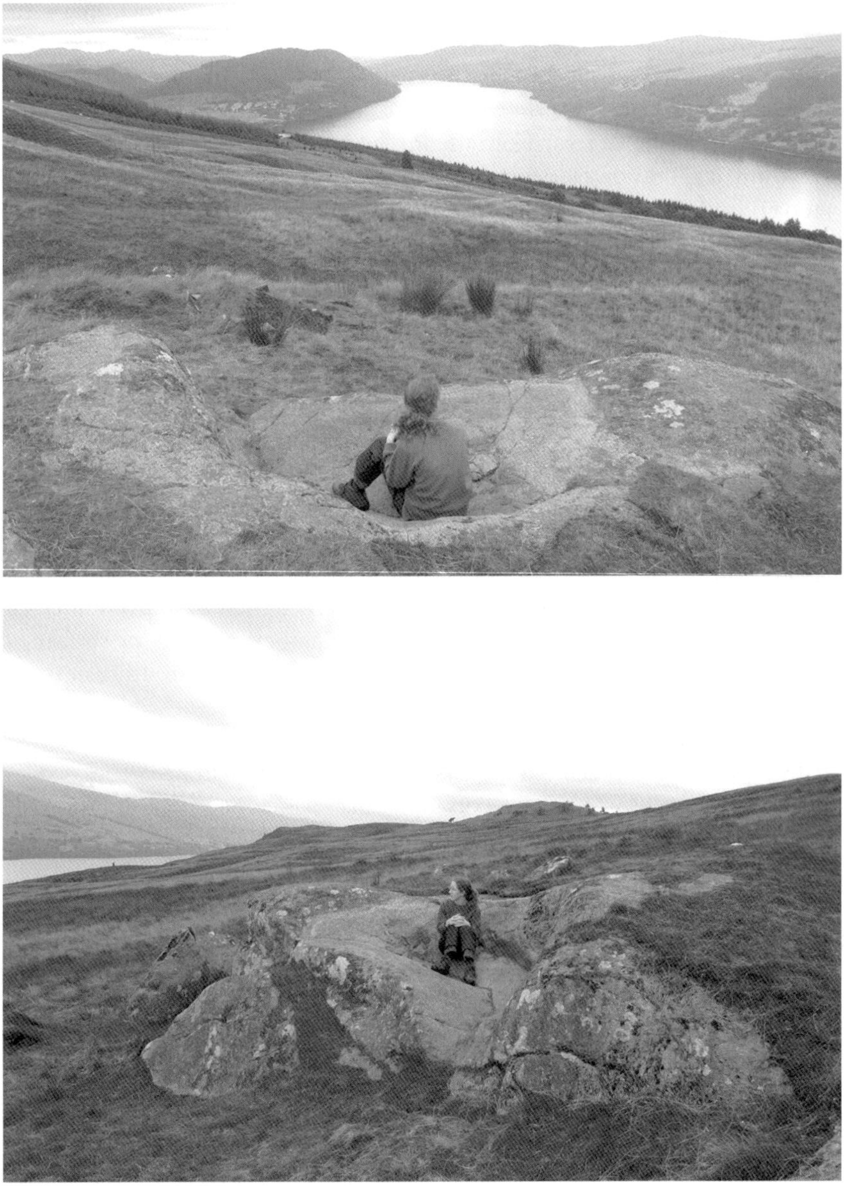

Figure 41. Two views of a decorated outcrop on Ben Lawers, Scotland. It was decorated with non-figurative designs and associated with a deposit of worked and broken quartz.

Taken in conjunction with the results of excavation, they provide the rudiments of a still more complex sequence. The earliest images were not the pecked decoration for which the site is famous, but a network of incised lines forming zigzags, triangles and chevrons. The circles, arcs and spirals that are so common in Irish megalithic art are not represented and may be a later development. They are a special feature of the outer section of the passage and the kerb delimiting the monument. Eogan (1998) believes that these structures were built afterwards, although there is curvilinear decoration on the backs of some of the stones, suggesting that they had been taken from a more ancient structure or had been decorated menhirs.

Other observations have been made in Orkney chambered tombs (Bradley, Phillips, Richards, and Webb 2001). The main designs inside the passage graves were linear patterns strikingly similar to the oldest motifs at Knowth, but in this case they also occur on the walls of Neolithic houses. They resemble the motifs associated with the earliest Grooved Ware. The later pots in this tradition have plastic decoration more akin to the pecked designs occasionally found in Orkney passage graves. Again they feature a few curvilinear elements.

Chapter 3 has already referred to the positioning of decorated panels in the Irish monuments. If Eogan (1986) is correct, the kerb of the principal monument at Knowth was built at a developed stage in the structural sequence. It follows that the associated decoration should also be late in date. This chronological evidence is significant as very few of the kerbstones at the seemingly earlier cemetery of Loughcrew had been embellished. That could be explained because those monuments are exposed to natural weathering, but another possibility is that the exteriors of these buildings were only elaborated towards the end of the Irish sequence. Although there is little to suggest that the kerbs at Newgrange and Knowth were dominated by curvilinear decoration, just outside them was a series of small circular stone settings containing numerous fragments of quartz (Bradley 1998b: 104–9). Their best parallels are arrangements of boulders laid out on the surface before they were covered by mounds. Similar features have also been identified on top of some of the smaller tombs at Knowth. In each case their configuration recalls the circular imagery associated with these extraordinary monuments.

Although most scholars concede that certain motifs are shared between megalithic art and open-air rock art, there are two objections to treating them together. Both concern major features of the designs.

The first objection is based on the use of linear decoration in megalithic art. It is certainly true that lozenges, triangles, and zigzags play a prominent part in the Irish tombs, but are rarely represented among the decoration on natural outcrops. Eogan (1997 and 1998) has suggested that they were associated with an early stage in the development of the principal monument at Knowth, and possibly with a phase before the curvilinear designs were made there. Even so, some of the angular patterns were later renewed by pecking and became a major feature of the finished structure. In one respect the evidence from Orkney is revealing. It seems possible that the oldest elements in the local passage graves were geometric motifs like those at Knowth, and that they were supplemented by curvilinear designs at a later stage. In this case the sequence depends on comparison with pottery decoration and is not based on superimposed designs inside the monuments. On the other hand, the linear motifs inside the Orkney passage graves had a specialized character and are closely comparable with those within the houses of the same date (Bradley, Phillips, Richards, and Webb 2001). Others are found on portable artefacts in the settlements there and on the Isle of Man (Burrow 1997: fig. 6.3). All the designs associated with domestic life were conceived on an intimate scale. They required close attention from the viewer and could never have been seen by many people. The same applies to the linear decoration inside the tombs. Perhaps they emphasized the links between the architecture of the dwellings and that of passage graves. There is no direct evidence of the same relationship in Ireland, but the cemetery at Knowth was certainly built over the sites of older houses (Eogan and Roche 1997).

The other motifs in Irish tombs—particularly the concentric circles and spirals—may have made other references. They occur throughout these monuments, but their closest counterparts were created on natural surfaces in the wider landscape. The same images occur in other media, so that chambered cairns, henge monuments, and settings of monoliths all adopted a circular ground plan. The contrasts with the angular designs can be revealing. Thus the interiors of the houses at Skara Brae and Barnhouse followed a rectilinear layout, while the exterior appearance of these buildings was roughly round or oval (Richards 2005). Is it possible that the linear designs associated with megalithic tombs referred to the domestic arena, whist the circular designs were associated with the world outside?

The second objection to any analysis which combines megalithic art and open-air rock carvings concerns these curvilinear motifs. Jeremy Dronfield (1996) has drawn comparisons between the circles and spirals carved at Irish megaliths and the passage leading into the chamber. He suggests that they evoke the sensation of a tunnel or vortex experienced in altered states of consciousness. Those designs are subtly different from their nearest equivalents on natural surfaces. Spirals are much more common at the passage tombs, while the circles associated with those monuments rarely have a central cup mark and are never breached by a radial line. Those are exactly the features that characterize the decorated outcrops in Britain and Ireland.

There is another way of thinking about the relationship between these designs. The radial line which is so often found with cup and ring carvings shows a path extending to the centre of the image from outside. It could represent a tunnel leading into the solid stone. This interpretation suggests that the rock face was a permeable membrane through which people could pass (Lewis-Williams and Dowson 1990). Where such a tunnel was represented by a solid structure it might be associated with circular images, but in that case there was no need to depict a passage in the design. On the other hand, where no such feature existed, it was suggested by using the convention of a circle and a radial line. It may be that these supposedly separate motifs were used to express the same idea.

To what extent can the evidence of open-air rock art illuminate the role of the decorated monuments? As happened with Iberian Schematic Art, there are similarities between these media.

The main sources of variation among the open-air rock carvings are the size and elaboration of the circular designs. They were apparently influenced by a number of different factors: their distance from the main areas of settled land; their proximity to major groups of monuments; and their positions along the routes leading towards these places. Other elements may have a made a smaller contribution. The motifs that are shared with megalithic art tend to be found on steeply sloping or vertical rocks, unlike the other petroglyphs that were normally on level surfaces. Those unusual designs may also be found in increased numbers close to monument complexes like that at Kilmartin, and can occasionally be carved on the monoliths of stone circles (Bradley 1997a: chapter 7). In each case it seems as if these designs were composed with some understanding of the wider contexts of such places within the Neolithic landscape.

At the same time, it remains unclear how such imagery is to be interpreted. The close relationship between the more complex carvings and groups of major monuments might suggest that they were addressed to a larger audience than the others. That may be so, but there is no way of telling whether the visual complexity of the motifs imparted a greater amount of information. Whether or not certain designs referred to altered states of consciousness, the fact that they were entirely abstract could have protected their meanings from strangers, conveying certain messages to the appropriate people and restricting their availability to others.

If the size and visual complexity of the circular images varied according to the contexts in which they were viewed, it seems possible that the same applies to their counterparts in megalithic art. Here the images are often larger and more ornate than those carved on natural surfaces. There is no absolute break between these separate contexts, but there is an obvious contrast. As much as anything else it was expressed by the virtuosity with which these monuments had been built and their component parts had been decorated. Alfred Gell's reference to 'enchantment' is surely apposite here.

Access to the open-air rock carvings may have been controlled by social conventions that cannot be documented by archaeology, but in the case of passage graves there could have been physical as well as intellectual restrictions on those who would encounter the images. Chapter 3 made the point that the art of the Boyne Valley passage tombs was directed towards two different audiences: the large groups who might have circulated around the decorated kerbs of these monuments, and those people who were allowed inside the passage and the chamber. Not only would they have encountered subtly different images, the designs were organized in rather different ways. Andrew Cochrane (2005 and 2006) has made the interesting point that the abstract motifs within these buildings have a fluid character; it is hard to grasp any overall design as some of the motifs are hidden, and the evidence of superimposition suggests that the array of visual images was constantly changing (Figure 42). That would be consistent with the idea that such designs referred to altered states of consciousness. The people who remained outside would not have shared these impressions, for there is less evidence that the designs on the kerb were modified. What has been interpreted as a series of successive phases in the development of megalithic art may have been a more dynamic process in which the images were always in flux. On the other hand, the superimposed designs inside the monument could still be recognized: that is how they have been identified during modern fieldwork. Andrew Jones suggests that it was one way in which past uses of the monument might have been recalled (2007b: 173–80). At the same time, the increasing use of pecking to roughen the surface of the orthostats means that each successive layer of images was obscured, and in the end some of them may have been obliterated. In a sense each set of designs receded into the past. The same might have applied to memories of the people whose remains had been buried inside these buildings.

Such arguments apply mainly to the stones in the chamber and passage. Nevertheless the interior and exterior decoration share on important characteristic, for many of the most striking images feature both angular and curvilinear motifs, which were often brought together to form unusually complex designs. If these motifs referred to the domestic sphere and the wider landscape respectively, the tombs themselves would provide a microcosm of the Neolithic world (Figure 43). Rather than presenting models of a three-tier cosmology, they may have been places where categories that were kept apart in daily life were synthesized in architectural form. Mortuary rites would provide an appropriate setting, for this was where the social order was unmade and brought into being again.

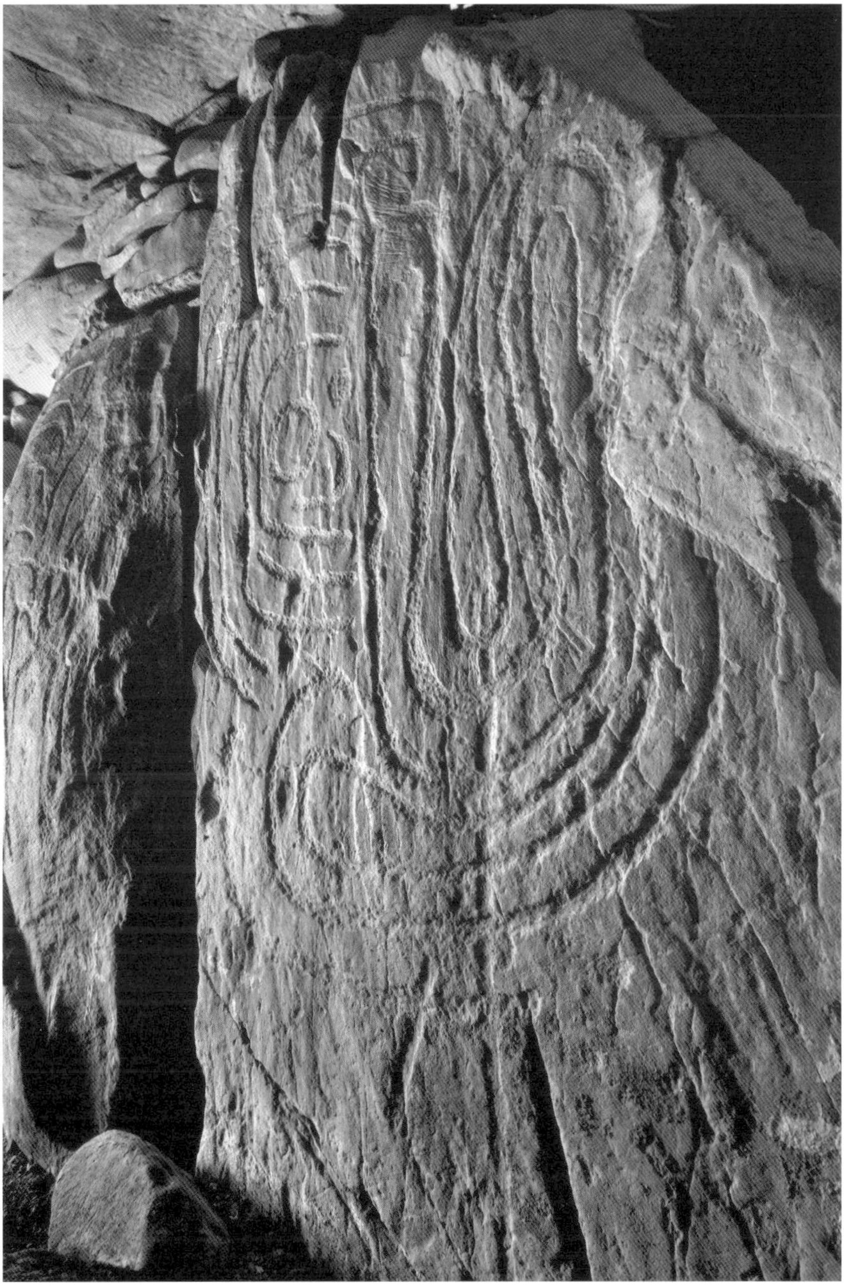

Figure 42. Pecked motif on the wall of the eastern passage of the main tomb at Knowth.

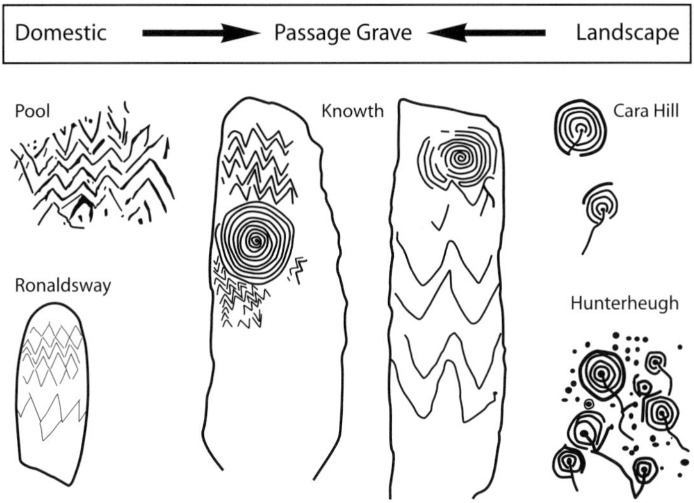

Figure 43. The megalithic art of the Boyne Valley as a synthesis of the wider world. The angular designs on the left are associated with a Neolithic house at Pool (Orkney) and with a decorated plaque from the settlement at Ronaldsway (Isle of Man). The curvilinear designs on the right are found on rock outcrops in northern Britain.

In that sense the greatest of the decorated tombs encapsulated the qualities of the landscape around them. The idea may seem far-fetched, but it would certainly explain why the tombs of the Boyne Valley incorporated raw materials that had introduced from much of the eastern seaboard of Ireland (Eogan 1999). Some of the stones were simply pebbles that could have been brought to these monuments as offerings. Others, like the great deposit of quartz at Newgrange, played a role in the design of these buildings. Again the process of creating and changing these places may have performed a vital part in public ceremony, and it could even be why so many of the structures that can be recognized today were built out of the decorated fragments of buildings that had been destroyed. That is another topic which requires more research.

This chapter—and Part II of the book—ends by emphasizing the intimate and intense relationship between the images within stone-built tombs and the people who encountered them. It is not clear that 'megalithic art' is a particularly useful term, but the juxtaposition of such evocative imagery and such extraordinary places would have provided an almost unparalleled experience in the Europe of earlier prehistory. It is right to acknowledge this, even if the archaeological evidence is still too fragmentary to take the reader very far inside the Neolithic mind.

Part III

Image and Audience in Bronze Age Scandinavia

6

Ships on Bronzes: Ships on Stones

BRONZE AGE IMAGES IN SOUTH SCANDINAVIA: A READER'S GUIDE

Part III of this book is concerned with the distinctive images created between about 1600 and 300 BC in Denmark, Sweden, and Norway. It is a study of how they were used and of the audiences who encountered them. These designs are particularly suited to this kind of analysis as they contrast in many different ways with the repertoire of megalithic art (Figure 44).

The most important contrast is that the Bronze Age images are largely figurative, in contrast to the decoration found inside Irish tombs which is abstract. That distinction is still more striking as naturalistic designs were a new development in parts of Northern Europe at the beginning of the Bronze Age. Another difference is significant, too. 'Megalithic art' is defined less by its style than by its context, although Chapter 5 showed that were some connections between the motifs associated with passage graves and those on artefacts and rock outcrops. The visual culture of the Nordic Bronze Age is even more diverse. It is represented by decorated metalwork in northern Germany, Denmark and southern Sweden (Kaul 1998). Further to the north, some of the same elements are a feature of open-air rock art (Malmer 1981), while there is more limited evidence for the use of similar designs in stone settings or geoglyphs, many of which are recorded on the Baltic island of Gotland (Artelius 1996). To some extent the distributions of all three phenomena overlap, but there are also elements which are peculiar to each of these media (Figure 45).

Few of the designs are non-figurative, although there is disagreement over the identification of individual images. It is generally accepted that among the commonest elements shared between bronze artefacts and rock carvings are boats (many of them with their crews), sun symbols, and horses. Portable artefacts also depict sea creatures, while human figures, weapons, and other species of animals are found in open-air rock art. The comparatively rare geoglyphs have a smaller repertoire and represent ships and the sun.

Although the rock carvings have attracted most attention—since 1994 those at Tanum in western Sweden have been a World Heritage Site—some

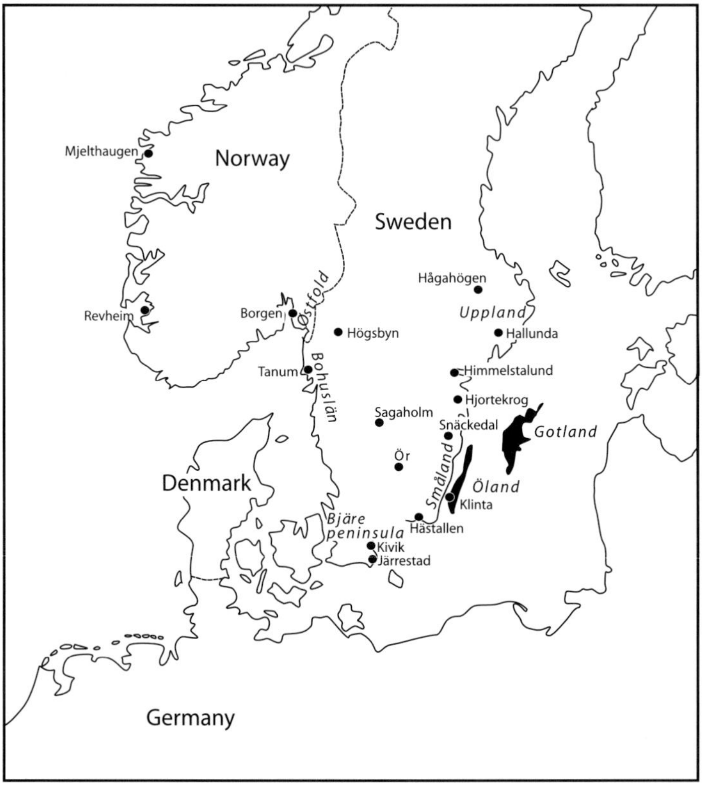

Figure 44. The sites and regions discussed in Part III.

of the most detailed studies have been of the metalwork which carries similar decoration. Many of the artefacts have been found together with other objects in graves and can be related to the chronology worked out by Oscar Montelius in the late nineteenth century (Gräslund 1987). Sometimes they can also be compared with well-dated objects in Central Europe (Kaul 1998). At the same time, it is only recently that much excavation has been undertaken at rock carvings, and so far they have provided less chronological information than had been hoped. Indeed, a number of the burnt deposits associated with these sites are rather later than the dates attributed to the images (Bengtsson 2004; Kaul 2006a). This problem has still to be resolved. At present the chronology of the petroglyphs, particularly those depicting boats, is based on comparison with the designs found on the metalwork. There are also cases in which distinctive kinds of tools or weapons are depicted on the decorated outcrops. In that case they are dated according to the same principles as the objects themselves (Malmer 1981).

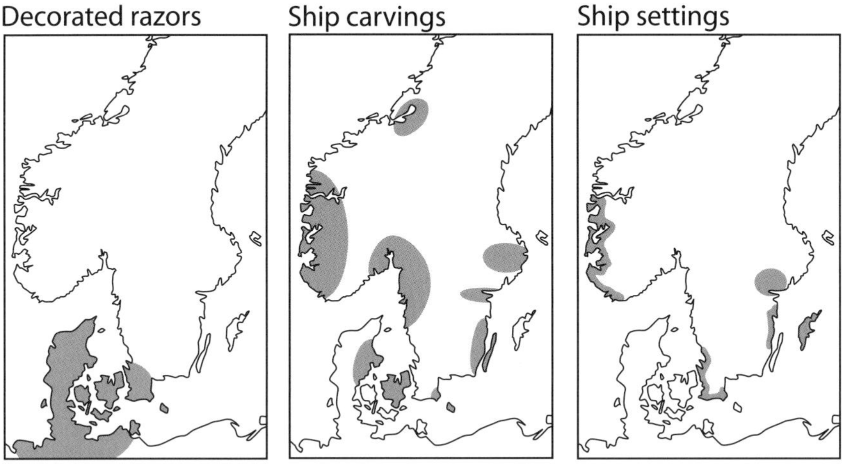

Figure 45. Outline distributions of Bronze Age decorated razors, carvings of ships, and stone ship settings in Southern Scandinavia.

The images had a very long history, extending from the beginning of the Bronze Age into the Early Iron Age, but the dating evidence is unevenly distributed. Few Early Bronze Age artefacts carry any figurative decoration, but there is enough evidence to define some types of boat which also feature among the rock carvings (Kaul 1998: chapter 6). Artefacts of the same date are depicted at these sites. Far more images date from the Late Bronze Age when they were a particular characteristic of the razors found with cremation burials. The designs have been compared with those on metal artefacts in north Germany and Central Europe, but again they also occur in rock art. Most of the stone settings depicting ships and the sun were constructed during the same period (Kaul 2004). The rock carvings include drawings of boats which can be dated by another method, for they show a distinctive type of vessel which is not illustrated on the decorated artefacts. Instead it is represented by the well-preserved wooden vessel from Hjortspring on the island of Als in Denmark which was deposited in a pool during the fourth century BC (Randsborg 1995; Crumlin-Pedersen and Trakadas eds. 2003). Although ships no longer appear on metal artefacts, it is obvious that they were still being pictured on rock outcrops.

On a broad geographical scale the distributions of decorated metalwork, rock carvings and geoglyphs overlap, but they can also complement one another. With only a few exceptions, they extend from northern Germany through Denmark, southern and central Sweden, as far as sub-Arctic Norway. Most of the designs are found in a series of regional groups, but, taken together, their distribution runs from Hamburg to Trondheim.

SHIPS ON BRONZES

Two of these media (the metalwork and the stone settings) feature a small number of distinctive images, while the third shows much more variety. Perhaps the most coherent group is represented by the decorated artefacts, although most of the naturalistic images date from the Late Bronze Age. These drawings have been analysed by the Danish archaeologist Flemming Kaul (1998), whose study has the evocative title *Ships on Bronzes*. The interpretation put forward in his book provides the starting point for any account of the visual images of South Scandinavia (Figure 46).

Ships on Bronzes is concerned with the decorated metalwork of Denmark, but it sets this material in a wider context through comparisons with artefacts and rock carvings over a larger area extending from Norway to Central Europe and even to the Mediterranean. These analogies are explored in more detail in another book by Kaul which is concerned with Bronze Age religion (Kaul 2004). One of the strengths of his analysis is that metalwork can be closely dated. It follows that the designs found on these objects can be placed in chronological order.

Although some Early Bronze Age rock carvings may be identified through comparisons with dated metalwork, the images were unevenly distributed between these two media. During that period metalwork was rarely decorated with naturalistic motifs, although some of the curvilinear imagery has been interpreted by Klavs Randsborg as representations of the sun (Randsborg and Christensen 2006: 59–93). Ships of Early Bronze Age type seem to be more frequent among the petroglyphs, which also feature artefacts of the same date: axes and swords. In the Late Bronze Age, however, much more metalwork was

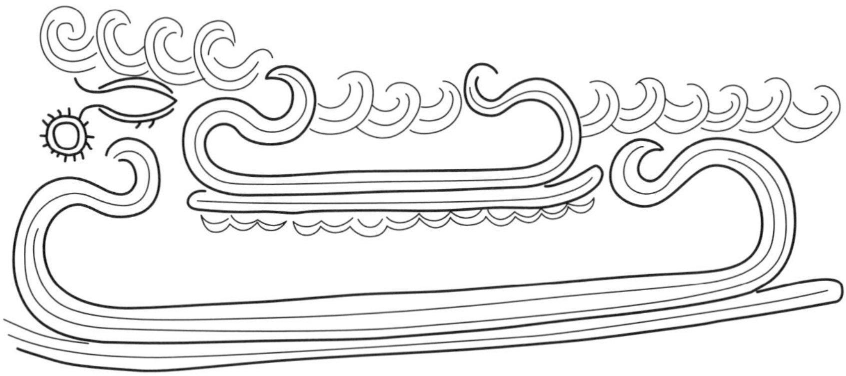

Figure 46. Two boats, a fish, and the sun on a Late Bronze Age razor.

embellished with figurative designs. As Kaul (1998) has argued, they often include the same few elements: boats, together with their crews; drawings of the sun; horses, fishes, and snakes. Other more specialized motifs are occasionally depicted on or above the boats (Figure 46).

These designs can be found on weapons and personal ornaments, but they are more common on the bronze razors that were buried with the dead. Such artefacts had been used on more than one occasion as their blades are often worn, but they must have played a specialized role in the mortuary rite for they are associated with cremations but do not seem to have passed through the pyre (Kaul 1998: 130–57). One possibility is that they had been used to prepare the corpse for the funeral. In that respect they may have played a similar role to the knives and tweezers with which they are commonly associated. On the other hand, it would not explain why the razors had been used more than once. Kaul suggests that they might have been presented to young men on their initiation as adults. The first time that they shaved could have marked an important change of status. A similar idea is suggested by Paul Treherne (1995), who argues that artefacts of this kind were used to create an ideal image of the masculine warrior. That was not always true, as a study of bronze razors in the east of Sweden has shown that some of them were placed in women's graves. Susanne Thedéen (2003) considers that they were employed in other rites of passage. Perhaps the razors, and the items associated with them, were used not only for the removal of hair but for scarification and tattooing. It was because they were so closely linked to the identities of certain individuals that they accompanied them in the grave. As artefacts connected with body decoration, they may have played a similar role to the sets of personal ornaments in the votive deposits of the same period.

Kaul suggests that the main source of inspiration for the Late Bronze Age decorated metalwork came from the Urnfield Culture of North-Central Europe, but in the Early Bronze Age, he argues, the symbolic importance of the ship may be explained by more local concerns (1998: 84). It seems as if the metal used in Scandinavia had to be imported. Many of the styles of artefact employed in Northern Europe were first developed in regions further to the south. That connection is plausible as amber was exported from Scandinavia during the same period. It seems possible that furs, pelts, and seal oil were also provided by hunters in the north, but this remains hypothetical.

The long distance movement of such materials depended on travel by water, and, for Kaul, it explains why the boat took on a special significance in the visual culture of the Early Bronze Age. It would have provided the means of communication between the Danish islands and Sweden, and between Jutland and Norway. It was often the most suitable method of travelling through inland areas, using the rivers and fjords that communicated between areas of high ground which were difficult to cross in summer and impassable in winter. Kristian Kristiansen (1987) has drawn attention to the chains of Early Bronze Age barrows and cairns that follow the coast of the Baltic and the North Atlantic, from Denmark into remote parts of Sweden and Norway. Some were located on small offshore islands, and Kristiansen suggests that they were used as seamarks by navigators travelling from the south.

ORIGINS AND WIDER CONNECTIONS

It would be wrong to look for an entirely pragmatic explanation for this emphasis on the ship in the visual imagery of Early Bronze Age Scandinavia. Like many other apparently mundane activities, the process of travelling by water was ritualized in the ancient world. That could account for the striking similarities between the symbolic significance of the ship in South Scandinavia and its importance in other regions. It is revealing to compare the European evidence with that from the Pacific, where the purely archaeological material can be interpreted with the help of ethnographic sources.

Here archaeologists confront a similar problem (Ballard, Bradley, Nordenborg Myhre, and Wilson 2003). Over an enormous area extending across South-east Asia and Micronesia the ship provides a means of transport vital to long distance trade. At the same time, the boat is used as a metaphor for the organization of individual communities, and a means of passing between the worlds of the living and the dead. Just as the ship is a symbol associated with Bronze Age cemeteries in Scandinavia, in the Pacific people may be buried in stone settings in the form of seagoing vessels. There is even a case in which the same word is used for a coffin and a boat. Ships may be depicted on elaborate metal objects just as they are in Northern Europe, and in both regions they figure prominently in rock art. At times the resemblance between these unrelated traditions is even more arresting, for the association between the ship and the sun identified on Bronze Age metalwork by Kaul is evidenced in the Solomon Islands.

This comparison is so suggestive because there is no possibility of contacts between these two areas. The striking resemblance between them is due to the special significance of travel by water and the various ways in which it has been ritualized. That is important as it provides an alternative explanation for some of the links that have been suggested between the Early Bronze Age of South Scandinavia and the Mediterranean. Such ideas played a fundamental role in Montelius's studies of Bronze Age chronology, but they have been discussed more recently by Kristian Kristiansen and Thomas Larsson (2005) in their book *The Rise of Bronze Age Society.* For them, the ship provides a metaphor for the long distance connections between the Northern Bronze Age and a vast territory extending from Egypt and Mesopotamia through Anatolia to Greece. Of course such arguments are controversial as they depend on comparisons that range widely across time and space, but the subtitle of their book is revealing: *Travels, Transmissions and Transformations.* Following the work of the American anthropologist Mary Helms (1998), they emphasize the social power that can be gained by travel, and by access to exotic goods and knowledge of unfamiliar beliefs. It is not surprising that sea transport plays such a prominent role in this interpretation.

SHIPS ON STONE

The proponents of this hypothesis do not confine themselves to the long distance connections suggested by Bronze Age metalwork. They also consider the distinctive images found in South Scandinavian rock art (Figure 47). Sometimes the designs play a direct role in their interpretations. For instance, Kristiansen (2004) suggests that some of the drawings of non-local artefacts recorded the visits of chiefs from distant areas. Similarly, Johan Ling (2004) argues that concentrations of rock carvings on the west coast of Sweden identify the places from which local elites had embarked on journeys of their own. *The Rise of Bronze Age Society* considers a series of exotic artefacts among the petroglyphs. They include the relatively rare designs associated with burial cists (Jellestad Syvertsen 2002).

Such arguments are based on a comparatively small sample of the rock carvings, whose overall distribution extends over a wider area than the decorated metalwork. The range of images certainly overlaps with those on razors and other artefacts, but it is much more varied. In fact the carved designs differ to a significant extent from one region to another. Not surprisingly, the closest links with the decorated bronzes are found towards the south where their distributions overlap. Further to the north they diverge (Malmer 1981). It follows that South Scandinavian rock art cannot be treated as a unitary phenomenon.

Which features connect the rock carvings with the decorated artefacts? Drawings of ships are the most important element, while the sun symbols that are found on the metalwork are not particularly common. The same applies to depictions of horses. Drawings of snakes and fish also appear on bronze razors but are rarely found in South Scandinavian rock art.

By contrast, there are important elements that are represented among the rock carvings but are rarely or never found amongst the designs on metalwork. The

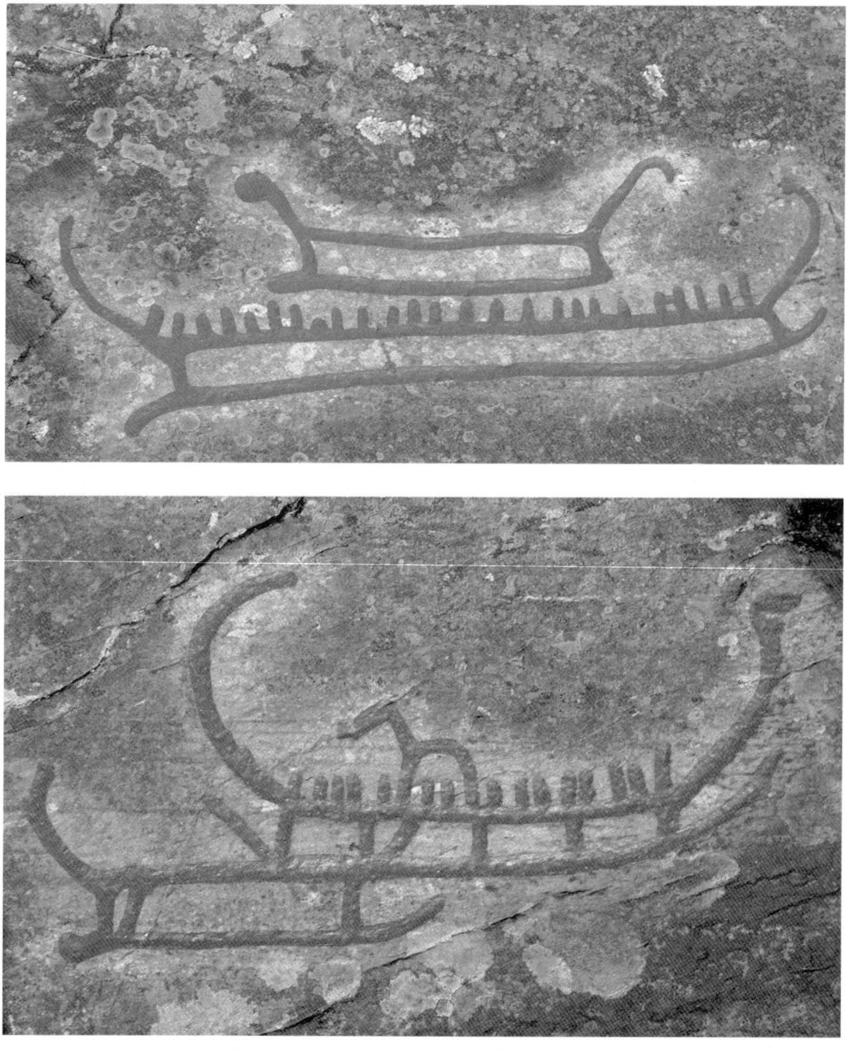

Figure 47. Carvings of ships at Himmelstalund, Sweden.

commonest are the drawings of human figures, which are more common on the decorated outcrops than are on bronzes. The petroglyphs also include wheeled vehicles (many of them drawn by horses), footprints, and cup marks, but they do not appear on portable artefacts. Other designs that seem to be peculiar to the rock carvings include wild and domesticated animals, weapons, ploughs, axes, and musical instruments. A still more important distinction is that the rock carvings illustrate complex scenes in which many of these elements are combined. Thus they show people farming, hunting, fighting, dancing, and moving in procession across the decorated surface. Any one panel may feature several different scenes, and sometimes they are 'framed' by natural features like running water, cracks or mineral veins in the rock (Hauptmann Wahlgren 2000). By contrast, a Late Bronze Age razor illustrates only one scene. There is another important difference between these media: the razors were formed in a single operation, whereas some of the rock outcrops were decorated incrementally over a substantial period of time. New designs might be superimposed on older ones and certain of the existing images were recut (Hauptmann Wahlgren 2002).

There are marked regional variations in the composition of South Scandinavian rock art, and not all these elements are found throughout its distribution. Thus the motifs that are interpreted as sun symbols are more common towards the south where most of the decorated razors are found. Drawings of weapons are most often recorded in southern and eastern Sweden, while outsize human figures, unambiguously male, are a particular feature of Bohuslän on the west coast (Malmer 1981). The same applies to the drawings of wheeled vehicles. Carved footprints, or foot soles, occur very widely but are particularly common in sub-Arctic Norway, among the northernmost carvings made in this tradition (Soggnes 2001). These are general trends, however, and are subject to numerous exceptions. In any case strikingly different combinations of motifs may be found on nearby rocks, or even on different parts of the same carved surface.

The associations of these carvings have attracted attention during recent years. They can be linked to particular environments, to rocks with distinctive characteristics, to settlement areas and also to Bronze Age monuments.

A common pattern is for the rock carvings to be associated with water (Bengtsson 2004). This relationship can take many different forms. Although they may be some way inland today, a large number of the decorated rocks followed the Bronze Age coast: a relationship that has been obscured because the land has risen. A few sites may have been located at the water's edge, but many more were within sight of the sea. At Tanum in Bohuslän most of the sites were within 100 metres of the contemporary shoreline; of these, the majority were less than 20 metres from the tidal margin (Ling 2008: 148). The sea was retreating during the course of the Bronze Age so that places that might once have been close to water were eventually located towards the limits of marshes or bogs. A graphic demonstration of this relationship is provided by Johan Ling's work in the west of Sweden. Here he has identified a series of carvings of ships which can be dated by comparison with the decorated metalwork studied by Kaul. The earliest vessels are represented on the upper part of the rocks, while the later forms are lower down. In this case it seems as if these designs were meant to be as close as possible to the water—as the sea level fell, the carvings followed suit (Ling 2008: 101). Other sites were around the margins of freshwater lakes and bogs or were situated beside rivers and springs. The close relationship between some—but not all—of the rock carvings and water recalls the importance of boats, but other factors might be equally relevant. During the Scandinavian Bronze Age such environments were among the principal locations for offerings of metalwork.

Away from the coast rock carvings can take another form. Three detailed studies illustrate this point. In Stjørdal, near Trondheim, some of the inland sites are dominated by drawings of footprints (Soggnes 2001). In the same way, fieldwork in the interior of Småland in southern Sweden recorded a very different series of rock carvings from the well-known sites along the Baltic coast. Instead of the familiar drawings of ships, the commonest motifs were circles, cup marks, and foot soles. There were occasional 'ring crosses' which might have been drawings of the sun, and possible depictions of carts or other vehicles, but in the course of this project just one drawing of a boat was identified (Skoglund 2006). There is similar evidence from the raised ground of the Bjäre peninsula in south-west Sweden. Here cup marks and footprints are particularly important. Although there are boat burials and a stone ship setting in this area, very few vessels features in the local rock art (Nord 2007).

The rock itself might also be important. Several factors are relevant here. In certain cases an outcrop might have been selected because of its distinctive shape. For example, a number of rocks in south-west Norway resemble an upturned boat (Nordenborg Myhre 2004: 144 and 178–9). That relationship is particularly obvious at Revheim (Figure 48), but it is also illustrated by an enormous outcrop at Himmelstalund, on the edge of the Swedish city of Norrköping (Hauptmann Wahlgren 2002). Both these sites feature numerous drawings of ships. Revheim introduces another issue, too. The position of the decorated cliff allowed people to observe the midwinter solstice as the sun rose and set by two landmarks visible on the horizon (Vinsrygg 1980).

The micro-topography of the outcrop could be equally significant. It determined which of the images would be visible, and the optimum positions for seeing them. In some cases it also constrained the viewer's path around the decorated surface. Again the contours of the rock should be considered in relation to the position of the sun, for it could emphasize the locations of certain of the designs. As John Coles (2006) has pointed out, many of the carvings are best inspected in low light. Some of them would be seen most clearly at sunrise, while others are illuminated by the setting sun. They could often be recognized because they were wet, and it is no accident that a number of these images were washed by shallow streams (Figure 49). Others were highlighted because they made use of mineral veins or natural basins in the surface of the rock (Figure 50). This served to pick out some drawings rather than others, but it also made them appear more realistic (Hauptmann Wahlgren 2000). There are cases in which depictions of boats cluster in the areas covered by running water, or where they

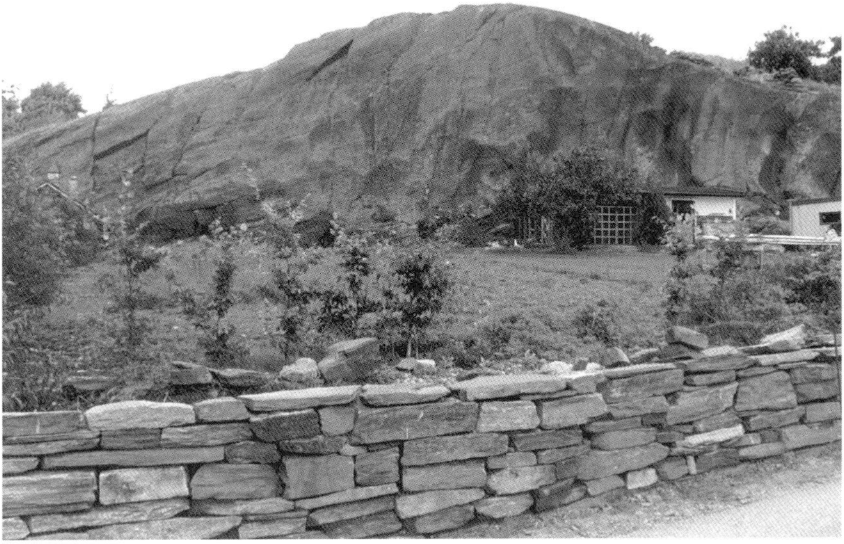

Figure 48. The decorated outcrop at Revheim, Norway. The form of the rock resembles an enormous upturned boat.

travel along veins of quartz which resemble the surface of the sea (Bradley, Jones, Nordenborg Myhre, and Sackett 2003).

It is more difficult to discuss the relationship between rock carvings and the wider pattern of settlement, but at one time the solution seemed obvious. The case was best set out by Jarl Nordbladh (1980) and Ulf Bertilsson (1987) in their accounts of the Bronze Age landscape of Bohuslän. The rock carvings were located by unusually productive grazing land and overlooked the main settled areas. By contrast, burial cairns of the same date were on higher ground. The interpretation seemed to be supported by the discovery of burnt stones and occasional artefacts at these sites.

That attractive interpretation cannot be accepted today. The fertile soils associated with the rock carvings are often the marine sediments left by the retreating sea, and some of these places would have been located on the shoreline when the drawings were made. Others would have been associated with tracts of salt marsh that were unsuitable for farming. In fact they were not settled until the Iron Age (Ling 2008: 111–13). The finds of burnt stone seem to be associated with the rituals performed on and around the decorated outcrops and should not be confused with the remains of settlements. They are better compared with the contents of more specialized sites with evidence of cremation pyres, feasting, and bronze production. Where domestic buildings have been excavated, as they

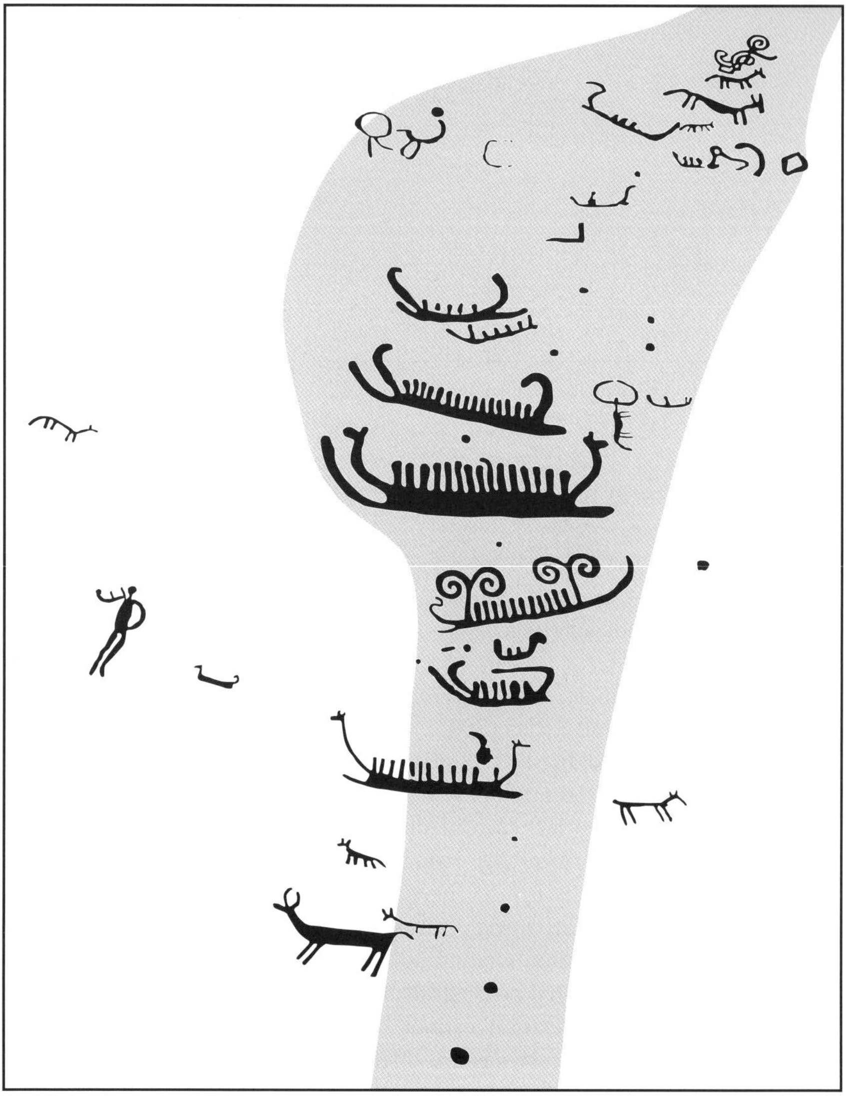

Figure 49. Carvings of ships on the part of a decorated panel at Tanum, Sweden, affected by running water (shaded). The presence of surface water is often thought of as a threat to the preservation of the designs. Here it is treated as part of the composition.

have at Pryssgården near to Himmelstalund, they seem to have been established some distance away from the rock carvings (Borna-Ahlqvist 2002; Nilsson 2005). In Bohuslän, the nearest settlements were between 500 and 1000 metres from the main carved rocks (Ling 2008: 5).

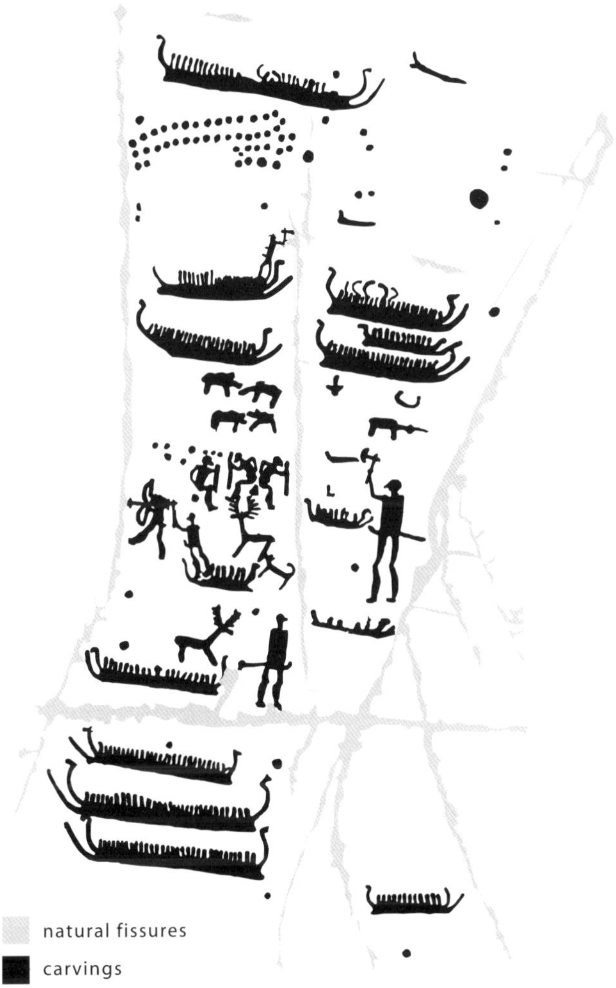

Figure 50. The framing of carved designs at Tanum, Sweden by natural veins in the surface of the rock. Geological elements like these should be regarded as parts of the composition.

Lastly, a small number of the designs found in South Scandinavian rock art are directly associated with burials. This evidence takes two forms. There are decorated surfaces associated with Bronze Age cairns, and there are a small a few cases in which parts of those monuments had been decorated in the same style.

The first of these relationships depends on the juxtaposition of rock carvings and Bronze Age cairns. This is not convincing in itself, but there are some instances in which a direct connection seems obvious. At Järrestad and Ör in southern Sweden files of human footprints extend from two such monuments and lead down the rock towards a bog (Coles 1999; Skoglund 2006: 29–33). At Hjortekrog in the same region, a Late Bronze Age burial cairn was superimposed on a series of carved ships (Widholm 1999), and at Unneset in the west of Norway similar vessels are depicted travelling between a cairn and the water's edge (Wrigglesworth 2002).

The second case is where carved stones formed part of the fabric of such monuments (Figure 51). In some cases the details are obscure, but there are instances in which the carvings were inside burial cists, as happened at Kivik in southern Sweden (Randsborg 1993) and Mjeltehaugen in the west of Norway (Linge 2005). Another arrangement is for the decoration to be created

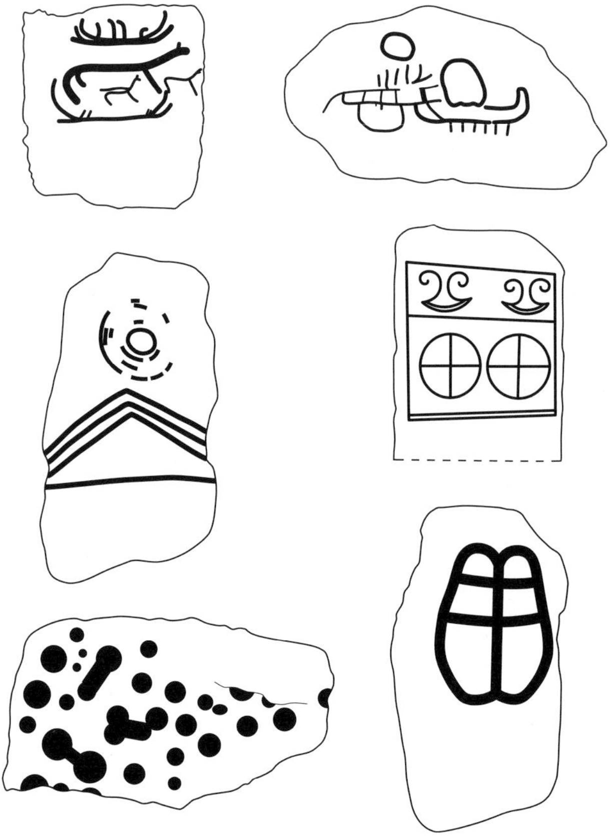

Figure 51. The range of motifs associated with decorated burial cists in Sweden and Norway.

on the kerb of a burial mound. This occurred at Sagaholm, where the decorated stones were concealed as the monument was extended (Goldhahn 1999). There have been attempts to interpret the organization of the decorated panels at Kivik and Sagaholm but they suffer from the disadvantage that finds of this nature are rare. At this stage it may be enough to say that they suggest that certain of these images, in particular ships, horses, and wheeled vehicles, could be associated with the dead.

The images inside the cist at Kivik have played a major part in discussions of the long distance connections of the Scandinavian Bronze Age, even though their exact date is uncertain (Kristiansen and Larsson 2005: 186–99). This raises a question that has already been asked in relation to the decorated metalwork. To what extent were images in the rock carvings of local inspiration, and how far were they influenced by contacts with other parts of Europe?

ORIGINS AND WIDER CONNECTIONS

In the past the carved rocks of Southern Scandinavia have been described as Farmers' Art to distinguish them from the Hunters' Art that occurs further to the north. That procedure is unsatisfactory, and today those traditions are usually described in neutral terms as the Southern and Northern styles respectively (Soggnes 1998). Their distributions overlap, particularly in western Norway, but it is uncertain whether the same applies to their chronology (Figure 52). Images in these two styles were created in very different settings from one another, although there are a few outcrops at which they were superimposed. Most of the designs were carved, but the Northern Style also includes some paintings whose distribution extends over a larger area than the petroglyphs. As its original name suggests, these pictures feature hunting scenes, wild animals, and sea creatures. It is clear that that the Northen tradition originated during the Mesolithic period, but it is not known when it went out of use. Kalle Sognnes (1995a and 2001) has suggested that in the region where both styles are represented they may have been used concurrently for a thousand years.

Most scholars agree on the chronology of the Southern style of rock art, but less is known about the circumstances in which it was first adopted. As was the case with the decorated metalwork, it is easy to invoke connections with Southern Europe, and specific designs play an important part in the thesis put forward by Kristiansen and Larsson (2005). There are difficulties with this approach, for the real problem is not to identify stylistic links with distant areas but to show why foreign imagery should have been so acceptable

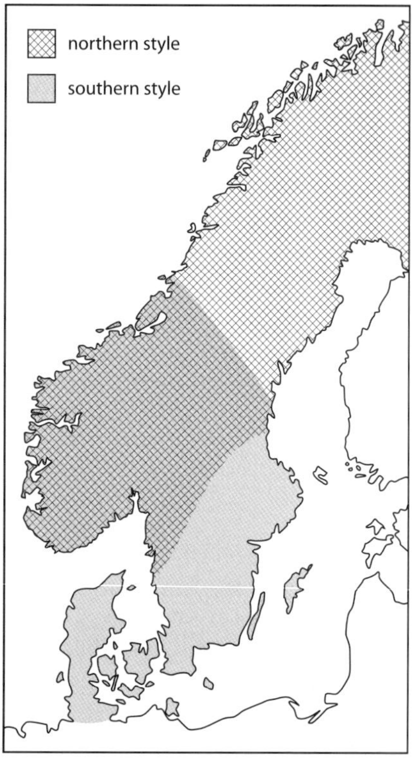

Figure 52. Approximate distribution of the Northern and Southern styles of Scandinavian rock art, showing the area of overlap between them.

in Scandinavia. These authors believe that it happened because local leaders wished to emphasis their access to restricted knowledge and their contacts with remote areas. A simpler explanation could have something to offer.

The chronology of the Northern Style may be rather uncertain, but a number of writers have suggested that some of its characteristic imagery can be interpreted in relation to Circumpolar ethnography (Zvelebil and Jordan 1999; cf. Jordan 2003). That is to say, the belief system documented in these drawings and paintings had not changed beyond all recognition when it was first recorded in the seventeenth century AD (Lahelma 2008). By then, paintings and carvings had not been produced for many years, although similar images were present on Saami drums (Helskog 1987). If these connections are real, it follows that the same beliefs had a very long history. If they maintained their integrity between the Mesolithic period and the Christian era, they must have been current during the Bronze Age. At one time they could have been important throughout Scandinavia. It may be because traditional ideas were so tenacious that they provided a context in which a new set of symbols could be interpreted.

That would explain the similarities between the rock art of Northernmost Europe and some characteristics of the Southern Style. They have less to do with the images than with their contexts (Mandt 1995; Bradley 2007b).

Nevertheless a few motifs do seem to be common to both of these traditions. The most important is the boat. Seagoing vessels were portrayed in Northern rock art at an earlier date than any of the images in South Scandinavia, although the latest examples at sites like Alta and Nämforsen may be of similar age. They are not represented in every group of rock carvings. One feature which these traditions share is an emphasis on bodily transformation. In the north, this is shown by drawings which combine the attributes of boats and elks, or those of humans and fish. In the south, the same applies to a comparatively few drawings in which people take on the characteristics of animals or birds. Here some of the ships have a horse's head on the prow.

Much closer connections are suggested by the siting of these images. To a certain extent the carvings and paintings in the Northern Style appear in different contexts. The petroglyphs were often associated with rivers, springs, cataracts and the sea, while the paintings were sometimes placed on vertical rocks overlooking bodies of still water (Bolin 1999: 146). In each case the association with the water's edge is a significant factor, for in Arctic ethnography it is where the three layers of the cosmos—the earth, the sky, and the sea—all meet (Mulk and Bayliss-Smith 2006: chapter 8). Cataracts are of special importance in this scheme, and some of the largest groups of rock carvings were located on small islands in the midst of a series of rapids.

Rock carvings in the Southern Style illustrate the same emphasis on water and the seashore. Many of the drawings of ships were intimately associated with the coast, and others were located beside rivers, bogs, and lakes. In some cases the carvings were set back from the sea but commanded a view of the water's edge. One of the exceptions was the decorated outcrop at Himmelstalund which overlooked a major river in between two cataracts (Hauptmann Wahlgren 2002).

Other elements in Circumpolar ethnography may be reflected by the Bronze Age archaeology of Southern Scandinavia. One is the burial of the dead on islands (Zvelebil and Jordan 1999). This is a feature of the Baltic and North Atlantic coasts and has already been interpreted by Kristiansen (1987) in relation to long distance navigation. The ethnographic evidence suggests another perspective. Some of those islands are small and isolated, and it seems unlikely that they could have been inhabited in prehistory. In that case it would have been necessary to transport the dead by boat. It is another element that features in the ethnographic record, but in this case it is clear that the ships of the dead were not equipped with oars, paddles or sails; instead they were allowed to drift (Zvelebil and Jordan 1999). In that respect they would have been very different from the vessels used by the living.

Again there is a link with South Scandinavian rock art. Although ships are among the commonest motifs, only rarely were they provided with any means of locomotion. Although most of the vessels do have crews, they appear curiously passive, as if they were unable to influence the outcome of their voyage. The carvings of ships suggest that there were important changes during the course of the Bronze Age. The earlier vessels are more often depicted with crews, but a greater proportion of those dated to the Late Bronze Age and Early Iron Age appear to be entirely empty (Ling 2008: chapter 10). The connection with northern beliefs is tenuous but plausible, yet it may help to explain why drawings of this kind can be associated with burial cairns.

In contrast to Kristiansen and Larsson, Sognnes (2001) suggests that this style first developed around the northern limit of its distribution where the importance of rock carvings was already well established. That is not to overlook the connections that have been suggested with Central Europe, which are based less on the definitions of boats then on other designs. It might even suggest why the Bronze Age inhabitants of Southern Scandinavia would have been peculiarly receptive to the visual images inspired by contacts with remote areas. Unfamiliar elements could easily have been interpreted in terms of local beliefs and preoccupations. Such beliefs were extremely tenacious and may have developed during the Mesolithic period. In the Arctic they retained their influence for much longer, so that they were still important at the time of the Christian missionaries.

SHIPS MADE OF STONE

Decorated metalwork and petroglyphs share a common feature, for both are characterized by drawings. A third medium is less often considered in accounts of Bronze Age Scandinavia. Small stone-built monuments make use of similar designs. They cannot be described as sculptures as they were built rather than carved, and yet they portray some of the same elements. There are rings of boulders, and there are low stone settings in the form of a ship (Capelle 1986 and 1995; Artelius 1996). The latter are sometimes accompanied by the circular monuments, but they can also be found with platforms or walled enclosures whose plan resembles that of a small house.

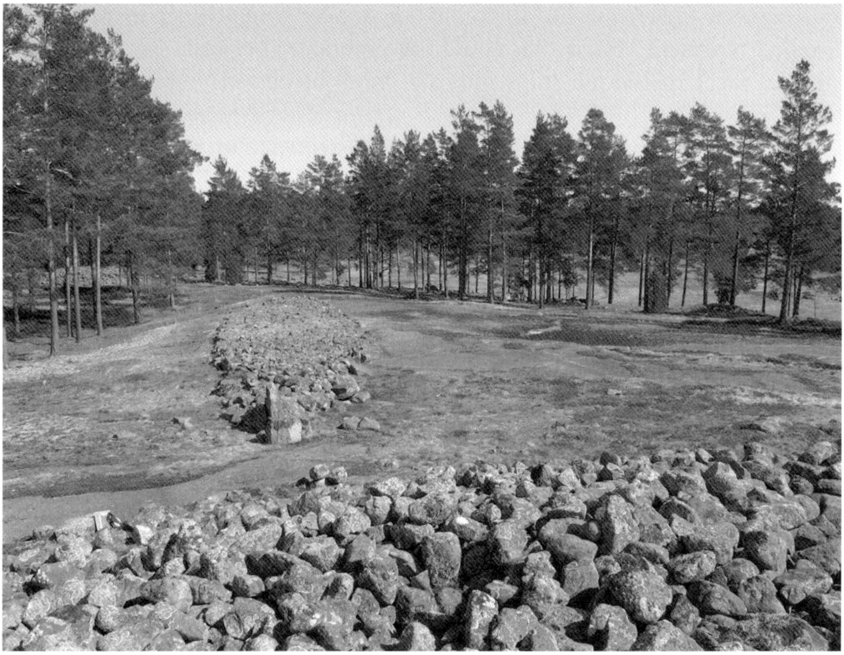

Figure 53. The largest of the Bronze Age ship settings at Snäckedal, Sweden.

The most distinctive of these structures are the ship settings, the majority of which date from the Late Bronze Age (Figure 53). They are quite different from the more impressive arrangements of monoliths built during the first millennium AD and occur in small numbers close to both the Baltic and the North Atlantic. The greatest concentration is on Gotland, where there is little evidence of rock art (Hallin 2002). Another major group is on the east coast of Sweden in an area with easy access to that island (Widholm 1998). These monuments are associated with cremation burials, a few of which include the bronze razors discussed earlier in this chapter.

It seems likely that Late Bronze Age ship settings were full size copies of actual boats, and the best preserved monuments even represent details of the deck, the prow and the stern. Rausing (1984) and Capelle (1995) have concluded that these vessels were of two different types: the smaller ones were suitable for short journeys, but there were longer, narrower craft which they identify as warships (Ellmers 1995). A minimum amount of space would be needed for a vessel to be paddled or rowed, and comparison with surviving prehistoric boats—especially those from Dover (Clark 2004) and Hjortspring (Crumlin-Pedersen and Trazadas eds. 2003)—makes it possible to estimate the sizes of their crews. In that case the smaller ship settings in south-east Sweden represent vessels that could accommodate between six and sixteen people; the larger stone ships indicate crews of between twenty and forty (Bradley 2008).

These figures can be compared with the evidence of rock carvings and decorated metalwork, both of which depict members of the crews. Since the vessels are drawn in side view, each 'crew stroke' should represent a pair of individuals, one sitting opposite the other. The rock art of south-east Sweden—one of the regions with a concentration of ship settings—shows boats with crews consisting of approximately ten, twenty and thirty-six people. They are not unlike the estimates based on the stone monuments. In Bohuslän, the Early Bronze Age boats usually carry between twelve and twenty-four people, although occasional vessels are much larger. The figure for the Late Bronze Age is similar: the commonest estimate is fourteen (Ling 2008: 191–7). On the other hand, the number of crew strokes depicted on the decorated metalwork from Denmark—the only country for which a comprehensive catalogue is available—is considerably higher, suggesting that many of these artefacts depict ships with crews of between twenty and sixty people; the most common estimate is forty (Bradley 2008). Hardly any of these vessels can be compared with the smaller boats represented by rock carvings and ship settings. Instead the drawings on the metalwork are probably pictures of warships.

Many of the Bronze Age ship settings on Gotland are located close to the shoreline (Hallin 2002). They are unevenly distributed, with four concentrations of monuments along the east coast and another three to the west. Only one major group is found in the interior. All the local concentrations of ship settings are in the same areas as round cairns. Like their counterparts in eastern Sweden, the stone boats were of various different sizes, although the overall range is similar, suggesting that they represented the same kinds of vessels. Where they differ is in their arrangement on the ground (Capelle 1986). Although they can occur singly or in pairs, there are other cases in which a series of stone vessels was constructed side by side, as happened at Liffride. There are also sites like Rannarve where the ship settings were laid out in a line, leaving no space in between them. These small fleets are not unlike those portrayed in Scandinavian rock carvings (Figure 54).

On the Swedish mainland ship settings are often found together with other constructions. The most distinctive are either square or rectangular. Perhaps some were open enclosures before they were filled with rubble. Like the stone ships, they may be based on a familiar prototype, for they have similar proportions to Late Bronze Age and Early Iron Age houses, although they are not as large as those buildings (Widholm and Regnell 2001; Artursson

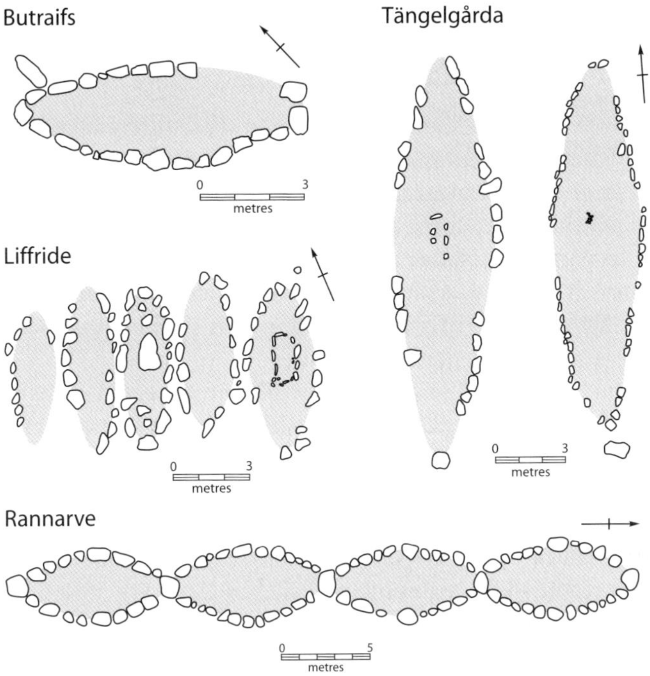

Figure 54. The variety of Bronze Age ship settings on the island of Gotland.

2005). They can also be compared with the small wooden cult houses known at ceremonial sites of the same date (Victor 2001 and 2002).

Ship settings are frequently associated with round cairns. The circular monuments are very common and come in a variety of sizes; smaller rings of boulders also appear during the Bronze Age and Iron Age. They present more of a problem, for they were occasionally buried beneath later monuments; in other cases they may have delimited those structures. Like the rectilinear monuments, some were platforms rather than cairns, and in a few cases they were constructed around a prominent boulder. Other monuments incorporate several concentric rings of stones, not unlike motifs found in the rock carvings. In most cases these circles were built in sequence, but the cumulative design was occasionally visible in the fabric of the completed monument. Other rings of boulders are divided into segments in an arrangement that resembles the ring cross pecked on the decorated outcrops (Hyenstrand 1969). Little is known about such features. The oldest dates from the Early Bronze Age, but, like the latest of the petroglyphs, similar structures may have been used during the Late Bronze Age and Iron Age. Some of the circular stone settings were still being built as late as AD 500.

ORIGINS AND WIDER CONNECTIONS

Compared with metalwork and rock carvings, these monuments are not well dated. Individual examples are associated with diagnostic artefacts, but in the absence of large scale excavation there is little to establish the lifespan of the cemeteries of which they form a part. All too often these structures must be attributed to particular phases according to their surface appearance. In the circumstances it is best to assign them to an extended period that combines the Bronze Age and the Early Iron Age. It seems possible that Scandinavian rock art was used for an equally long time.

Rock carvings and decorated metalwork incorporated ideas that were introduced from other areas. That is less likely in the case of stone settings. Each of the separate elements may have had a more local source.

The stone ship settings are associated with cremation burials, but are the direct successors of smaller structures buried beneath Early Bronze Age barrows and cairns. They are not especially common, but monuments of this kind are recorded from a number of sites in Denmark (Artelius 1996). In the west of Sweden and Norway the use of such features for burials continued into the Late Bronze Age (Skoglund 2005), but in other areas it ran in parallel with the creation of freestanding monuments. The link between boats and the dead is of even greater antiquity, and during the Mesolithic and Neolithic periods there are cases in which human bodies were buried in actual or model vessels (Skaarup 1995). There are even underwater 'burials' associated with Mesolithic canoes (Skaarup and Grøn 2004: 36–40).

The new development in the Late Bronze Age was the construction of ship settings which were no longer covered by a cairn. Often they were displayed as part of a larger cemetery. The same is true of the stone settings that resemble a domestic building. During the Early Bronze Age, wooden houses were covered by burial mounds in Denmark and occasionally in Sweden. The layout of the monument was obviously influenced by that of the older structure (Svanberg 2005). In the Late Bronze Age, however, such buildings provided the prototype for the features described as 'cult houses' (Victor 2001 and 2002). They were rubble enclosures of the same size as dwellings in the settlements, but do not appear to have been roofed. Most examples lacked an entrance, and their orientations differed significantly from those of domestic buildings. They are mainly associated with evidence of fires, metalworking and cremation burials. Outside one example in Denmark there was a row of decorated slabs (Kaul 1987). Smaller wooden structures may have been used in similar ways and could have been the prototypes for the rectangular platforms that are often found with ship settings. It seems as if features that had originally been concealed from view became important elements of Late Bronze Age and Early Iron Age cemeteries.

The circular monuments can also be associated with ship settings, and there are even examples in south-west Norway in which such vessels seem to travel through a gap in the kerb (Nordenborg Myhre 2004: 216). The closest equivalents for these cairns and platforms are known in other media. Either they appear in rock carvings, where they are commonly interpreted as sun symbols, or similar designs are depicted on Bronze Age metalwork. Although Kaul (1998) identifies the circular devices on bronze razors as drawings of the sun, another comparison is with more elaborate artefacts studied by Randsborg and Christensen (2006: 59–93). Like Kaul, Randsborg interprets the concentric circles as solar imagery. It may be that the rings of boulders in Bronze Age and Iron Age cemeteries expressed the same relationship between the dead and the sun.

FROM IMAGES TO AUDIENCES

So far this account has emphasized the features that were shared between images in three different media. The commonest designs on the decorated metalwork were drawings of ships and the sun. They are among the comparatively few elements portrayed by the Bronze Age stone settings. Their distributions overlap, and among the artefacts associated with these monuments there are a small number of razors. Ship settings and rock carvings are rarely found together, but again they share certain elements. Boats figure prominently among the petroglyphs, and circular symbols appear on many of the same sites. These three media might have been treated as local manifestations of the same ideas, so that the stone settings on Gotland might be viewed as the regional equivalent of the rock carvings. The same could be true on the coast of south-east Sweden. In Sonja Wigren's study of Södermanland, further to the north, the same features have mutually exclusive distributions (Wigren 1987).

That overlooks an important factor. The designs may illustrate similar ideas, but they cannot have been directed to exactly the same audiences. The images on the decorated metalwork were extremely small, as were most of the artefacts themselves. By contrast, the carved panels could be very extensive, although the individual motifs varied considerably in size (Burenhult 1973; Coles 2000 and 2005). Many of the components were displayed in miniature, but the most impressive human figures in Bohuslän were larger, and were often on higher ground than the others (Ling 2008: 146). Similarly, the footprints and foot soles depicted on the decorated outcrops may have been life-size (Brox Nilsen

2005). Many of the carved designs were organized into compositions that could be seen from a single viewpoint. By contrast, the geoglyphs were often located within large cemeteries, where it would be necessary to move between the separate monuments in order to inspect them. It seems likely that the ship settings depicted real vessels. They probably follow the actual dimensions of these boats, and the same may be true of the stone 'cult houses' which apparently represented buildings. Goldhahn (2007) has argued that they were used by ritual specialists and may have been associated with beliefs about the ancestors. The rectangular platforms that are often found with stone ships were conceived on a far smaller scale, but the circular stone settings come in a variety of sizes. The same is true of their closest equivalents among the petroglyphs and the decorated metalwork.

These differences of scale have important implications for the ways in which the images could be viewed. The designs on the decorated metalwork are very small indeed. They could only be recognized at close quarters and probably by one person at a time. Although decorated razors were commonly associated with the dead, it is most unlikely that anyone could have construed these drawings while the body was displayed during a funeral. Since the razors show signs of wear, it seems possible that the designs had been addressed to the dead person at an earlier stage in his or her career. Kaul suggests that that they referred to a mythology that was taught to particular people during the rites of passage (1998: 154–7). That is entirely plausible, although it no longer seems likely that such knowledge was restricted to young men (Thedéen 2003). Perhaps the drawings on these objects were small in order to protect them from scrutiny. In a sense they codified 'secret' knowledge. That could be one reason why these artefacts were taken out of circulation when someone died.

Kaul also suggests that the rock carvings expressed the public aspect of the same beliefs. These locations were readily accessible, although the more complex sites seem to have been distanced from the settlements of the same period (Nilsson 2005). In contrast to many of the decorated surfaces discussed in Chapter 5, these images were created in places which were easy to find and which could normally accommodate a large audience. At the same time, the designs might be divided into a series of separate panels, so that it would have been necessary to move around them in order to see all the pictures (Frontispiece). It raises the possibility that they acted together as a narrative that had to be followed in sequence. The drawings were normally arranged along a horizontal axis in relation to a viewer standing at the edge of the decorated surface. Recent fieldwork has established that ceremonies had been conducted on some of these sites. That could account for the finds of pottery and burnt stones, and even for the identification of walls or platforms in front of the rock face (Kaul 2006a).

In Bohuslän they are most common with the simpler carvings (Bengtsson 2004; Ling 2008: 6). This evidence will be discussed in detail in Chapter 8.

Although Kaul suggests that the carved rocks were employed in public ceremony, it is important to remember that many of the decorated surfaces built up over a considerable period of time: in some cases up to a thousand years. Only a few motifs might have been carved on any one occasion. They would soon fade from view unless the older designs were painted—a practice for which there is currently no evidence. Otherwise that process could only be arrested if the designs were recut. That may have happened with the major panels at Himmelstalund (Hauptmann Wahlgren 2002), and in south-west Norway it seems as if carvings of ships may even have been renewed in a more up to date style (Nordenborg Myhre 2004: chapter 6). The problem is that such details have not been recorded until recently, and in older records of Scandinavian rock art it is hard to tell the motifs that are boldly carved and may have been maintained for a long time from images that were more tentative or could have been used over a shorter period (Coles 2003a). The modern practice of painting the designs in order to display them to the public is misleading as it treats all of them in the same way. In fact it is an open question whether the people who visited these places in the Bronze Age attempted to trace the outlines of drawings that had been made in the past, or whether the newest motifs were the only ones with much significance. If the viewers had shown a concern with drawings that were becoming obscured, their visits would have provided an opportunity for tracing the histories of the people who had made them. That is suggested by the fact that carvings were made on the same rocks long after the sea had retreated (Ling 2008). On the other hand, the fact that some of the pictures were superimposed could equally suggest that those who formed the new designs were rejecting the past.

The comparatively rare stone settings raise yet another possibility. Like the rock carvings, they present the 'public' face of some of the beliefs recorded on the decorated metalwork. At the same time, these monuments had a permanence that was not necessarily shared with the decorated outcrops. Most of the geoglyphs formed part of cemeteries that had been established before the Late Bronze Age. Moreover, the use of these sites often continued into the Iron Age. The positions of successive monuments acknowledged one another, so that these were places where histories were put on display. It was only by moving between the different structures and comprehending the relationships between them that their full significance could be appreciated. That contrasts with the 'secret knowledge' expressed by the designs hidden on the decorated metalwork, and, perhaps, with the fading of the narratives recorded in rock art. Yet all three media had their basis in the same beliefs. The myths that they expressed are considered in Chapter 7.

7

Crossing the Water

LINES OF ENQUIRY

There are several ways of interpreting the Bronze Age images of Southern Scandinavia, but they lead to very different conclusions from one another. It is essential to know their strengths and weaknesses, since the nature of those designs has obvious implications for the circumstances in which the pictures were made.

Two of these approaches draw on literary evidence from other periods or areas. The first treats the images as reflections of Indo-European mythology, evidenced by written sources from regions as far away as India. Thus beliefs concerning the special importance of fire in Scandinavia have been reconstructed by reference to the Rig Veda (Kaliff 2007); and the unusual pairs of human figures depicted on Bronze Age metalwork are explained by the institution of the Twin Rulers (Kristiansen and Larsson 2005: 271–82). The separate pictures in the rock art of western Sweden have even been identified with scenes in Indo-European mythology (Fredell 2003a).

There are serious problems with this approach. The chronology of these separate elements is controversial, yet the analysis proceeds on the basis that there was some kind of Indo-European 'horizon' that allows researchers to combine elements from different regions and to treat them on equal terms. No doubt it provides a useful source of ideas, but there is a danger that this approach will emphasize the similarities between past communities rather than the contrasts indicated by archaeological evidence. Given the chronological problems that beset historical linguistics, it is hard to see how both kinds of study can be brought into alignment.

In the same way, the Northern European evidence has been interpreted by comparison with later literary sources. Although the sagas were written down in Iceland during the Christian era, it is clear that they relate to an earlier phase and often describe events that had happened in Scandinavia. They usually refer to the pagan period and provide the principal source of information about Old Norse religion. Like Indo-European myths, they have been used to interpret the visual images of the Bronze Age. At first sight this is anachronistic, as the texts were collected almost two thousand years after the designs were made, but at one time there was a historical justification for this procedure (Mandt 1995). Until prehistoric chronology was better understood, the drawings of boats were identified as Viking warships. For a while it seemed as if scholars were comparing features that were contemporary with one another.

The problems posed by this method are evident from *The Chariot of the Sun*, an influential book by two British authors, Peter Gelling and Hilda Ellis Davidson (1969). It is divided into two parts. Gelling wrote the first section: a disciplined analysis of the visual culture of the Bronze Age, much of which is still valid today. He makes little reference to later literary sources and, where he does offer wider comparisons, they are usually with Central and Southern Europe. Davidson summarizes the main components of Late Iron Age art and their interpretation in relation to literary evidence. Like Gelling, she makes few comparisons with material of other periods. It seems as if two unrelated studies have been printed end to end. The reader is left with the impression that Davidson feels that comparisons between these sources are not particularly useful. Gelling is even more circumspect. If wider relationships are to be considered, they are with societies in the first millennium BC. There is no meeting of minds between these writers, or between the traditions of scholarship they represent. It is obvious that direct comparisons of this kind have not fulfilled their promise. More recent studies have recognized that Old Norse religion was a hybrid of ancient beliefs and newer elements that may have developed during the Viking Age (Andrén, Jennbert, and Raudvere 2006).

In the circumstances it is better to begin by interpreting the images using archaeological sources. Such research has led in a different direction. Two of the most widely quoted interpretations are based on metalwork and rock carvings. The first emphasizes the relationship between some of these drawings and the dead. Ship settings are found in cemeteries, and decorated razors in graves. Related imagery is recorded at a number of funerary monuments. Thus some of the most distinctive carvings are on cists, and other decorated panels are associated with burial mounds. Nearly all the key images of the Scandinavian Bronze Age occur in these specialized contexts, including footprints, ring crosses, cup marks, and boats (Kaul 2004: chapter 6; Figenschou Simonsen, and Vogt 2005).

An alternative is to emphasize the importance of fertility (Almgren 1927). The most obvious visual evidence is provided by drawings of phallic males among the rock carvings in the west of Sweden, but there are also scenes of cultivation and domesticated livestock. Sometimes these elements are combined, as in the drawings of naked ploughmen in Bohuslän, or in rock carvings which seem to portray sexual intercourse between people and animals. Another picture has been identified as 'the cosmic wedding' and features a human couple (Johnsen 2005). Prehistorians who postulate a fertility cult also consider depictions of the sun.

That provides the starting point of *Ships on Bronzes* (Kaul 1998). It contrasts with some of the approaches mentioned earlier because it is far more sensitive to the details of the artefacts themselves. Kaul's starting point is the Early Bronze Age 'Sun Chariot' from Trundholm which gave Gelling's and Davidson's book its name (Figure 55). The vehicle is drawn by a horse and carries a decorated disc. One surface is gilded and reflects the light, but the other is dull. It has always been interpreted as an image of the sun. Perhaps its different faces show the sun during the day, when it provides a source of light, and during the night, when it disappears from view. Kaul's achievement is to identify the same principle among the decorated razors and other artefacts, most of which date from the Late Bronze Age. They feature four main designs—ships, the sun, fishes, and snakes—which are combined in quite specific ways.

His analysis depends on a simple observation. In the Northern Hemisphere the sun can be observed crossing the sky from the left where it rises, to the

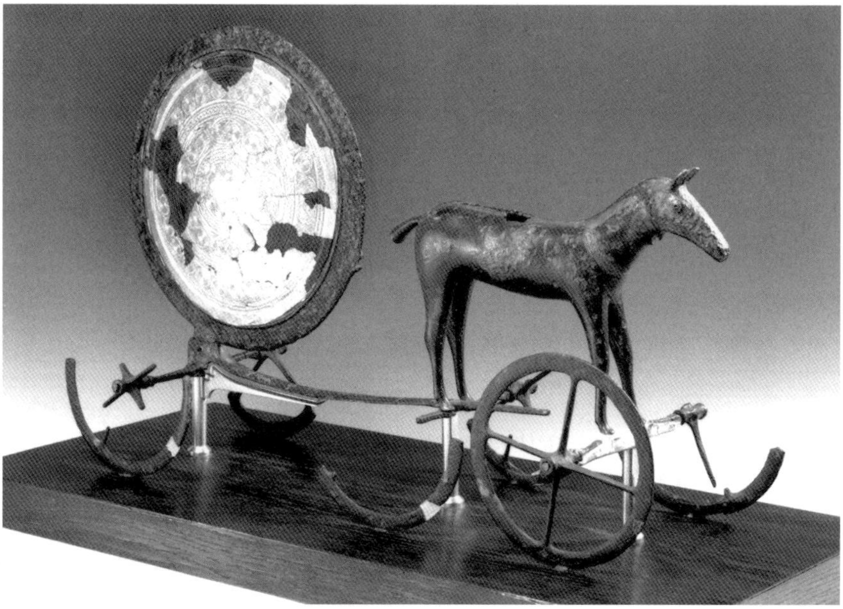

Figure 55. The Trundholm 'Sun Chariot'.

right where it sets. For people who lacked a notion of scientific astronomy, that would have posed a problem. If the sun had moved across the sky during the course of the day, how did it return to its original position to repeat its journey the next morning? In many parts of Northern Europe the sun appears to emerge from the sea and to sink into the water at dusk. Was it possible that during the period of darkness it travelled beneath the ocean to break the surface at dawn? That contrast between day and night is illustrated by the two faces of the Trundholm disc. Kaul suggests that the same narrative is illustrated by other kinds of metalwork.

The Trundholm disc is mounted on a wheeled vehicle, but on many of the artefacts studied by Kaul a circular image is conveyed by a ship. Most of these vessels are depicted in sufficient detail for the viewer to work out the direction in which they are travelling. Some of them carry the sun from left to right, so they should record its passage during the day. Like the Trundholm disc, these vessels are accompanied by horses. Where the ships bear the sun from right to left, they have different associations, and in this case they are often found with fishes or snakes. These symbols would be especially appropriate if the journey took place underwater. The 'night ship' is carried through the hours of darkness between the sunset and the sunrise. The fish is an ideal companion on this voyage, for it passes between rivers and the sea. Perhaps the snake identified by Kaul is actually an eel, for eels are common in Denmark and travel between sea and land (cf. Berntsson 2005: fig. 33) The decorated metalwork would have summarized the movement of the sun through the sky during the day, and its passage below the surface at night. Kaul's analysis is meticulous and well documented, and his interpretation is widely accepted (Figure 56).

Further connections are worth mentioning here. Some of the decorated artefacts take the form of a ship, and a number of them even have a horse's head on the prow. This recalls the role of the horse that draws the Sun Disc. At the same time, the wheels carrying that vehicle have four spokes. The same motif occurs in isolation in Southern Scandinavian rock art and is usually described as a ring cross, or *wheel cross.* There is linguistic evidence from many regions that connects wheels with the sun (West 2007: 201–3).

There are other cases in which the ships depicted on Late Bronze Age metalwork are embellished with birds' heads. On one level, this is a reference to the visual images of the Urnfield Culture (Kossack 1954). On another, it contributes to Kaul's interpretation because, like eels, birds move between land and sea. In this case they are also linked with the sun because they fly through the air.

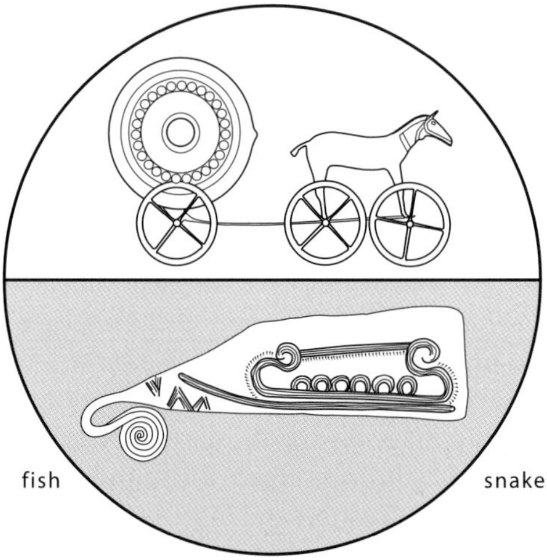

Figure 56. Outline of the solar cosmology postulated by Kaul (1998).

FROM METALWORK TO STONE

Were the same conventions followed in the rock carvings of South Scandinavia?

The scheme identified by Kaul on decorated razors and other artefacts has its closest equivalent on a carved rock found in a Bronze Age cairn at Klinta on the Baltic island of Öland (Burenhult 1973: 66). It is not clear how the stone had been used, but the decoration is organized in three layers, with a frieze of cup marks along the edge that encloses most of the decorated surface. The lowest layer includes two ships, one of them carrying horses and the other with a human crew. Although the direction of travel is not entirely clear, they seem to be moving in opposite directions to one another. The middle layer contains a solitary horse walking from right to left, while the upper part of the stone features a set of concentric circles and another group of cup marks.

Comparison with Kaul's scheme suggests an interpretation (Figure 57). There are just two drawings of boats. The lower one appears to be moving from left to right. The other vessel travels in the opposite direction and is shown with its crew. It seems possible that in fact the drawing depicts a single vessel crossing the decorated surface and coming back again. The same argument applies to the drawings of animals. As Kaul's interpretation would

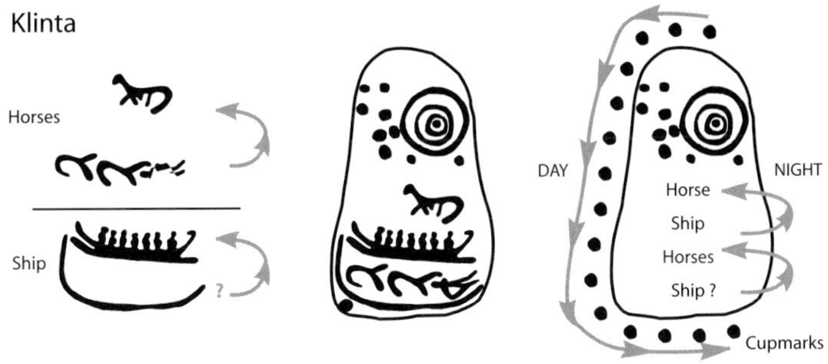

Figure 57. An interpretation of the decorated stone from a burial monument at Klinta, Öland.

suggest, the 'day ship' at the bottom of the panel is accompanied by horses. Like the boat, one of them changes direction and returns towards its original point of departure. It is overlooked by what is surely the sun. The left-hand edge of the stone is embellished with cup marks; if the decoration conformed to the same scheme as the decorated bronzes, it would be associated with the day. Similarly, the right side, which was left undecorated, would be connected with the night. The panel is rather like a clock face in which boats and horses are shown as they pass through a twenty-four hour cycle. This is not the only way of interpreting the design, but its similarity to the decorated razors is very striking indeed.

Many of the same elements can be identified on a small rock outcrop at Borgen in south-west Norway (Marstrander 1963: pl. 24; Coles 2005: fig. 250). In this case there seem to be four sun symbols on the stone. The more complex examples (two cup marks ringed by concentric circles) are higher up the rock than the others—a wheel cross and another cross which is not enclosed. A group of carved ships is shown travelling from left to right across the decorated surface. It includes both the large circular motifs and a solitary animal which could be a horse. These are 'day ships' in Kaul's terminology. By contrast, the two crosses are associated with vessels travelling from right to left; the edges of the decorated panel include further examples. In this case the drawings of the sun are in two different styles, each of which is associated with vessels sailing in one direction. The simple scheme identified on the Danish metalwork is no longer apparent, yet the decorated surface seems to be formed out of similar components (Figure 58).

The same is true at a much larger scale. There is an important distinction between the images on the decorated metalwork and those in the open air. The drawings on bronze razors and other artefacts are not only small, they are

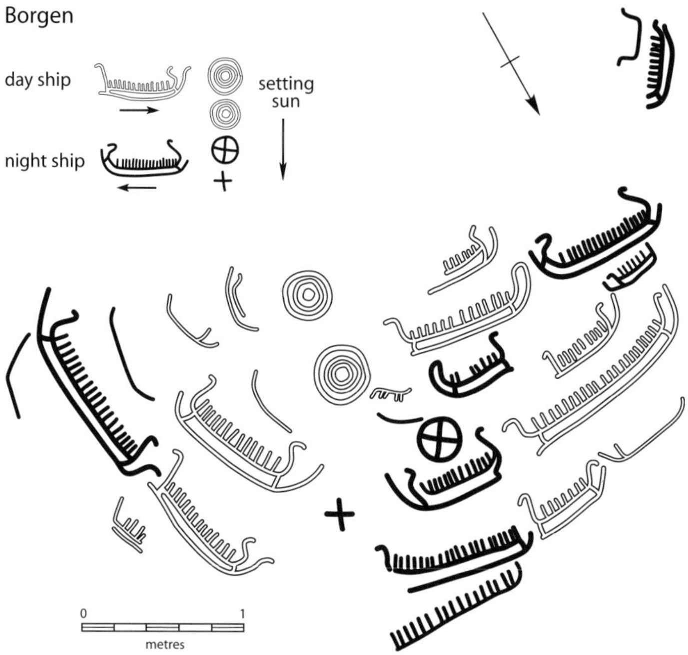

Figure 58. An interpretation of the designs on the decorated outcrop at Borgen, Norway.

entirely two-dimensional. Many of the petroglyphs in Southern Scandinavia are located on prominent boulders, on outcrops, or on sheets of rock that slope down towards a former shoreline. The gradient can vary, and so can the orientation of the decorated surface, but it is important to appreciate that these are three-dimensional structures. This is recognized by the best modern surveys, and it is unfortunate that so few drawings published in the past include this information.

THE HORIZONTAL AND THE VERTICAL: TWO AXES IN SCANDINAVIAN ROCK ART

The form of the rock contributes to the organization of the carvings. In the Swedish regions of Bohuslän and Uppland where the images are recorded in detail (Coles 2000 and 2005), they are probably organized in relation to two distinct axes. The first was briefly described in Chapter 6: many of the drawings extend along the contours of the stone. It suggests that the viewer stood at the lower limit of the decorated panels. The second axis extends at right angles to these designs and normally runs up and down the sloping surface of the outcrop. If the drawings of ships observe the 'horizontal' axis, the 'vertical' axis is represented by less common motifs: by wheeled vehicles (normally drawn by horses), and by footprints of various kinds (Bradley 2006).

The horizontal axis features many boats. In a sense this visual device makes the drawings look more realistic, for the surface of the water itself appears to be level. By drawing the vessels on a single plane, the people who carved them gave the impression that the ships were crossing the sea together (Bradley 2000: 141). There is more variety in these scenes than is commonly recognized. In some panels the boats are of different sizes from one another; they also vary in the amount of detail provided, and in the depths to which the drawings had been pecked into the surface of the rock. Some motifs are quite ephemeral, but others are much bolder and could have been renewed many times. A number of the vessels have crews, but others are quite empty. Kaul's research on the decorated metalwork has drawn attention to the directions in which they are travelling. Now this feature assumes a new significance.

In a few instances the drawings of ships follow certain conventions (Bradley 2006). The most important resemble the rules of perspective. Some vessels are shown in detail, as if they were close to the viewer. Their outlines are boldly carved; they can be larger than their counterparts elsewhere on the same surface; and they are normally shown with their crews. There are other cases in which the opposite happens. The boats are rather smaller, they are less deeply cut, and sometimes their outlines are left incomplete. In extreme cases, such vessels are represented by faint curving lines that seem to represent the hull; usually, there is no one on board. These visual devices could be meant to draw attention to certain carvings rather than others, but they also suggest that the ships are moving away from the viewer. The vessels recede into the distance until the details of their structure are lost (Figure 59). These designs might have been suggested by watching craft setting out to sea, but in this case they travel across the panel until they disappear.

Just as the boats move away from the viewer, they can also approach from a distance. Here the same visual devices are reversed. Vessels may be found at the limits of the decorated surface, apparently making their way towards its centre. As they do so, they increase in size and definition. Again it suggests that the voyage commenced beyond the limits of the panel.

It is rare for the largest panels of rock art to show only one axis of movement. More often ships travel in two directions. Some, like Kaul's 'day ships', move from left to right; others pursue the opposite course. Borgen offers a simple illustration of this pattern, but it can also be found in more

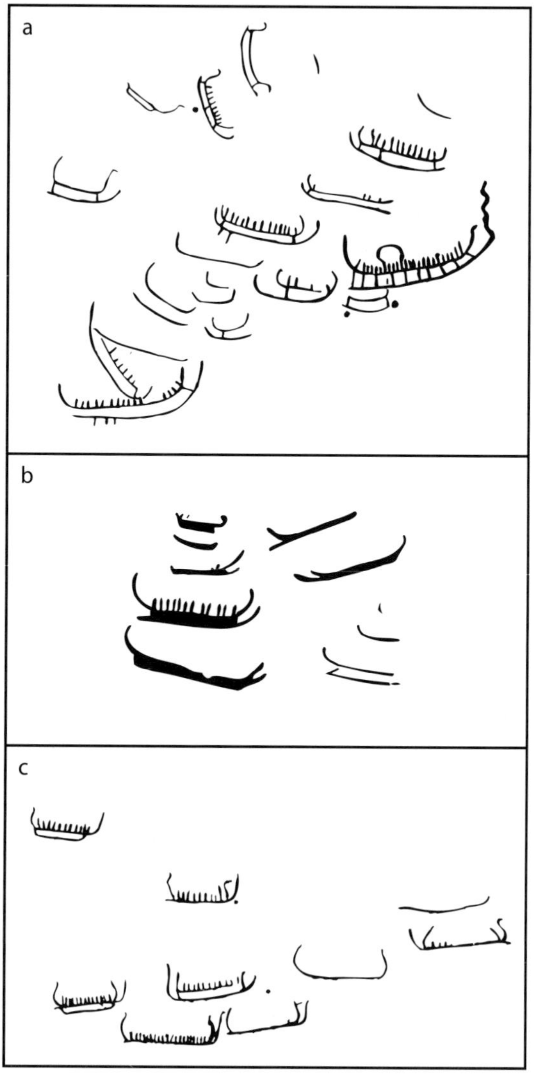

Figure 59. The movement of ships as depicted in Bronze Age rock art. In (a) the vessels enter the panel from the left; in (b) and (c) they leave it, travelling towards the right-hand edge of the decorated surface.

extensive compositions. The obvious explanation for these images is that they depict only one section of a longer voyage. Perhaps these conventions are meant to suggest that the vessels are moving in both directions, vanishing into the distance where the carvings cease and occasionally reappearing on the opposite side of the decorated surface. If some of the boats circumnavigate the panel (or even the entire rock), only their arrival and departure are recorded. This idea is necessarily speculative, but it is based on the evidence of the carvings themselves. The only obvious comparison is with the movement of ships illustrated by Bronze Age metalwork.

The vertical component of these carvings can be defined in two ways. Where the micro-topography of the rock has been recorded, wheeled vehicles and footprints may be shown climbing or descending the decorated surface. Where that detailed information is not provided, the frieze of ships provides a datum. In that case other motifs are offset from it at about ninety degrees.

The carvings of wheeled vehicles pose fewer problems than those of boats. They are generally drawn by horses and cut across the contours of the rock (Figure 60). The bodies of these carts can be represented by circular motifs, not unlike a drawing of the sun, while the vehicles themselves are carried on wheels which can be compared with the isolated ring crosses found in

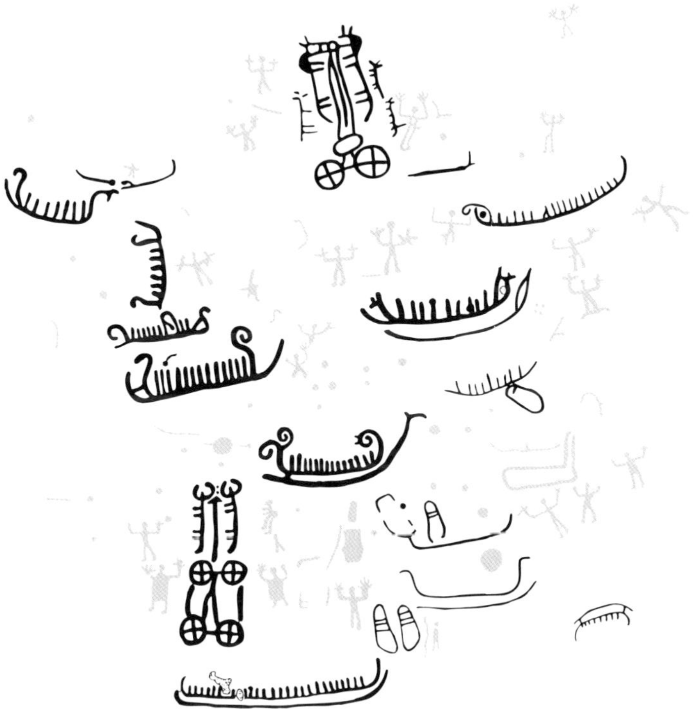

Figure 60. The movement of carts in Scandinavian rock art. Here they are contrasted with drawings of boats and footprints. The remaining designs on the same surface are shown in light tone.

Scandinavian rock art. They recall the construction of the Sun Chariot, but similar designs are also associated with the carvings of ships (Kaul 1998: 195–9; Coles 2002). Another point of comparison is that at Trundholm the disc was drawn by a horse. Horses draw the vehicles depicted in Bronze Age rock art, and on the decorated metalwork they are also associated with the 'day ships' that carry the sun through the sky. A similar connection is present in the petroglyphs where some of the carved ships have a horse's head on the prow.

Carvings of footprints are more frequent (Figure 61). They are of two different kinds; the distinction is based on the presence or absence of shoes. These motifs pose many problems of interpretation, for they are not related to the carvings of men and women in the same panels. In some cases the carved footprints might indicate paths leading up or down the rock, although these

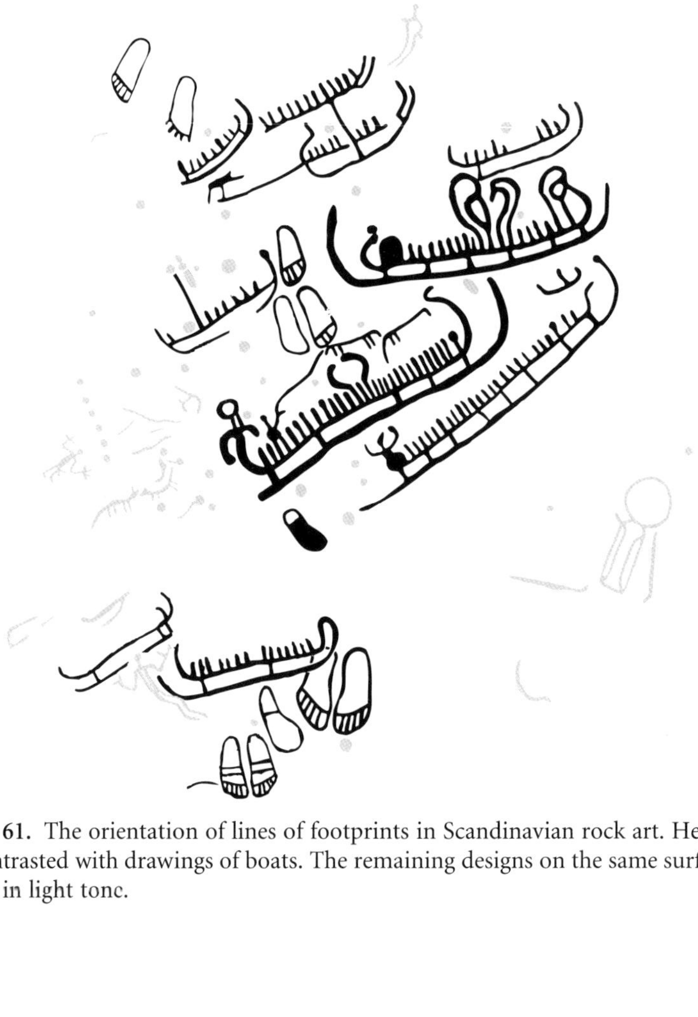

Figure 61. The orientation of lines of footprints in Scandinavian rock art. Here they are contrasted with drawings of boats. The remaining designs on the same surface are shown in light tone.

drawings are usually arranged in pairs. It is not clear whether people had walked across the decorated surface or whether they stood in single file, as if they were in a queue. If the footprints do represent trails, those paths may be continuous or incomplete (Bradley 2006).

In any case it is not obvious where the paths begin, or even where they end. There are certainly examples in which files of carved footprints lead towards bogs or pools, just as there are occasional sites where they appear to emerge from Bronze Age cairns: a connection which is emphasized by similar designs inside the cists in south-west Norway (Jellestad Syvertsen 2002). In other instances lines of footprints may lead towards the highest point on the rock. This is where many of the cup marks can be found. As John Coles has observed, they face directly into the sky (2000: 35). Although it is too simple to claim them as drawings of the stars, the association is important. These features are occasionally associated with wheel crosses which seem to represent the sun. Just as common are isolated pairs of footprints which suggest the presence of someone standing on the decorated outcrop. These positions often command extensive views.

There may be a connection between the carvings of feet and those of vehicles. For the most part the pairs of foot soles are shown a short distance apart, but sometimes they are run together to form a single design. Each half represents the outline of a shoe and the strap by which it was held in place, but, when this happens, the overall design is difficult to distinguish from the ring crosses that are interpreted as drawings of the sun (Figure 62). It is unlikely that it came about by chance. Perhaps the idea of moving up and down the decorated rock recalled the motion of the sun as it climbed the sky in the morning and descended in the late afternoon.

To sum up, while it is easy to think of the rock carvings as a series of static components rather like prehistoric artefacts, some of the more elaborate panels were organized around the idea of *movement.* The ships were not presented like a display of trophies; they were shown in motion, travelling towards the viewer or receding into the distance. Their voyages may have extended beyond the limits of the panel, or even beyond those of the rock. Like the vessels shown on Bronze Age metalwork, they may have illustrated a series of fundamental beliefs, although fewer examples appear to be carrying the sun. That may not be true of the carts which, like the Trundholm 'chariot', are drawn by horses. In some cases the structure of the vehicle resembles a drawing of the sun. More often, the vehicles are supported on 'wheel crosses'. They are taken up and down the decorated outcrops in the same way as the sun rises and sets in the sky. Their movement across the decorated surface follows a similar course to the footprints which have always been difficult to explain. Now it appears that some of the pairs of foot soles were brought

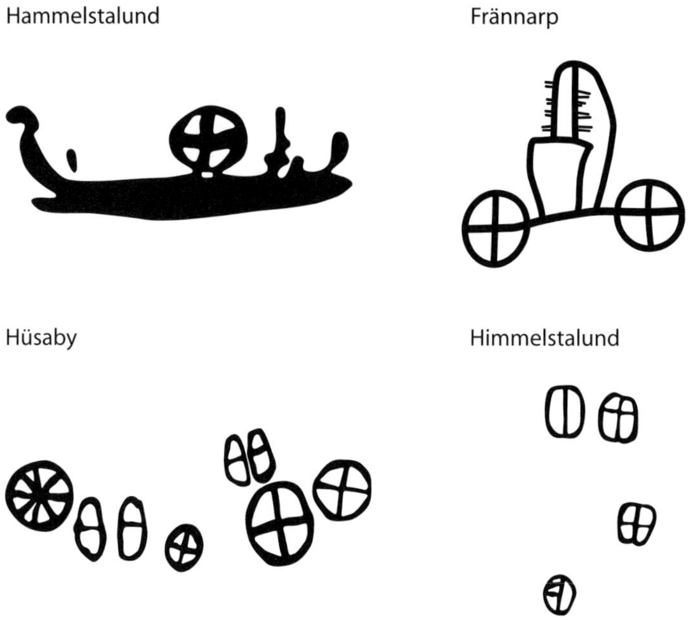

Figure 62. The overlap between drawings of 'ring crosses', wheels, and pairs of footprints in South Scandinavian rock art.

together to create a design that could have been understood as another reference to the sun. The movement of these different elements across the stone and beyond it shares certain elements with the cosmology identified by Kaul (1998 and 2004).

THE SEA, THE SKY, AND THE LAND

One fundamental contrast between the two media has not been considered so far. The decorated bronzes are interpreted in terms of a narrative that accounts for the passage of the sun through the sky during the day and its journey under the sea at night. The common element is that it is carried by a boat, but that vessel is accompanied through the air by a horse and through the water by a fish and possibly by an eel. The key transitions occur where the sea meets the sky and where the sun rises and sets. The horse may be a domesticated animal—albeit one with a special significance during later prehistory (Ullen 1996)—but at no stage does *the land* play any part in this cycle.

The land is what distinguishes the decorated metalwork from the rock carvings of the same period (Bradley 2006). On those sites closely associated with water the horizontal axis may be dominated by drawings of ships, but the vertical axis has a very different character. It is represented by various kinds of footprints and by vehicles drawn by horses. They are directly related to dry land. The same applies to a whole series of images, not discussed so far, which feature in the rock carvings but are not present on metal artefacts. They include human beings (some of whom dominate these scenes), wild animals, and domesticated livestock. There are also groups of people hunting, fighting and farming. They are only the most common elements, but all these figures are securely located on the ground.

The beliefs investigated by Kaul concern the relationship between two important elements: the sky and the sea. The rock carvings, on the other hand, record the complex relationship between three different layers: the sea, the sky, and the land (Figure 63). That is why there are so many differences between these separate media. At the same time, elements of all three may be represented on some of the largest carved surfaces. The sea is represented by drawings of boats and occasionally of fish; the land accounts for numerous drawings of people, animals and artefacts; and the sky is surely referenced by circular designs on the highest part of the decorated surface. Those patterns can be identified at sites in Bohuslän and Uppland (Coles 2000 and 2005),

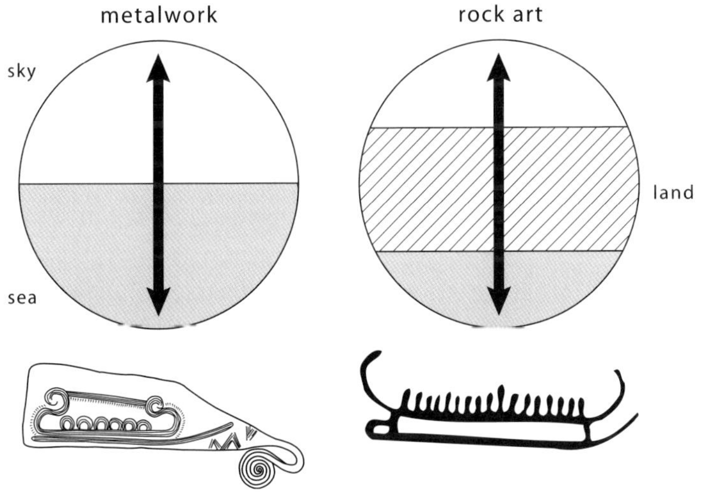

Figure 63. Contrasts in the imagery associated with decorated metalwork and rock carvings in South Scandinavia. The designs on portable artefacts concern the relationship between the sea and the sky. The images associated with rock carvings also refer to the land.

but they can also extend across a wider area in which certain components feature in one set of carvings and different elements in another. Thus drawings featuring ships are mainly a feature of the coastal regions, while carts, wheel crosses, cup marks, and other circular motifs are quite common at inland sites (cf. Burenhult 1980: fig. 3). The same is true of footprints. Thus the scheme that can be identified on some of the larger outcrops by the coast can also extend across the landscape as a whole (Bradley 2006).

The metalwork studied by Kaul illustrates the relationship between the sky and the sea. The introduction of a third component complicates the situation, but it may help to explain the special significance of sites located on the shoreline. Of course this is the ideal position from which to watch the sun rising out of the sea in the morning or setting there at night, but it is also the only place where all the elements represented in the rock carvings come into contact with one another (Figure 64). Chapter 6 suggested that it is why the seashore plays such a crucial role in Circumpolar ethnography. It seems possible that it was just as significant in South Scandinavia. In some ways this idea recalls the interpretation of megalithic tombs discussed in Chapter 3 (Lewis-Williams and Pearce 2005), but in this case a tripartite cosmology is postulated on the basis of the images and their siting rather than the workings

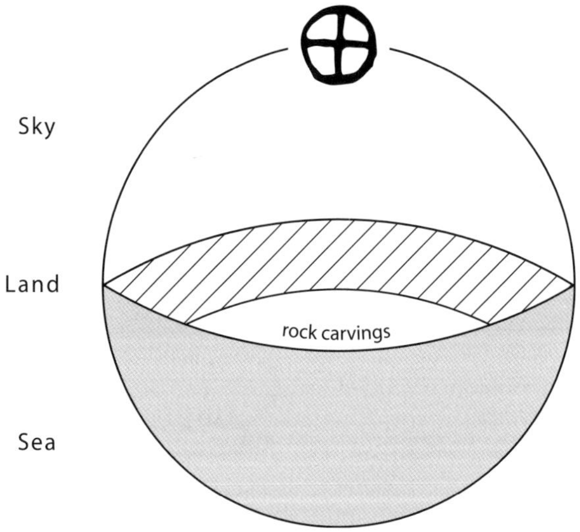

Figure 64. The relationship between the sea, the land, and the sky, emphasizing the movement of the sun, and the location of many of the carved rocks close to the seashore.

of the nervous system. The same interpretation is proposed by Kaul (2005) in a recent study of the significance of the wheel cross.

There are other reasons for supposing that the shoreline had a special significance during prehistory. During the Middle Neolithic period it was where megalithic tombs had been built in the west of Sweden. They were often placed very close to the sea, by the shore or even on small islands (Bradley and Phillips 2004). Although these areas had an unusually abundant supply of fish, it is possible that coastal resources were less important than they had been in earlier periods. There is evidence that the people who were buried at these sites occupied settlements that were located further inland and that they supported themselves mainly by farming (Sjögren 2003). In that case the positioning of the cairns may have been a reference to a way of life that had been followed in the past. Similarly, in the Early Bronze Age the coastal barrows and cairns discussed by Kristiansen (1987) were sometimes located on offshore islands which could not have sustained a resident population. They can be difficult to identify from a vessel sailing on the water, so it seems unlikely that they were intended as aids to navigation. In the north of Sweden, Baudou's work has shown how similar monuments were close to the water's edge. Again it suggests that the coastal margin enjoyed a special significance (Baudou 1968). Its importance was already established by the period when most of the decorated metalwork was used, and cannot be explained entirely in functional terms.

At the same time, the special importance of the shoreline could be expressed in other ways. One of the problems of interpreting Southern Scandinavian rock art is the seemingly chaotic organization of the motifs on certain of the decorated surfaces. Although there are fleets of boats, wheeled vehicles, and trails of footprints, the carvings feature numerous drawings of people and animals which are interspersed with the other images (Frontispiece). At first sight this undermines any notion that the sea was distinguished from the land, for humans and their livestock are depicted alongside many of the boats. One explanation is that the carvings are really palimpsests and that not all of them were contemporary with one another; when the ships were pictured, for example, the other motifs may have faded from view. It is true that the Late Bronze Age carvings contain a rather wider range of motifs, but there is another way of reading these scenes which does not imply a complex sequence. Perhaps the drawings of ships and of creatures that live on land were mixed together in order to emphasize the importance *of the shoreline itself*, for it is the only place where these all separate elements would have been found (Bradley 2006). If so, panels that appear entirely unstructured today may originally have possessed a special significance.

The same idea could be expressed by the stone settings. Here two rather different patterns are important. There are the large cult houses studied by Helena Victor (2001 and 2002). They were first built during the Early Bronze Age, but their history extends into the following period. The form of these buildings referred to that of the domestic house, but a number of more impressive examples are paired with exceptionally large barrows and cairns located by the sea. Typical examples of such pairings are the famous site at Kivik and the enormous mound at Hågahögen. In southern Sweden the distribution of cult houses extends from the Mälar valley near to Stockholm as far as Göteborg on the west coast. Rock carvings occur in the same areas, but not on the same sites. These places may have been the power centres of local elites whose main contacts with one another would have been by sea. At the same time, the association between rectangular ceremonial buildings, circular cairns and the coast referred to more arcane beliefs.

The cairns with which the larger cult houses are associated present a special problem. On one level they form part of the series of coastal monuments identified by Kristiansen, but occasionally they make a more specific reference. The decorated cist at Kivik includes drawings of ships, horses, and ring crosses (Randsborg 1993), all of them images that might be linked to the solar cosmology postulated by Kaul. A substantial round barrow at Sagaholm was located near an inlet of Lake Vättern. It had a decorated kerb which also featured drawings of boats and horses, but in this case there was no picture of the sun. It would have been necessary to move around the mound in order to view these designs, and Joakim Goldhahn (1999) suggests that in this case the circular array of decorated kerbstones supplies the missing element. Perhaps the entire monument was understood as a solar symbol. It is an interpretation that might be extended to other sites.

The same relationship is indicated by a series of smaller structures whose chronology appears to be limited to the Late Bronze Age and perhaps the Early Iron Age. Most were built of stone, but they also include rectangular cult houses made of wood. A series of cemeteries located on or near to the coast combine three different elements (Widholm 1998). There are the ship settings that can be associated with cremation burials, but there are also square or rectangular platforms whose form echoes those of ceremonial structures and also of domestic buildings. Each is associated with circular stone settings. Two arrangements are common at these sites. There are well preserved ship settings where it is possible to decide the direction in which the boat is moving. Some of these are aligned on the circular cairns, as if an actual vessel was travelling into a tomb. Others appear to emerge from circular monuments. There are also cases in which these structures are apparently attached

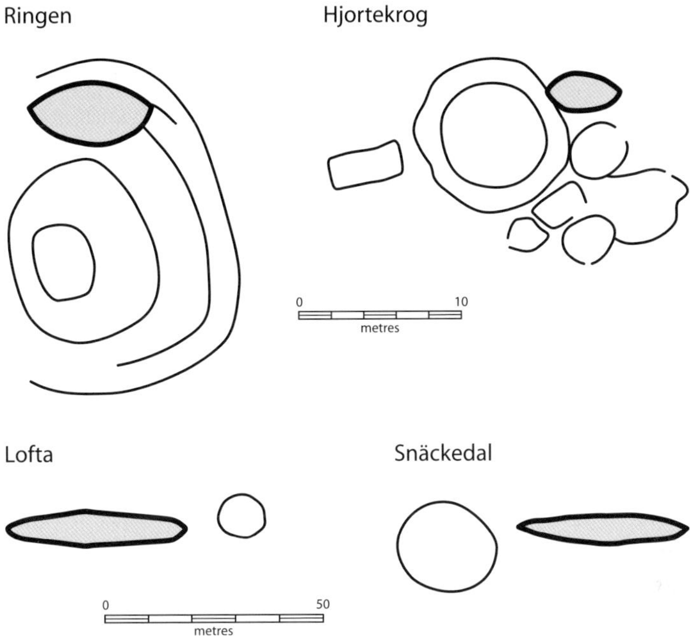

Figure 65. The relationship between ship settings (shaded) and round and rectangular cairns or platforms in Bronze Age cemeteries in Scandinavia.

to the ship in a way that recalls the sun symbols engraved on Bronze Age metalwork (Figure 65).

The ship settings can also be paired with rectangular monuments whose closest parallels are in domestic architecture (Widholm and Regnell 2001; Artursson 2005). They may abut one another, or they can be separated by small circular structures. The organization of these sites seems to be based on the complementary relationship between a seagoing vessel and a building constructed on land. The combination of both these elements provides a striking image of the seashore. It seems as if coastlines—both real or metaphorical—played a major part in the rock carvings of Bronze Age Scandinavia; perhaps the same was true in some of the cemeteries. In that case it is noticeable that images in these two media are rarely found together. Their distributions are almost mutually exclusive, as if each represented a different way of expressing the same ideas.

Again it appears that common concerns may link the visual images that were created in separate parts of Scandinavia. The decorated metalwork, whose distribution focuses on Denmark and the southernmost part of Sweden, emphasizes the complex relationship between ships, the sun, and the sea. The rock carvings of the same period, the largest examples of which tend to be further to the north, illustrate a similar concern with boats and water. Sometimes they include motifs that have been identified with the sun. Most of the petroglyphs with complex images of ships are within sight of the sea, and a number of them were probably by the water's edge (Ling 2008). It seems likely that the combination of motifs associated with these sites was intended to evoke the distinctive character of the shoreline. The same connection is illustrated by a small number of stone settings or geoglyphs. They combine circular designs that may have been meant to represent the sun with images of ships and rectangular buildings. The latter are sometimes juxtaposed, as if to emphasize the importance of the seashore.

THREE EXAMPLES

This chapter concludes by considering three sites in greater detail. All are located in Sweden: Snäckedal, Himmelstalund, and Högsbyn. The cemetery at Snäckedal contains numerous stone settings, one of them associated with a bronze razor, but there are no carved rocks in the vicinity. The site at Himmelstalund is an important decorated outcrop, but in this case the nearest cairns are some distance away. The remarkable complex at Högsbyn, on the other hand, includes both these components and constitutes a miniature landscape in its own right.

Snäckedal is a cemetery of over thirty Bronze Age monuments: the largest and most distinctive of a series of structures overlooking the margins of a bog a kilometre from a former inlet of the Baltic (Bradley and Widholm 2007). It is distinguished from most of the other monuments in the vicinity because it includes a number of square or rectangular stone settings, and seven other structures in the form of a ship; two more stone ships are recorded beyond the limits of the site. In addition to these specialized structures, there are considerable round cairns, and a series of smaller circular monuments (Figure 66).

The cemetery has two main components. The earliest feature appears to be a line of four large cairns, each of them located on the highest available ground. The biggest was in the middle of the site. There was a similar monument beside it. In a subsequent phase, four small groups of stone settings were constructed within the cemetery, two of them in relation to the existing cairns at its centre, and one beside each of the others. An enormous ship setting was also built. It is one of the longest in Scandinavia and divided the site in half. It ran up to the base of the largest cairn.

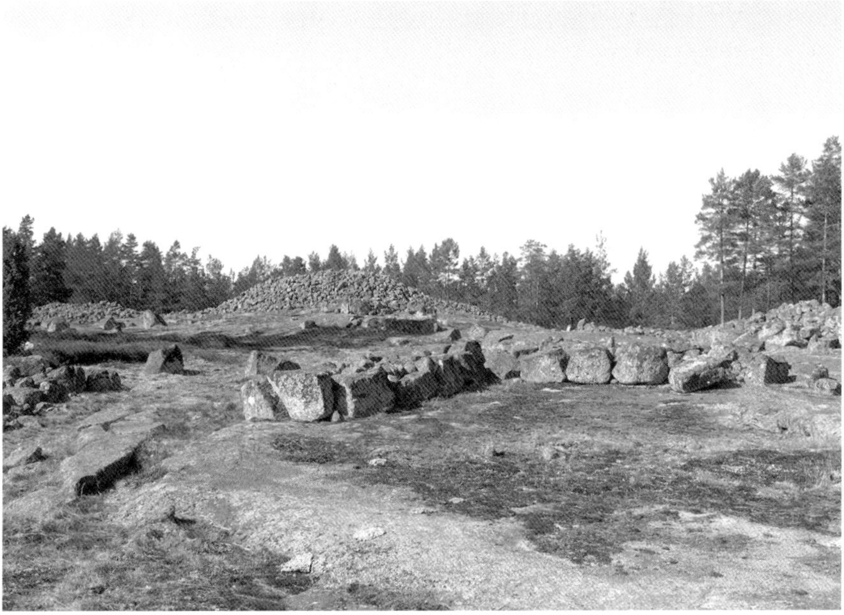

Figure 66. General view of the Bronze Age cemetery at Snäckedal, Sweden, with two rectangular stone settings in the foreground.

Every group of monuments includes circular structures, but the small ship settings are all located in the northern part of the cemetery, and all but one of the rectilinear monuments are in the other half. If their wider references have been interpreted correctly, the site is subdivided between one section in which the structures relate to the land and perhaps to the domestic world, and another which refers directly to boats and the sea (Figure 67).

The ship settings have further implications. Almost all of them are aligned on the large round cairns which appear to be the oldest structures on the site, but they do not run right up to them, nor do they approach their centres rather than their flanks. One way of explaining this observation is to suggest that the vessels were attached to these monuments in the same way as sun symbols are connected to ships in the rock carvings. At the same time, two of the stone ships at Snäckedal are well enough preserved to establish the direction of movement. They seem to be paired with one another, yet they are obviously travelling in opposite directions. In Kaul's terminology, the smaller structure would be a 'day ship', and the larger vessel a 'night ship'.

Although their alignments differ by about thirty degrees, both these ship settings are orientated approximately east–west. That contrasts with the north–south alignment of all the remaining vessels, as well as two isolated

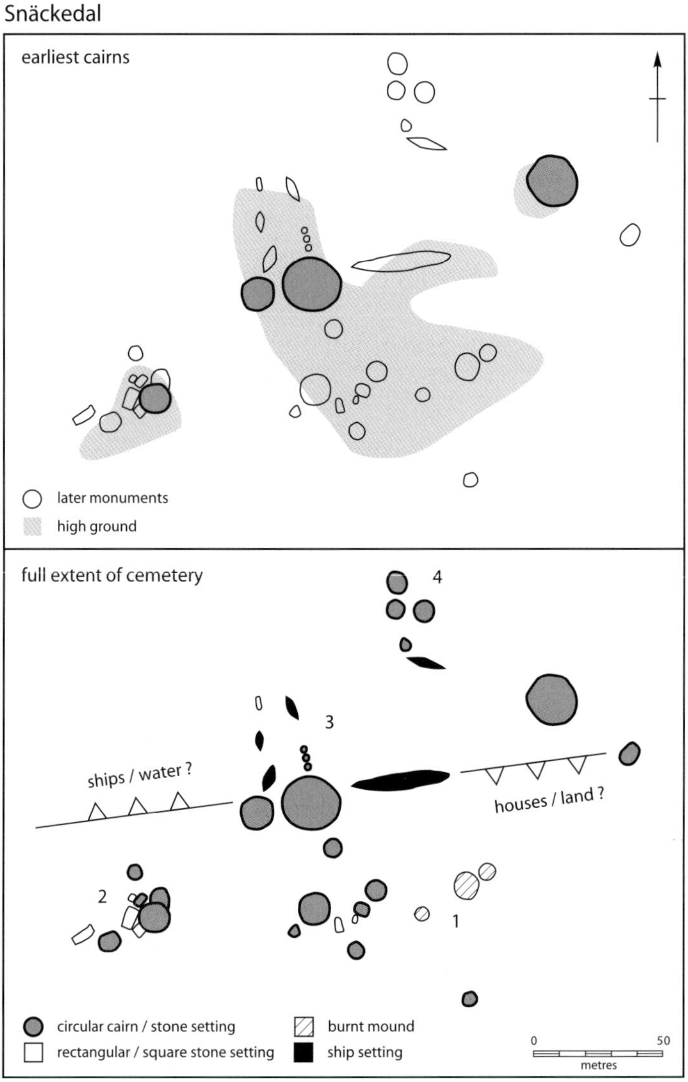

Figure 67. The development of the Bronze Age cemetery at Snäckedal, Sweden. The upper plan shows the four cairns attributed to the earliest phase of activity. The lower plan shows four clusters of smaller (and later) monuments, each focusing on the position of one of the older cairns. It suggests that the cemetery was divided between one group of stone settings in the form of ships, and another in the form of domestic buildings.

examples outside the cemetery itself. In most cases it is impossible to distinguish the prow from the stern, but in one instance it is clear that a stone ship is departing from the site. The boats that followed a rough east–west orientation could have been aligned on the position of the summer sun as it travelled above the local horizon; but the example that was sailing towards the north was directed into an area where the sun would never appear.

The second site is the large rock outcrop at Himmelstalund which was briefly described in Chapter 6 (Hauptmann Wahlgren 2002). It was not on the coast but overlooked a river communicating between a major lake and the sea. The principal carved rock was located in between two sets of rapids. Here questions of orientation are most important. The river flows from west to east towards the Baltic Sea. The outcrop shares the same alignment. It is long and relatively narrow and has two major groups of carvings on its flanks, one facing north and the other south. There are fewer designs along the top of the stone. There were other rock carvings in the vicinity but they are not considered here; nor are more isolated panels towards the western limit of the site.

Perhaps unusually, there are differences between the designs created at different levels on the main section of the decorated outcrop. This is most apparent on its northern flank. In contrast to some of the patterns considered earlier, here there is little overlap between marine and terrestrial imagery. The drawings of boats tend to be located on the lower parts of the decorated surface, and drawings of animals are generally higher up. It even seems as if domesticated livestock were closer to the base of the rock than the pictures of wild species, for along the top of the decorated surface there are the tracks of a bear. Drawings of weapons can be identified in a similar position (Figure 68), although Katherine Hauptmann Wahlgren suggests that they may have been among the earliest elements at Himmelstalund. In some respects these images represent a world in miniature, for the ships cluster around the foot of the outcrop. Higher up there is more of an emphasis on creatures that live on the land, but there are also foot soles and a wheel cross.

The main carved surfaces face north and south respectively, but in each case virtually all the ships are shown sailing down the river to the sea. Those on the northern side of the rock would receive less illumination from the sun than their equivalents towards the south. In the summer it would rise to the north-east and set in the north-west, but for part of the year the decorated surface would often be in shadow. By contrast, the designs that overlooked the river to the south would have been illuminated. Although the drawings of vessels show them travelling downriver, those on the north face of the outcrop are moving from right to left. In Kaul's terminology they should be 'night ships'. On the same argument those on the opposite face can be interpreted as 'day ships'.

There are significant contrasts between the two groups of vessels. The largest 'night ships' are towards the base of the outcrop; smaller craft tend to be higher up the rock face. Most ships are shown with their crews, but this is less common further up the slope, where some of the vessels are apparently incomplete. Those on the northern side of the outcrop are associated with sun symbols, mainly in the form of a wheel cross.

These patterns contrast with the drawings on the south side of the rock. The 'day ships' are closer together than the 'night ships'. On the whole they are rather smaller than the other vessels, and there is no clear distinction between boats with crews and those that are apparently empty; in some cases they may even be paired with one another. The distribution of the ships overlaps with that of drawings of wild and domesticated animals. There are also a few cup marks, but sun symbols are not represented.

In this case it is possible to compare two groups of images. Those on the north-facing slope share features in common with the 'night ships' identified by Kaul. They would not have faced directly into the sun for part of the year and are associated with wheel crosses and other solar symbols (Figure 68). The nature of these vessels seems to have varied with their height above the

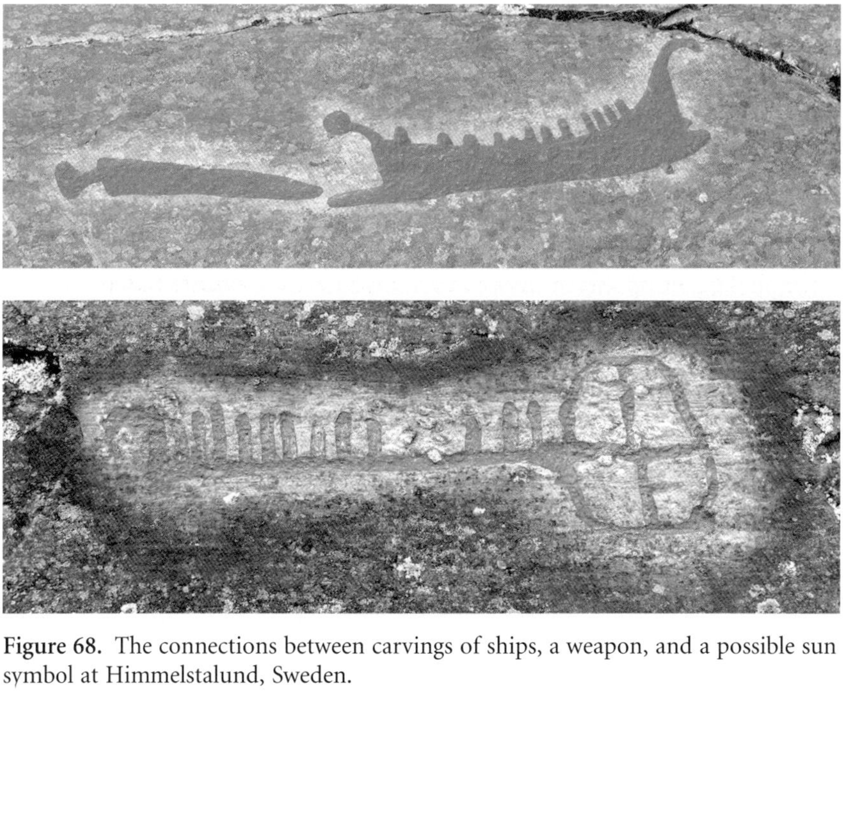

Figure 68. The connections between carvings of ships, a weapon, and a possible sun symbol at Himmelstalund, Sweden.

foot of the outcrop, and there are signs that drawings associated with land were generally further up the decorated surface than those connected with the water. Domesticated animals were distinguished from wild species by means of the same device. The carvings that face south are very different. They are directly lit by the sun and do not adhere to the same scheme. Here boats with crews are interspersed with empty vessels, and wild animals with domestic species. A major contrast is that solar symbols are not represented. These associations are not like those on the decorated metalwork, but they still suggest that the differences between day and night, and those between light and shadow, remained a fundamental concern.

The last of these three sites is Högsbyn where a series of carved rocks is distributed between an inland lake and an area of higher ground with a Bronze Age cemetery (Svensson 1985; Tilley 1999: 133–73).

The rock carvings extend down the hillside towards the edge of the lake. Further upslope there is a cemetery which includes the largest cairn in the region. Another cairn overlooks the water's edge. Its characteristic profile is reflected by a small island not far from the shore where some of the carvings were made; there are carved rocks on other islands in the lake. The Högsbyn complex is subject to important seasonal variations. The carved rocks are covered by snow between November and March, and those by the edge of the lake are sometimes underwater. This site has been studied by Christopher Tilley who argues that people would have visited the images in a prescribed sequence (1999: 153–71). He suggests that they followed a path leading upslope from the shoreline towards the cairns.

If the rock carvings were only visible during the summer months, it is worth considering the position of the sun at that time of year. It rose in the north-east, moved south as it climbed the sky and would eventually have been seen above the lake. After it had crossed the water, it returned to dry land where it set towards the north-west. It would have moved around the zone of rock carvings from dawn to dusk before it disappeared from view on the high ground behind the petroglyphs, to reappear the next morning close to the position of the cemetery.

The importance of the sun is illustrated by the distribution of Late Bronze Age images at Högsbyn. There are two groups of circular motifs at either end of the zone of rock carvings. This is where the main concentrations of ships are found. The largest vessels are towards the shore, where most of them are travelling towards the lake. They are associated with large wheel crosses and similar devices as if they are carrying the sun. There are other ways in which the carvings suggest a direction of movement. Most of the ships travel towards the water, and a few footprints follow the same course from north to south.

The main emphasis seems to be on the movement of the sun between the high ground and the water.

There are fewer ships travelling away from the lake in the general direction of the cairns, but this axis does seem to be marked by a larger number of isolated footprints. More important is a striking pattern identified by Tilley. The human figures depicted on the rocks change their character from one end of the complex to the other. Towards the lake these figures are diminutive and do not display any obvious characteristics. Further upslope they are larger,

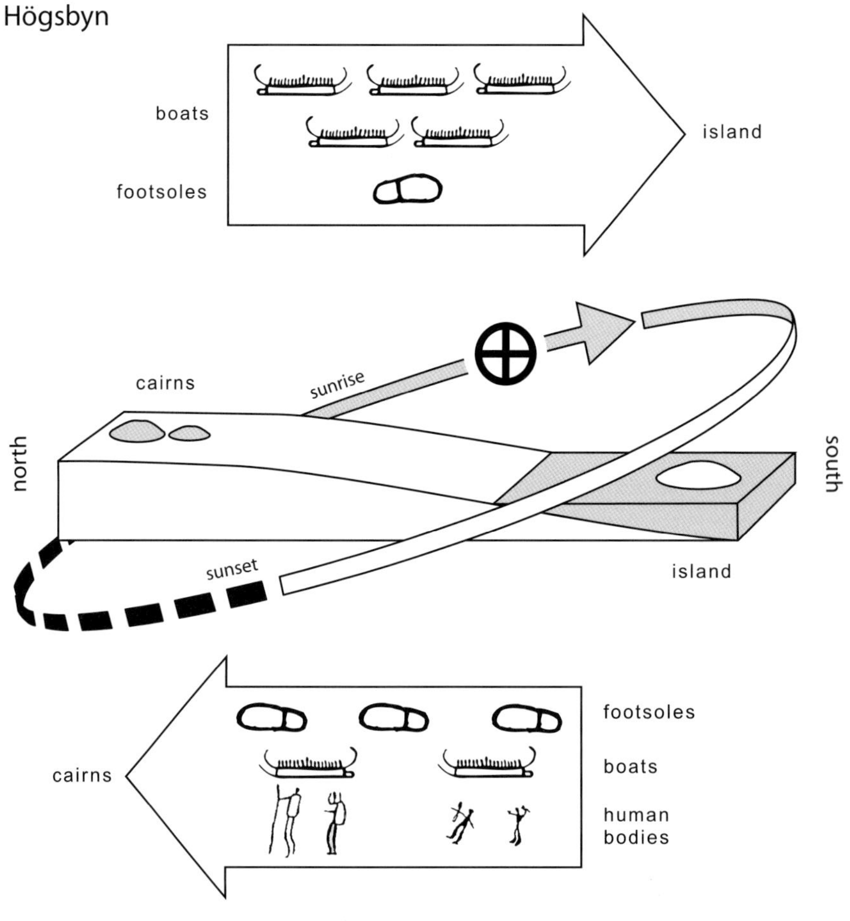

Figure 69. An interpretation of the rock art and nearby monuments at Högsbyn, Sweden in relation to the movement of the sun around the site in summer. The diagram summarizes the axes of movement of the carved ships, people, and footprints in relation to the position of a Bronze Age cemetery and an offshore island with a strong resemblance to a cairn.

and those towards the northern edge of the site carry weapons and are clearly male. Tilley is right to describe this as 'a narrative about becoming human' (1999: 171).

His interpretation works best when it considered in relation to the passage of the sun around the site (Figure 69). During the summer months it moved from land to water and then back again. It also connected the sunrise with an important cemetery, and with an offshore island that resembled another cairn. Some of the carvings record a similar passage between land and water, while others follow a course leading upslope towards the burial ground. Again that is not unlike the distinctive cycle described by Kaul.

All three examples share certain features in common, but they do little more than suggest that the different images reveal similar concerns. The solar cycle may have influenced the organization of these designs, but it simply provides a framework for the remaining elements. It does not exhaust their significance. There is immense variety, just as there are other components that have not been considered here. No doubt many different narratives were embedded within this overall scheme. They may have varied from one region to another and could have changed over time.

The uses of these places would have been equally diverse. Chapter 8 develops this point by discussing the relationship between the different images and the people who originally encountered them.

8

The Origin of Fire

THE HELIOS OVERTURE

In 1903, the Danish composer Carl Nielsen was on holiday in the Mediterranean. While he was staying in Athens, he completed one of his most famous works, the orchestral overture *Helios*. Nielsen explained that the music evoked the sun rising out of the sea and travelling across the sky before it set. The piece has a special significance more than a century after it was written, for it is performed on Danish radio to mark the beginning of a new year. It seems that even now the passage of the sun is an important event.

In one sense Nielsen's overture is a celebration of light and warmth. It can also be understood as part of a more general phenomenon, as Scandinavian artists and scholars have often been attracted to the cultures of Southern Europe. Perhaps it is why there are so many Classical archaeologists in the Nordic countries. It may also help to explain why their prehistorians have emphasized the links between the Northern Bronze Age and the Mediterranean.

The *Helios Overture* traces the same process as Bronze Age cosmology. It portrays the sun as it rises out of the sea, travels across the sky and descends into the water at dusk. That is a familiar sight in Northern Europe where it gains an added significance because in many places it can be seen for a comparatively short time during the winter. The sun is visible for much longer in the summer months.

The contrast between summer and winter is even more apparent in the Arctic and plays a significant part in local mythology. The Finnish national epic, *The Kalevala*, includes a poem called 'Fire from heaven' which describes how the land is in darkness because the sun and the moon have been captured. Fire has been stolen from people's homes. This is a challenge to the authority of the most powerful god:

> Therefore was night unending,
> And for long was utter darkness,
> Night in Kalevala for ever....
> Likewise in the heavens was darkness...

Ukko, then, of Gods the highest,
In the air the great Creator,
Now began to feel most strangely,
And he pondered and reflected,
What strange thing the moon had darkened,
How the sun had been obstructed

(*Kalevala* 47; translation Kirby 1907)

Ukko restores order, using his sword to make fire. The poem surely reflects the concerns of people who were aware of the annual cycle, and of their dependence on the heat and light of the sun. Such beliefs appear to be of considerable antiquity, and some of the scenes depicted in prehistoric rock paintings have been interpreted using the oral poems recorded in *The Kalevala* (Lahelma 2008) The *Helios Overture* has a Finnish counterpart, for it happens that 'Fire from heaven' was set to music by Sibelius only one year before Nielsen wrote his piece. There is another link with prehistoric archaeology as Sibelius was the first person to identify ancient rock art in Finland (Lahelma 2008: 28).

Sibelius's cantata *The Origin of Fire* provides a useful reminder that complex systems of belief often develop out of everyday concerns. Just as the disappearance of the sun during the northern winter provides the basis for a narrative involving the gods, its relation to the sky and the sea was apparently explained by the cosmology recorded on Bronze Age metalwork. In the past, similar problems may have been presented by the relationship between land and water, and by the passage of the seasons.

THE COSMOS AND DAILY EXPERIENCE

The visual images of Bronze Age Scandinavia date from a time when the natural environment was changing rapidly and in unexpected ways. As the land continued to rise after the Ice Age, the sea gradually retreated. In some places the process was so rapid that it could be traced from one generation to another, and there are areas like Bohuslän in the west of Sweden where the water receded so far that sometimes it was no longer visible from places that had originally been on the coast (Coles 2005; Ling 2008). The presence of prehistoric rock carvings bore witness to these changes. They had originally been located on or near to the water's edge, and that relationship was recorded by numerous drawings of boats. Now they were some way inland. Sometimes new images were created closer to the shoreline, but more often the older designs were renewed at the traditional site, even though its connection with the sea was lost. The same applies to the carvings made on cliffs. Johan Ling has demonstrated that, as the sea level fell, new images were created lower down the rock (2008: chapter 7). The older carvings acted like a tidemark, showing how high the water had reached. Harbours, inlets, and channels gradually silted up, and many places were no longer accessible by boat.

At the same time conditions changed out at sea. Small offshore islands increased in size as submerged rocks broke the surface. In time they developed into islands in their own right, so that the coastal archipelagos in both the Baltic and the North Atlantic gradually changed their configuration. This happened to a different extent from one region to the next as the land was not rising at a uniform rate; this process was more pronounced in some areas than in others, and there are certain regions where any change of level was minimal. Even so, these developments might have been extremely important, for it was where the land met the sea that Bronze Age cairns were constructed. Some of the most conspicuous were built on offshore islands.

The rocks that were rising from the sea had been sculpted by glaciers long before they were submerged. As a result, they often have rounded profiles. That is important, for they bear a striking resemblance to Bronze Age monuments of a type that was already associated with islands (Figure 70). Rather than supposing that land was emerging from the seabed, people might have thought that cairns were rising out of the water (Nordenborg Myhre 2004: 179). That would be particularly apparent as ships were taking corpses for burial in the archipelago.

The appearance of new islands would have been apparent to generations of sailors as they travelled these waters, and the rocks themselves would have been more useful as seamarks than many of the monuments that had been constructed off the coast. Nevertheless such places could still be associated with the dead. Chapter 7 argued that the meeting place of land and sea enjoyed a special significance in Northern prehistory. Now there is another factor to consider—perhaps the emergence of small islands along the east coast could be compared with the appearance of the sun as it rose from the underworld every morning.

There were more rapid developments, too. Certain experiences would have posed problems for travellers in these waters, especially if they were engaged in the long distance voyages postulated by Kristiansen and Larsson (2005). As mentioned earlier, the contrast between day and night became more pronounced in northern latitudes. The climate was probably similar to that today (Keith Bennett pers. comm.), so that seasonal variations would be significant. Large bodies of water could be frozen, and much of the land might have been buried under snow. Movement was much more difficult. Sometimes the

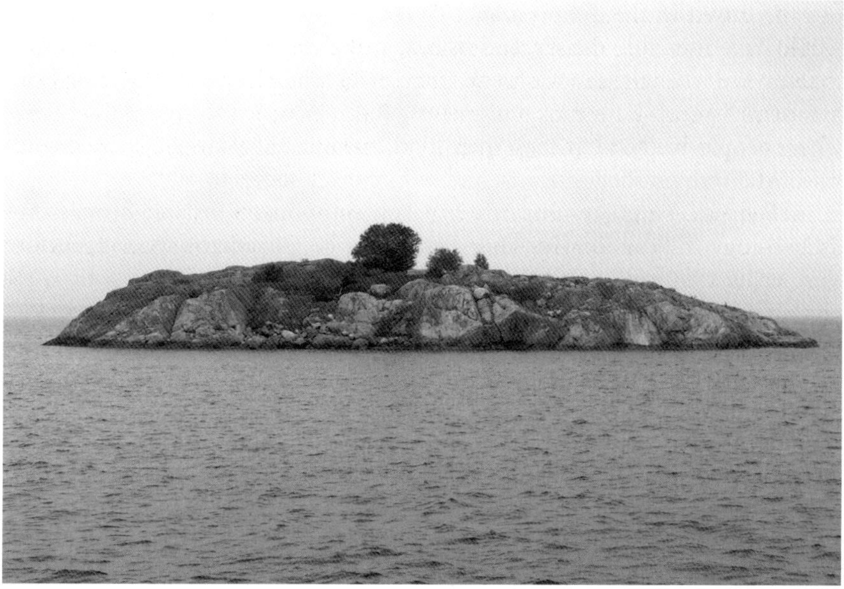

Figure 70. A small island in the Stockholm archipelago.

coastline was free from ice because it was warmed by the Gulf Stream, but there were inland areas which would be almost impassable.

As the temperature increased and the days became longer, profound changes came over the Northern landscape. They would have presented their own problems of interpretation. Ice and snow melted, and streams and rivers flowed across the countryside. It was then that waterfalls and rapids had their greatest impact. Knut Helskog (1999) has pointed out that decorated outcrops on the shoreline would be the last to be affected by snow and the soonest to reappear. When winter ended, rocks that had been covered over became accessible again, and small stone-built monuments and petroglyphs could be clearly identified for the first time in months. The colours and textures of the bedrock would be immediately apparent. For a while these places were largely free of vegetation. The harsh winters only emphasized the dramatic contrasts between the seasons, which were still more apparent as one travelled from south to north. All these changes could be attributed to the movements of the sun during the course of the year.

In the circumstances it is hardly surprising that fire became so important in the ritual life of Bronze Age Scandinavia (Kaliff 2007). On one level it was closely linked to the importance of the sky and the sun; both provided a source of heat and light, and in the extract from *The Kalevala* quoted earlier the theft of fire is directly linked to the disappearance of the sun and moon. Smoke from fires would have risen into the sky, and its heat would have melted the snow and ice that formed when the sun was weak, or even absent, in the winter. Fire was both a creative force and a means of transformation. It was used to heat the houses where people lived and to cook their food, but it could also split stone, change raw metal into finished artefacts, and reduce dead bodies to ash.

In fact sea, sun, sky, and fire are key components of the Bronze Age archaeology of Scandinavia. They deserve to be considered in detail before this account returns to the visual images of the same period.

WATER, SKY, SUN, AND FIRE

In Southern Scandinavia there are cairns on offshore islands and others on high ground near the coast, but their distribution extends into the interior (Hyenstrand

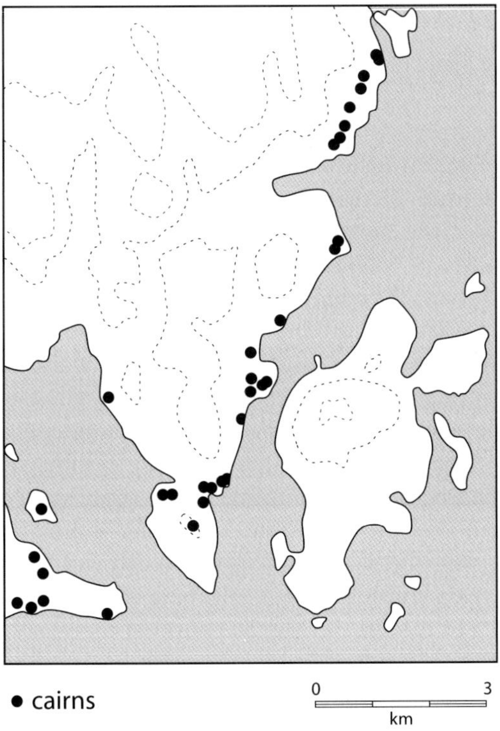

Figure 71. The distribution of cairns in part of Ångermansland, northern Sweden in relation to the Bronze Age coastline.

1984). Thus the concentration of sites along the shoreline forms part of a wider phenomenon. Further to the north, the situation changes. Here the cairns are confined to the seaboard and have not have been found in inland areas, even though those regions are associated with other kinds of monuments (Figure 71; Baudou 1968). The distinction appears to be a real one.

The distribution of the northernmost cairns has always been considered in terms of contacts with the south, and what little excavated evidence is available suggests that they do date from the Bronze Age and Early Iron Age. They have been connected both with traders visiting these areas from Southern Scandinavia and with the establishment of agricultural settlements beside the sea. The evidence for this interpretation is very limited. At the same time, it is thought that the absence of similar cairns in the interior was because it was occupied by a different population, who came in contact with exchange partners on the coast.

There are difficulties with both these arguments (Bolin 1999: 55–68). The northern cairns are not easy to characterize. They do not conform to standard types like those found further south, and there is structural evidence they had been used and modified at intervals. Moreover, few of these structures are associated with human remains; animal bones are just as often found on the sites. In these respects they have a distinctive character of their own. Baudou's fieldwork has demonstrated that they were located very close to the water's edge (Baudou 1968). In contrast, the cairns in Southern Scandinavia—even those near to the sea—occupied more prominent positions in the landscape.

If some of the cairns emphasized the distinction between land and sea, others were certainly directed towards the sky. Some of the largest monuments on the coast of Southern Scandinavia occupy the highest ground. It may have made them more visible, but this tendency can even be recognized within cemeteries like that at Snäckedal where differences of elevation are slight. Moreover, there are a number of cases where a large cairn had been constructed on top of a particularly small hill or outcrop, with the result that it collapsed (Figure 72). The material for its construction had to be taken to the site, a stone at a time, and there are sites at which it was necessary to build a kerb to hold this material in place. Sometimes the kerbstones were obtained by quarrying around the edge of a monument, which had the effect of raising it on a plinth (Bradley and Widholm 2007: 249). In such cases it seems as if height above the surrounding area was the most important consideration. Perhaps it was necessary to build these structures in relation to the sky (Gerdin 1999).

The hilltop siting of cairns is a special feature of the larger monuments, many of which are attributed to the Early Bronze Age. It is less apparent with the smaller and more specialized constructions which date from the Late

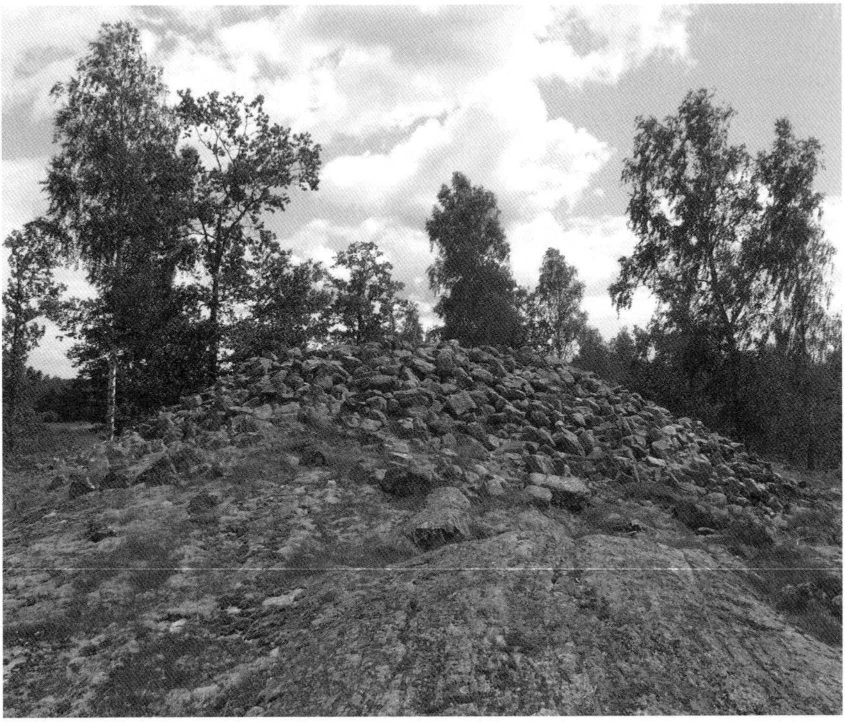

Figure 72. The siting of the Bronze Age cairn on top of a small rock outcrop near Gamleby, Sweden.

Bronze Age and Early Iron Age. Some of the same relationships were expressed in a different way. The juxtaposition of ship settings and rectangular monuments could have referred to the boundary between the sea and the land. Similarly, the small circular stone settings could have represented the sun and the sky. Chapter 7 argued that these structures illustrate similar themes to the carvings and decorated metalwork.

Another concern was with fire. At one time it was thought that mounds of fire-cracked stones marked the positions of Bronze Age settlements in South Scandinavia (Jensen 1985). That no longer seems likely. Many occupation sites have been identified during recent fieldwork. They are characterized by timber longhouses, but not all of them are associated with deposits of this kind; instead deposits of burnt rock are often on other sites. Burnt mounds have been reinterpreted in recent years and may even have changed their roles during the Bronze Age (Runcis 1999). Few artefacts are associated with the earlier examples, but those dating from the Late Bronze Age are found with metalwork and human bones. Their wider contexts are revealing, too. They can cover small circular stone settings. One example in the east of Sweden overlay four concentric rings of boulders, like the monuments recorded in cemeteries (Karlenby 1999). Deposits of burnt stone occur in other places. They are a notable feature of the cult houses described in Chapter 7 where they have similar associations. Here they can be found with human cremations, metalworking residues and querns (Victor 2002). Deposits of burnt stone are also associated with the long rows of hearths in South Scandinavia (Thorn 2007). They are usually interpreted as places where feasts took place, but it seems possible that they had been lines of bonfires. If so, they would have been particularly impressive at night.

Recent fieldwork has shown that deposits of burnt material are associated with South Scandinavian rock carvings. This evidence takes several different forms. There are accumulations of burnt stones around the base of the decorated outcrops, sometimes associated with rubble platforms or enclosures (Kaul 2006a and b). Similar material has been recorded on the top of the rocks themselves, where it could be used to fill cracks and fissures (Bengtsson 2004). It may even impinge on the carvings. There is also some evidence for the positions of fires, marked by blistered patches on the surface of the stone (Figure 73). Until recently they were attributed to recent vandalism, or even seen as a Christian response to the pagan imagery on display. Now that appears unlikely. Although the burnt surfaces have not been studied by scientific methods, the deposits of charcoal found on these sites have radiocarbon dates in the Bronze Age and Early Iron Age (Bengtsson 2004; Kaul 2006a; Lingaard 2006). An area of burning of this kind was sealed underneath a Late Bronze Age cairn at the Swedish site of Hjortekrog (Widholm 1999).

On one level this emphasis on the importance of fires reflects significant changes in the treatment of the dead (Kaliff 1997). Initially, the remains of the human body were preserved and buried, sometimes in a coffin or cist, and occasionally in a grave in the form of a boat. Although such burials could be aligned on the rising or setting sun, they were generally hidden from view beneath a mound or cairn (Randsborg and Nybo 1984). In the Late Bronze Age, however, there is evidence that bodies were burnt on pyres. The remains of this process have been identified in the course of excavation at Gualöv in southern Sweden: a site which includes the remains of three cult houses (Arcini 2005; Svanberg 2005). It is clear that what have been treated as cremation burials in the past are often a small selection of relics from such a pyre, the rest of which have been lost or distributed among other contexts, including the foundations of buildings, hearths, and cultivated fields (Oestigaard 1999). Bo Gräslund (1994) suggests that cremation was a way of freeing the spirit of the deceased. It is certainly true that this process would have accelerated the rites of passage.

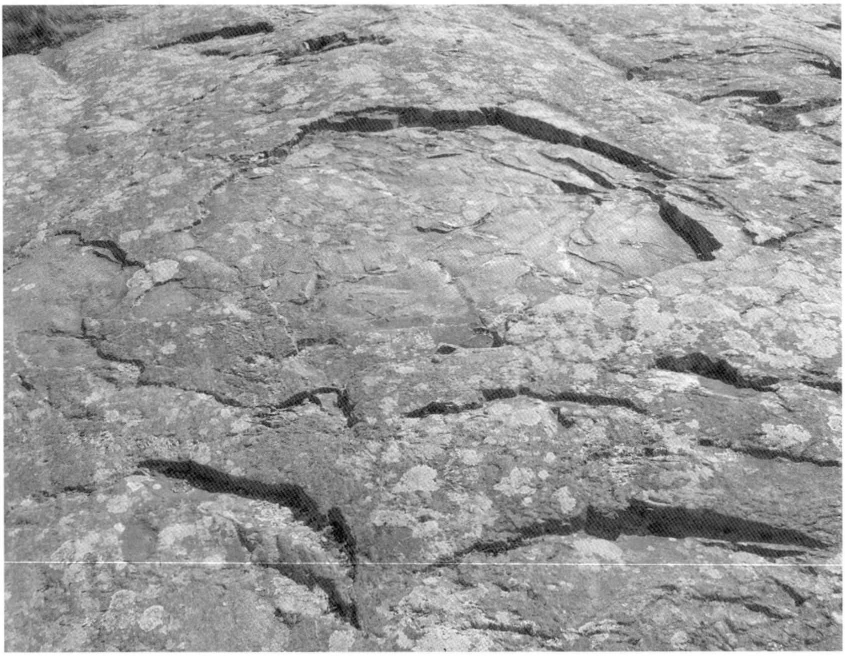

Figure 73. Blistered patches, apparently caused by fires, on top of the decorated outcrop at Himmelstalund, Sweden.

Some of the bodies were burnt at a very high temperature. There was only one context in which that could be achieved: the furnace used by a metal worker. For that reason Goldhahn (2007) and Oestigaard (2007) suggest that the smith was also the ritual specialist who conducted funerals. It is an attractive argument and would certainly explain why the residues of metal production are so often found in the same contexts as burnt human bones. A good example occurs in the settlement at Hallunda near Stockholm where cremations were found together with the largest bronze workshop excavated in Scandinavia. Six ovens were inside a possible cult house at this site (Goldhahn 2007: 293–306). There is also evidence that pottery was produced in the same places as metal artefacts and that both processes could be carried out together with the treatment of the dead. There is only one feature that unites these separate elements—that is the use of fire.

In fact fire is a vital element that connects nearly all the different aspects of Late Bronze Age visual culture. Cremation burials are directly associated with stone settings in the form of rectangular buildings, ships, and round cairns. All these monuments have produced finds of razors. Such artefacts can be embellished with drawings of the sun carried by a boat, while a few examples are shaped like a sea-going vessel. The large stone cult houses that were sometimes built near to round cairns are also associated with burnt material, as well as evidence of metal production. In the same way deposits of burnt stones are found in direct association with Bronze Age rock carvings and may have been deposited within a demarcated zone around the base of the outcrop. There are other signs of fires on top of the decorated surface, and it is possible that some of the burnt areas on the rock mark the positions of pyres (Goldhahn 2005: 59–9).

It seems likely that the Bronze Age 'art' of Southern Scandinavia was only one component of a more complex set of beliefs that placed a major emphasis on the importance of the sun, the sky and the sea. These elements can certainly be recognized in all three media considered in Chapters 6 and 7, but it is clear that they extend to other features. The relationship between land and water that is so obvious from the decorated metalwork is reflected not just in the rock carvings and stone settings of this period; it is also mirrored in the distribution of cairns along the coast. Similarly, the emphasis on the sun and the sky is not confined to the drawings on metal and stone, for it is illustrated by the hilltop siting of cairns. Their circular form may be related to the same body of ideas, while the special emphasis on fire in the Scandinavian Bronze Age celebrates its importance as a source of light and warmth and may be yet another reference to the sun. That is especially interesting as it seems possible that such beliefs owe as much to northern sources of inspiration as they do to ideas that first developed in the south.

FERTILITY AND DEATH

What light can these observations shed on the competing interpretations of the visual images of Bronze Age Scandinavia, briefly summarized in the previous chapter? How were they related to the passage of the sun? Were they primarily concerned with the fertility of people and animals, or were they really associated with the dead?

At this point it is necessary to distinguish between the different timescales discussed at the beginning of this chapter. The earliest images may be influenced by two different processes, each of which involves the sun. On a daily basis it rises from the sea, moves across the sky, and sets in the water. During the night it travels beneath the surface and then reappears. In that sense the sun *dies* and can be said to be *reborn*. That process is repeated every twenty-four hours. A second cycle extends over the course of a year. In the winter, the sun is visible for progressively shorter periods until the solstice when the hours of daylight increase. In the summer the period of darkness is curtailed. These distinctions are more pronounced in the north than in the south, and in the Arctic the sun may not be visible at midwinter, but at the height of summer it is present throughout the night. The process can be compared with the daily cycle, but in this case it extends across the year. It is directly related to the growth of plants which increases in the warmer months and dies back in the winter. In a sense both cycles describe the same idea—the death and rebirth of the sun—but in the first case it happens on a daily basis, while the second cycle extends over twelve months. It involves the *diminution of life* in the colder months and its *increase* after the winter. In that way it is related to fertility. Perhaps there is no need to distinguish between ideas of death and rebirth, on the one hand, and the importance of fertility, on the other. Both are aspects of the same set of beliefs, played out over cycles of different durations. The passage of the sun provides the most powerful symbol in the beliefs of Bronze Age Scandinavia.

Within Scandinavia such ideas—and the pictures that conveyed them in visual form—must have contributed to the performances associated with Bronze Age 'art'. Here the most detailed information is provided by the rock carvings. They are considered next.

WHERE WERE THE ROCK CARVINGS MADE?

One point is of fundamental importance. There was a direct relationship between what could be seen in the South Scandinavian rock carvings and their location in the prehistoric landscape and seascape.

It was essential that the sun should be visible to those who encountered these images. Without that connection, some pictures would not make much sense. That perhaps set a limit on the distribution of the Southern style of rock art. It is often been claimed that it follows the distribution of fertile soils–that, in the traditional sense, it was 'farmers' art' (Soggnes 1995b). Of course that could be true, but is it entirely coincidental that its distribution virtually runs out at a latitude where the sun never set during the height of summer? At the same time, in winter the sunrise and sunset could hardly have been seen from the carved rocks as they would usually be covered by snow.

There are more local factors to consider. Many of the carved rocks were beside, or near to, the sea (Figure 74), while some examples were attached to inland lakes and rivers. These are normally the sites which feature drawings of ships; different images occur in landlocked areas (Burenhult 1980). Where the evidence has been analysed in detail, the carvings that are connected with water tend to form local clusters along sections of the shoreline which would have commanded views towards the rising or setting sun. As Johan Ling has pointed out, these concentrations of carvings are often in places which provided sheltered harbours where boats could moor and their crews could disembark—in that sense the designs were readily accessible; some of them were equally easy to reach by land (2008: 232 and 235). It is not the fact that these places look out to sea that is important, but the observation that there are sections of the coast that were largely without petroglyphs. It appears that people chose to embellish groups of rocks within the same small areas and to ignore other potential locations. It is unclear how many of the decorated rocks were used simultaneously, but it is obvious that those within these concentrations would have commanded similar views. Their preference for east- or west-facing sections of the coastline is probably significant (Figure 75).

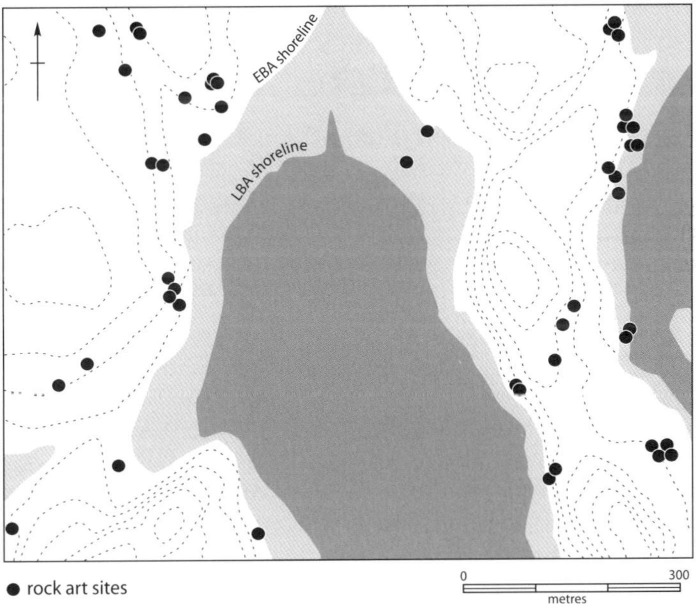

Figure 74. The relationship between the positions of the rock carvings and successive Bronze Age shorelines near Tanum, Sweden.

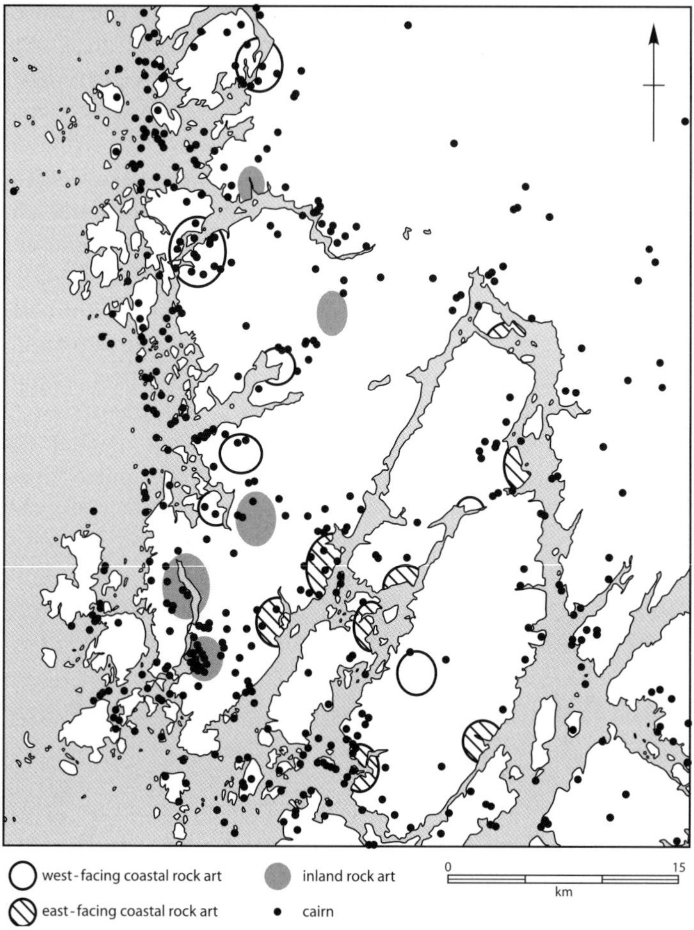

Figure 75. The siting of rock carvings and cairns in relation to the Bronze Age shoreline near Tanum, Sweden.

WHEN WERE THE ROCK CARVINGS USED?

If those factors influenced where the rock carvings were made, is there any indication of when they would have been used? Their chronology has already been discussed; what matters here is a different question. Could they have been in active use all year, or might they have been employed only at certain times?

It is difficult to approach this question where carved rocks were on the shoreline, for they might have been free from snow and ice to a greater extent, or for a longer period, than others found inland. Indeed, it is the sites with cup marks, footprints, vehicles, and wheel crosses that are most likely to have been covered by snow. That may be revealing, as these designs place a more direct emphasis on the sun and sky than the complex compositions near the water. At the same time, a number of carved rocks were seen to best advantage when they were wet, and this would certainly have happened at the end of winter; as the snow and ice melted, the decorated surfaces would be refreshed by running water. It goes without saying that the rocks themselves would have been more accessible at that time of year. As the hours of daylight increased, the carvings could have been seen for longer, and now that the sun was higher above the horizon the colours and textures of the stone would have been illuminated more intensely.

There is also a practical consideration to discuss. It takes a significant period of time to carve even a single ship (Ling 2008: 166), yet some of the panels contain many separate designs. Those beside the sea in Bohuslän would probably have been made in summer when the tidal range was smaller and there was less risk of storms. On the other hand, some of the completed designs might have been exposed to spray. A few examples on vertical surfaces could even have been carved by people standing in boats during calm weather.

WHO USED THE ROCK CARVINGS?

A tantalizing question is who would have encountered the carved rocks. The available evidence does not point to a single answer, and it seems unlikely that these images were used by only one kind of audience. Different activities took place there, and may have involved groups of people of different ages and genders.

Two main groups can be identified within the carvings themselves, although that is not to say that they were the only people permitted to see, or use, these places.

The first group consists of men, identified by an erect phallus. They have sometimes been interpreted in terms of human fertility, but Yates has pointed out that they are commonly associated with drawings of stags with a full set of antlers. Both may have been considered as symbols of masculinity (Yates 1993). The drawings of naked men have a restricted distribution within Scandinavia, and their bodies are out of proportion to all the other carved designs. Some of the men have been described a 'giants' and are depicted together with swords, spears, bows, axes, and shields. The reference to warfare is unmistakeable, but there is another sense in which these drawings may have been images of power, for a number of examples were clearly superimposed on already-existing drawings; often they are located on the decks of older boats. On the other hand, it would be wrong to treat the petroglyphs as an exclusively masculine preserve, although Ling estimates that 95 per cent of the human figures in the rock carvings of Bohuslän can be identified as male (2008: 218). There are a smaller number of images that probably portray women, and the scenes of heterosexual intercourse that are sometimes described as 'the sacred marriage' (Johnsen 2005).

A second group of individuals may be represented by the drawings of footprints (Figure 76). They are of much the same proportions across the entire distribution of South Scandinavian rock art and are much too large to belong to any of the humans depicted on the same sites. Their uniform character suggests that they were based on the bodies of people with access to these places. There is a wide range of variation, but if they were drawn at life size the majority should have belonged to children or adolescents (Brox Nilson 2005). This idea is supported by the comparatively rare images

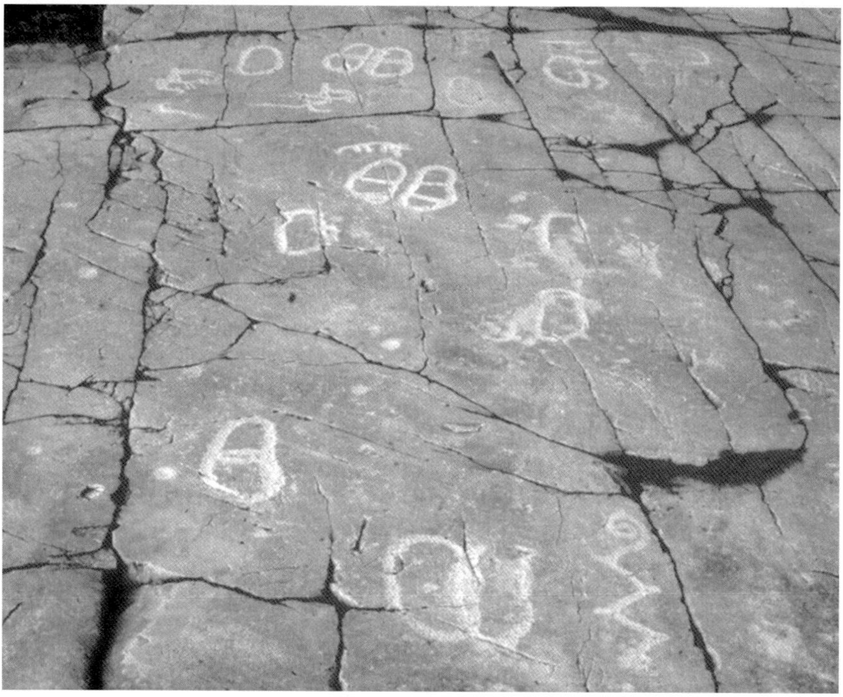

Figure 76. Trails of carved footprints at Järrestad, Sweden.

of bare feet, which can be considerably smaller. Perhaps some of these places were used in rites of passage similar to the rituals postulated by Thedéen (2003) and Kaul (1998). At the same time it is possible that individual carvings were used by people in different age groups. That can only be studied by comparing the sizes of the footprints carved on separate sites. Hauptman Wahlgren's study of forty decorated rocks at Norrköping certainly identified differences of this kind. She concluded that their prints may represent children, young people and women (2002: 223–9).

The most important rite of passage was, of course, the commemoration of the dead. That is also evidenced at these sites. There are two observations to consider here. The same carved motifs are found inside burial cists and in the open air (Jellestad Syvertsen 2002). At the same time, a surprisingly large number of Bronze Age barrows, cairns or stone settings are found on, or very close to, the rocks where the images were made. In Sweden, nearly 20 per cent of the decorated sites are within fifteen metres of a funerary monument (Joakim Goldhahn pers. comm.). There is even some evidence that cairns were built on top of a few of these drawings. Files of carved footprints seem to issue from cairns, and in other cases carved boats appear to travel between these monuments and the water's edge. Similar vessels were depicted on the kerb of the round barrow at Sagaholm (Goldhahn 1999).

There is one hypothesis that connects these different observations. Hauptman Wahlgren (2002) has suggested that it was the individuals who had been initiated into society at the carved rocks who were eventually buried in Bronze Age barrow or cairns. Wahlgren is not referring to the monuments in her own study area at Norrköping, which are some distance from the carved rocks, but the idea is worth considering for other sites. Thedéen (2003) and Kaul (1998) have both suggested that the small artefacts deposited with cremation burials carried a long history with them and were buried with the dead because they had played a crucial role in the rites of passage. Such rituals may have included initiation ceremonies. Perhaps the construction of cairns close to the carved footprints of young people resulted from a similar process. It can be compared with Christopher Tilley's interpretation of Högsbyn, where the carvings of human figures may pass from childhood to maturity as they move between a lake and a cemetery (Tilley 1999: fig. 5.14). Here there may even be evidence for a complex cycle, linking youth, adulthood, death, and rebirth with the passage of the sun.

These interpretations relate to some of the main protagonists in the use of the rock carvings: adult men or gods, young people and probably the dead. It only remains to be added that the audience for the images, and for the ceremonies associated with them, might have been much more diverse. There is no evidence to shed any light on this question.

WHAT HAPPENED AT THE CARVED ROCKS?

It may be more useful to concentrate on the activities associated with these places.

If the images are treated as works of art in a modern Western sense, the main activity would have been looking at the different drawings and attempting to interpret them. That is not surprising since it has been the main process followed by archaeologists in studying these sites. Most likely, both would have attempted to trace a narrative among the different drawings. There is no way of knowing whether those different interpretations, separated from one another by more than two thousand years, have anything in common. On the other hand, the organization of some of the individual panels seems to presuppose an audience located at the edge of the decorated surface (Tilley 2004: chapter 4). At sites where people had embellished a sloping rock it might be possible to survey the images from a single viewpoint. There are also places where the rock was too steep or slippery for that to happen, and images on vertical surfaces that may have been inspected from boats. Where the ground was more or less level, the audience may have had to move around the panel in order to examine its contents. The placing and orientation of the different images would have influenced the course followed by the viewer. Similarly, many of the larger outcrops feature several different panels. While the conventions discussed in Chapter 7 might have influenced the composition of individual scenes, it would have been necessary to change position in order to see them all.

This was probably what happened at Hästhallen in southern Sweden. This is a large flat rock, located at the centre of the Torhamn peninsula. There are three main panels of decoration which feature drawings of boats, sun symbols and footprints among other motifs. Lena König (2007) has observed that the foot soles towards the eastern limits of the outcrop point to the position of the rising sun. During the course of the summer it would have moved around the peninsula, emerging from the sea to its north-east and setting into the water to its north-west, where the only cairns in the region are found. König observes that, in contrast to the normal pattern, the three clusters of drawings at Hästhallen were not organized in relation to the position of an audience located beside one edge of the panel. Rather, 'the figures are placed in such a way that the observer is forced to move over the rock to be able to see all the figures from the [correct] angle' (König 2007: 68; Figure 77). The viewer passed around the drawings in the same way as the sun travelled around the peninsula.

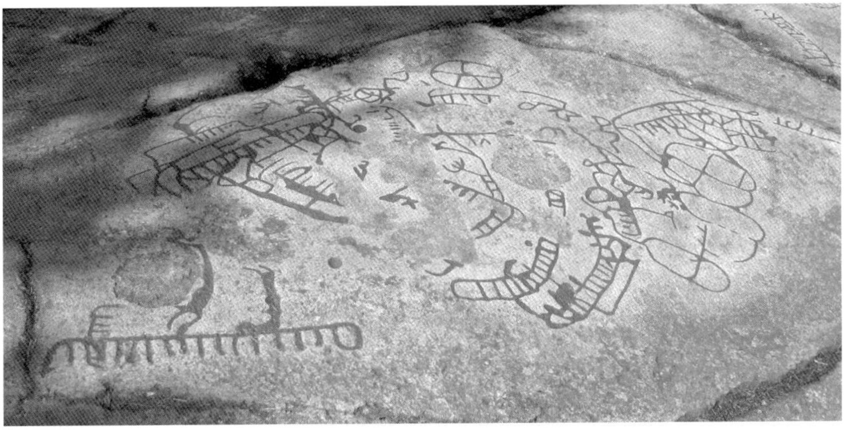

Figure 77. One of the decorated panels at Hästhallen, Sweden.

A different example is provided by the principal rock at Himmelstalund. On the northern side of the outcrop a series of 'night ships' travels towards the Baltic. These images were sometimes in shadow, but the largest vessels can be seen by an observer standing at the bottom of the panel. There are smaller boats further up the decorated surface, but it is necessary to climb the rock in order to view them. It is these vessels that are associated with drawings of the sun. Wheel crosses are also found in isolation on the higher part of the outcrop. It is surely no accident that the solar motifs can be identified at the point when the viewer sees the southern horizon for the first time—until then, it is concealed. The changing character of the motifs reflects the viewer's passage up the sloping surface. There is no evidence of a similar pattern on the opposite side of the outcrop, which faces the sun

In other cases an audience might need to pass between a series of different outcrops to see the images in context. The best example of this is at Högsbyn. In his analysis of the site Tilley suggests that people moved between the decorated surfaces from south to north, following a path between the edge of a lake and a cemetery on higher ground (1999: fig. 5.14). Chapter 7 suggested an alternative interpretation in which the audience followed the course of the sun, down to the water's edge and back again. It does not matter which of these readings is the more convincing, for both versions depend on the patterns of similarity and contrast between the different panels and on the process of moving between them.

On a smaller scale, the lines of footprints carved on individual outcrops may also indicate a kind of path, but on a site like Järrestad they assumed so much formality that it might be better to think in terms of a procession

(Coles 1999). The identity of the actors has already been discussed. Perhaps the carved footprints are less a representation of where people *had travelled* in the past than a series of cues as to where they should stand, or the appropriate pattern of movement. Was their main role to *choreograph* the passage of the actors across the rock? One reason for taking view is that processions are among the most distinctive scenes in South Scandinavian rock art (Coles 2003b). Whatever the occasions on which they happened, they were obviously of considerable importance.

If this is correct, it places a special emphasis on any contrasts between the top and bottom of the rock. Certain features might be found at both locations. Just as fires were lit on some of the decorated outcrops, they could have burnt around the borders of these sites, where their special significance might be emphasized by a platform or an enclosure wall. Artefacts might be placed inside the cracks and fissures in the decorated surface, but on some of the simpler sites (which may have been located near to settlements) the same kinds of material—pottery, burnt clay, and worked stone—have been found below the outcrop too (Bengtsson 2004; Kaul 2006a). Even so, there are important differences between these locations. People standing on the decorated surface would have been seen against the skyline, highlighted like the actors on a stage. Fires burning on the summit of a decorated rock would be visible from a greater distance than the others, and would have had a stronger visual impact. That would certainly have been true at Himmelstalund where the burnt patches extend along the crest of the main rock, approaching the positions of the nearest carvings but leaving them intact. Where the drawings end there are fewer indications of fires—hardly evidence for recent vandalism.

In such cases the topography of the rock would have raised certain actors—and the tasks they were performing—above the other people on the site, for the surface of the outcrop was like a platform on which movements, gestures, music and speech could all have been directed towards a wider audience. That is especially true at Revheim where one set of rock carvings is on top of a cliff and a second, much larger series at its foot. Both sets of images are closely related to one another, but there is no direct access between those two locations. The topography of the natural outcrop divided one group of participants from another as effectively as the architecture of a passage grave (Bradley, Jones, Nordenborg Myhre, and Sackett 2003).

At the same time, other activities might have been associated with the base of the decorated rock and the areas beyond it. There may be evidence of feasting at these locations, but at a greater distance there could have been deposits of Bronze Age metalwork, especially when the carved rocks were close to water. The evidence is much more limited, but two well-known examples illustrate this point. The rock carvings beside the river at Himmelstalund feature a number of drawings of Early Bronze Age swords and axes. Both kinds of artefacts are known from votive deposits in the vicinity (Hauptmann Wahlgren 2002). In the same way, there was a bog below the decorated cliff at Revheim (Bradley, Jones, Nordenborg Myhre, and Sackett 2003). At different times a sword, a dagger, and two of the musical instruments known as *lurs* have all been found there.

Observation

Revheim is important because the carved rock provided a vantage point from which to observe the midwinter solstice. That may explain the presence of a spiral and a wheel cross at its highest point. Two pairs of footprints are also located on the cliff edge looking out over the lower ground.

Isolated pairs of footprints are found so often that they require a specific explanation (Figure 78). They occur at several of the sites discussed in detail here. For example, they appear towards the top of the sloping surface at Järrestad next to two small mounds, one of which contained a cup-marked stone (Coles 1999). Their positions would have commanded a view towards the east, where there is a distant view of the Baltic. It is here that the sun would have been visible in the morning sky. Similarly, pairs of human footprints are a common feature at Högsbyn where they occur at intervals throughout the distribution of the rock carvings. Again they seem to be directed towards the summer sun at various points in its circuit along the eastern horizon. Others face the sunset (Bradley 2007c: 212–14). There is comparable evidence from the main outcrop at Himmelstalund, where pairs of footprints can be found near to the carvings of wheel crosses. For the most part they face north, with a concentration towards the positions of the summer sunrise and sunset.

The same pattern occurs throughout the well recorded rock art of Bohuslän, on the west coast of Sweden, and Østfold, across the Norwegian border to the north (Coles 2005). Here the isolated pairs of footprints face north-east, south-west, and north-west, with a slightly smaller group that is directed towards the south-east. There are practically no other alignments.

The same may be true of a smaller sample in south-west Uppland (Coles 2000), and a similar pattern can probably be recognized from Burenhult's tracings of Bronze Age rock carvings in south-east Sweden, but this evidence is less decisive because some of his drawings lack a north point and cannot be included in the analysis (Burenhult 1973). In all these areas the axes identified by the footprints correspond to the turning points of the year. North-east and north-west mark the directions of the midsummer sunrise and sunset respectively; south-east and south-west indicate the same events at midwinter

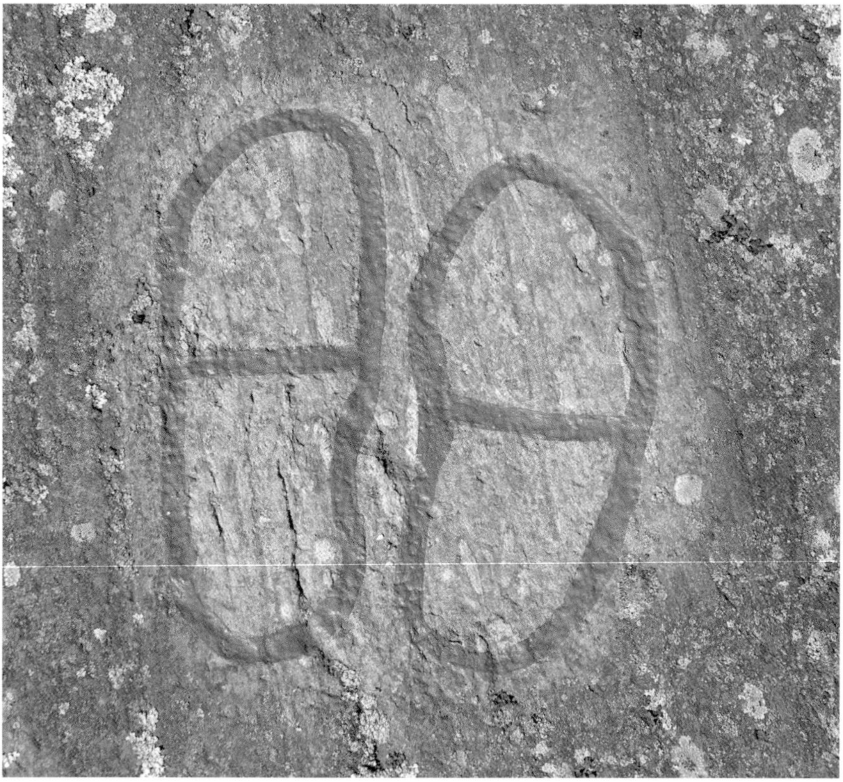

Figure 78. Carving of paired footprints at Himmelstalund, Sweden.

(Figure 79). The relationship is very striking indeed. The pattern probably changes in other areas. In the large group of carvings in south-west Norway, recorded by Eva and Per Fett (1947), all these images are orientated between south-east and south-west.

Of course such orientations are not as precise as the alignments of Neolithic tombs, but they do show an overriding concern with the movement of the sun through the sky, and with the places where it appears and disappears. If the files of carved footprints choreographed the passage of people across the decorated surface, surely these images mark the stances where observers celebrated the sun's arrival and departure at particular times of year. Indeed, it is even possible that that what look like paths leading across the rock were actually where groups of actors stood in rows to observe such phenomena. It is difficult to decide between these explanations, but in each case they would have been raised above a congregation at the base of the rock.

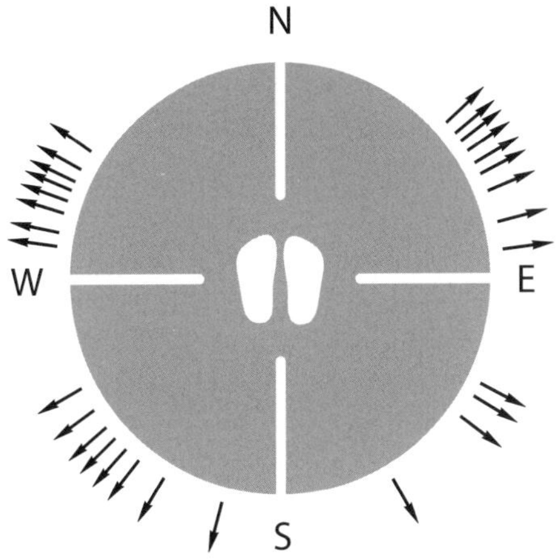

Figure 79. The orientation of carvings of paired footprints in Bohuslän and Uppland (Sweden), and Østfold (Norway).

Animation

Finally, discussions of prehistoric rock carvings give the impression that the drawings were directed exclusively to a human audience. That may be mistaken.

It is worth recalling some characteristics of the carved images. They are often quite ephemeral, yet there is no evidence that they had ever been painted. Unless they were recut on a regular basis, they would probably fade. They are best seen early in the morning, or in the evening when the sun is low in the sky and the drawings are highlighted by shadows (Coles 2004). They are easiest to recognize when they are damp, and some of the clearest drawings are crossed by running water. They can also be recognized because they make use of natural fissures or mineral veins running through the rock (Hauptmann Wahlgren 2000; Bradley, Jones, Nordenborg Myhre, and Sackett 2003). Some of the pictures would have been concealed by snow and ice during the winter months, and others might have been inaccessible. During the summer, however, the appearance of decorated surfaces beside the sea would have been enhanced by spray and by light reflecting off the water.

The images would be most apparent if the audiences were able to view them at the optimum times, perhaps moving between separate panels—or separate rocks—at intervals during the day. They might also have been illuminated by fires, which could have happened at night. The crucial point is that all but the freshest of the drawings would have been difficult to recognize without the aid of these processes. It was sun, water and, quite possibly, firelight that brought the pictures to life. In many cases this could only have happened at certain times. The spring would mark one important transition as carvings emerged from snow and ice and the designs were wet. It is this relationship between the carved rocks and the forces of nature that is too often overlooked. It raises the possibility that certain of the drawings were directed to the sun as much as to any human audience.

In fact the configuration of certain of the carved rocks suggests an important distinction between those on top of the outcrop watching the movements of the sun, and those lower down who were better placed to observe the drawings themselves. If the sun illuminated the carvings at the turning points of the year, this could have been seen by an audience who were located above the carved surfaces, looking towards the horizon. At other times the same places may have been used in quite different ways—for funeral ceremonies, or for other rites of passage. On such occasions the audience may have collected around the base of the rock, facing the carved designs, and some of the images may even have been animated by the light of fires.

IMAGE, PERFORMANCE, AND BELIEF

This chapter has considered all these elements. The beliefs that seem to have been important in the Scandinavian Bronze Age were closely allied to experience of life in parts of Northern Europe where the heat and light of the sun were an ever-present concern. Its movements seem to have been recorded in three quite different media—decorated metalwork, rock carvings, and geoglyphs—and may have provided the basis for a series of beliefs that considered such fundamental concerns as human and animal fertility, death, and the regeneration of life. They pervade the visual culture of later prehistory.

At the same time, such images were not meant for passive contemplation. The rock carvings seem to have been set apart from the settlements of the same period, and the more complex of them were in places which provide evidence of specialized performances, of which the most important was the commemoration of the dead. The same connection is illustrated by the decorated metalwork, much of which is associated with burials, and by the geoglyphs which generally occur in cemeteries. The siting of many of the images refers to the relationship between the sea, the land and the sky: one of the major themes illustrated in these three media.

The carved designs were directly integrated into the workings of the natural world. Many of them vanished and reappeared according to the cycle of the seasons. They could only be viewed at certain times of day and during particular periods of the year. Otherwise they were most accessible when they were illuminated by firelight or running water. It is a moot point whether the emergence of these figures from the stone was more significant than the details of the images themselves. In fact it is an open question whether members of the audience would have observed the creation of those designs in the first place.

In either case the designs were not treated in isolation, like the pictures in a gallery. They had to be viewed from particular positions, and perhaps in a specific sequence as people moved between the different panels and the sun travelled across the sky. They may have been consulted on special occasions—midsummer and midwinter seem to have been especially significant—and some of the images may even refer to specific groups, especially the adolescents whose footprints were engraved in the living rock. The organization of certain of the major sites suggests an important distinction between those who were allowed to walk across the carved surface and those who had to watch from a distance. There may have been a similar division between the people who observed the rising and setting sun from positions that were marked by petroglyphs, and those who saw its effects on the drawings themselves. Again it was never a passive activity. Fires were burning on and around the rocks; sometimes there were feasts; and valuable objects may have been sacrificed nearby. The images can only be understood in a wider context, and yet that context is forgotten when they are treated as works of art.

The same is true of the images that were associated with the Neolithic tombs discussed in Chapters 3 to 5. In the light of these observations, the closing section of the book considers some of the ways of rethinking 'prehistoric art'.

Part IV

Prehistoric Art and Archaeology

9

Losses in Translation

Two kinds of translation intervene between the artworks of the past and those of the present day. The first is the transformation of ancient objects through the antiquities trade. Once they are taken out of their original contexts they enter a new domain in which their associations are ignored and their visual appearance changes them into works of art. The second translation is where they provide a model for contemporary artists who may be equally unconcerned with the primary roles of those objects. That process is considered here.

PAST AND PRESENT

Chapter 1 made the point that exotic artefacts were studied and collected by modern painters and sculptors, like Picasso, Braque, Modigliani, and Brancusi. These objects suggested new ways of seeing and new sources of visual images. Sometimes their influence was even more direct, so that there are paintings in which it is possible to discern the original models among African masks or figure sculptures. The same process involved ancient objects, although the artists would not have been concerned with the ages of these artefacts as much as their appearance. In this way prehistoric images were incorporated into twentieth-century art.

These developments separated certain objects from their original contexts, and one aim of this chapter is to consider which elements were most obviously lost in translation. It is one way of distinguishing between the nature of the images in prehistory and their role in contemporary culture. A second aim is to reconsider some of the processes involving prehistoric 'art' itself and to compare them with the ideas behind Conceptual Art and Installation Art. This account suggests that both ancient and modern objects can be interpreted using the same body of theory. The links are not formed by the images themselves, but by the ideas that led to their creation. Here the discussion refers to Colin Renfrew's recent book *Figuring It Out*, which has the subtitle *The Parallel Visions of Artists and Archaeologists* (Renfrew 2002)

DRAWING ON THE PAST

The prehistoric figurines of the Cyclades provide one of Renfrew's examples. They are relevant here because it is known that they were admired by Constantin Brancusi whose work they obviously influenced. Renfrew comments that very few Cycladic sculptures come from well documented contexts. The majority have been obtained by illegal excavations and sold to collectors. They have been studied, classified and dated, not least by Renfrew himself, but all too little is known about the ways in which they were originally used (Renfrew 1993 and 2008). Indeed, the original roles of the life-size human sculptures remain completely obscure.

Renfrew summarizes the limited information that is available. Some of the smaller figures have been found in cemeteries where they occur in a few of the graves. Others are occasionally associated with settlement sites where they were probably made. Certain of the objects may be unfinished, while a number had been broken and repaired. The most striking information comes from a badly damaged site on the island of Keros which had been looted before it was investigated by archaeologists (Renfrew 1993: 23–4; Renfrew, Doumas, Marangou, and Gavalas 2007). This was not a settlement, although there was one nearby, and the surviving material was dominated by fragments of carved figurines which had been deliberately broken in the past. None of the remaining sculptures was intact, presumably because any whole objects had been removed by looters. It was the complete pieces that circulated through the art market and acquired a monetary value (Sotirakopolou 2005). The broken fragments had been left behind, and yet they provide the strongest clue to the original roles of these artefacts and even to the character of the site.

Renfrew argues that this was neither a workshop nor a dwelling place. It was most probably a sanctuary where sculptures were deliberately destroyed: a widely documented process which was discussed in Chapter 4. He compares their treatment with that of some of the figures found in graves. Of course that does not account for the undamaged pieces that dominate museum and private collections, nor does it explain the unusual life-size sculptures which lack an archaeological context. Nevertheless it does suggest that the motives of the people who made and used these objects were entirely different from those of the connoisseurs who acquire them today. Moreover, these objects had quite different connotations from the modern artworks which they may have inspired. It even seems possible that complete and undamaged Cycladic sculptures were the exception rather than the rule. Modern perceptions of these artefacts have been biased by the requirements of the antiquities trade.

There are other cases in which twentieth-century artists were influenced by prehistoric visual images. One is the work of the famous Catalan artist Joan Miró. His career shows just how complex these influences could be. His early works were largely figurative, but his mature paintings and sculptures deploy a series of largely abstract devices that owe something to the influence of Surrealism. At the same time, certain of these elements include drawings of the sun, eyes, humans and animals which resemble the repertoire of Iberian Schematic Art. There is evidence that he was influenced by these designs, although art historians have confused them with Palaeolithic cave paintings (Rowell ed. 1986: 3 and 203). That is incorrect, for Miró is known to have drawn on sites in southern Spain where nearly all the paintings are of postglacial origin. He also drew on Schematic Art in the south of France, where Palaeolithic images were not discovered until after his death (Hameau 2003).

His change of style was influenced by another factor which is documented in interviews. When he broke with naturalism, he based his paintings on what he called 'hallucinations', which he induced by starving himself. That may be why some of his work recalls the entoptic imagery discussed by Lewis-Williams and Dowson (1988). That is interesting, but it takes on an added significance when these motifs are compared with those in Schematic Art, for the caves and rock shelters where they are found may have played a specialized role in prehistory. They are sometimes in remote locations and could not have accommodated many people. Not all were living sites, and there are certainly cases in which the decorated caves and rock shelters were associated with human burials. It is possible that the painted surfaces recorded what Dronfield (1995a) calls 'subjective vision'. In that case Miró's images and their prehistoric counterparts may originate from similar sources in the nervous system. What is missing from Miró's paintings is any sense of the distinctive places where the prehistoric motifs occur, or of the special character of the activities that happened there. Again the most informative feature of the archaeological evidence has been ignored.

Both examples illustrate the same point. Perhaps the best way of characterizing ancient 'art' is by focusing on those features that do not have any obvious equivalents in the artworks of the twentieth century: the period when painters and sculptors tried to assimilate the material culture of the remote past. It is important to establish *which elements were left out* as prehistoric artefacts made the transition from their original settings to a new role in galleries and collections. The process is similar to that described by Howard Morphy (2007) in his recent account of Australian Aboriginal art.

MIXED MEDIA

There is an important distinction between portable objects and images that cannot be moved. On the whole the smaller artefacts have received more attention because they are easier to study. They may be found in association with other kinds of material; they can be placed in chronological order through their stratigraphic contexts; and their age can sometimes be measured by radiocarbon dating. In that respect the decorated pieces which have been treated as ancient art are investigated by the same procedures as any other objects. That is why they dominate accounts of Iron Age decorated metalwork. To some extent the same is true in the Late Bronze Age, but not in Scandinavia. During earlier periods, however, the balance shifts. Monumental art and open-air rock art predominate, and comparatively few small objects carry similar designs. Access to the earlier images depended mainly on the places where they were made.

At the same time, decorated tombs do have counterparts in quite different media, and so do rock paintings and carvings. Thus the repertoire of megalithic art overlaps with pottery decoration, and the motifs on the Bronze Age metalwork of South Scandinavia also feature in the petroglyphs of the same region (Kaul 1998). Similarly, Late Neolithic pottery in Orkney is decorated with the same motifs as stone artefacts, the walls of houses and those of chambered tombs (Shepherd 2000). The cross references between these different contexts provide the basis for defining particular *styles* of imagery, but they do more than that. One problem with studying decorated objects—however elaborate or rare—is that they appear in the archaeological record in only two contexts. They are found where they were taken out of circulation, and occasionally there is evidence of sites where they were made. The remainder of their history has left no trace behind. The artefacts from La Tène, which were discussed in Chapter 1, provide a typical example. Very little is known about the circumstances in which they were created, or the settings in which they were used. It is uncertain who would have had access to the more elaborate objects, or the extent to which decorated metalwork was exchanged between different people and different communities. All that has been established with any certainty is that at the end of their careers they were deposited in a river (Reginelli Servais 2007).

Rock art or decorated monuments offer a different perspective. They can rarely be dated directly, although surviving pigment has provided some radiocarbon samples, but the painted and carved surfaces do have the advantage that they have rarely been moved. In principle, their entire history can be traced by careful analysis. Again that statement requires some qualification, for there are certainly cases in which decorated stones were transported from one context to another, and even examples like the principal tomb at Knowth where a major monument was formed out of the remains of another structure (Eogan 1998). Such examples are exceptional and should be easy to identify. Otherwise it is the fixed component of prehistoric art that can shed most light on the contexts in which it was employed. That is why the Bronze Age rock carvings of South Scandinavia have been used to interpret the decorated metalwork of the same period. It is also why a book which might have been based on decorated objects has laid so much emphasis on images made in more durable media.

If the designs associated with portable objects are shared with tomb decoration, studies of similar contexts show how much information is overlooked when these artefacts are treated in the same ways as modern works of art. The same is true when they provide a source of inspiration for contemporary painters and sculptors. The following section considers some of the elements that have been lost in translation.

(RE)PLACING THE IMAGE

The title of this section can be taken in two ways. The first is perhaps the most obvious. It suggests that individual images should no longer provide the main focus for archaeological analysis. At the same time, those designs could be *re*-placed in another sense: the places where people encountered them might make an important contribution to the analysis. In that case the best procedure is to begin any discussion with images whose positions were fixed, before considering the much more limited evidence provided by portable artefacts. All the examples discussed here have been introduced in earlier chapters.

THE SOURCES OF THE IMAGES: PLACES, MATERIALS, AND PROCESSES

There are a number of factors that seem to have influenced the placing, and even the character, of the monumental images. Among the most important was the form of the natural landscape. Thus particular kinds of images were created in particular kinds of places—British and Irish rock art on inconspicuous outcrops (Bradley 1997a: chapter 6), Iberian Schematic Art in caves or rock shelters and at remote locations in mountainous country (Hameau and Painard 2006). In the southern Alps there is a similar contrast between De Saulieu's 'art discret' and 'art ostentatoire'; one was created on flat or gently sloping rocks, and the other on vertical surfaces (De Saulieu 2004). At times the very nature of the images was suggested by the local topography. Thus some of the carved ships on sites in south-west Norway are associated with natural features which resemble upturned boats (Nordenborg Myhre 2004: 178–9), and some of the stone vessels in Gotland run parallel to the coast (Hallin 2002).

The micro-topography of the decorated surface could have been as important as the designs that were painted and carved. In the west of Scotland, petroglyphs are associated with outcrops characterized by cracks and mineral veins, rather than those with a smoother surface. Not only were these features incorporated in the carved designs, they may have been considered as petroglyphs in their own right. Andrew Jones (2005) has argued that the configuration of these 'natural' features may even have determined which kinds of carvings were made. Thus a regular lattice of fissures and bands of quartz was interpreted as a design associated with megalithic art and new motifs were added, some of which would be appropriate in a chambered tomb. Where the available space was divided up in a less regular manner, different designs were created.

More examples of this connection have been identified in Northern Europe. They can be recognized on several scales. Individual images may have been integrated with veins of quartz which resembled snow or the surface of the sea. Separate panels could be enclosed by fissures, or were distinguished by folds in the surface of the stone. At the same time, the processes affecting the rock suggested the choice of images (Bradley, Jones, Nordenborg Myhre, and Sackett 2003). There are sites in Southern Scandinavia where drawings of ships were deliberately located where they would be covered by running water, and many others where the same motifs were within sight of the sea (Bengtsson 2004; Ling 2008). Colour was important, too. In northern Britain spirals like those in megalithic art are associated with deposits of red stone (Frodsham 1996). Like De Saulieu's 'art ostentatoire', they were often on vertical panels. Red rocks were also selected for the rock paintings in south-east Spain discussed by Margarita Diaz Andreu (2002).

Just as the images could be created in places that were more or less conspicuous, they could also be directed towards the sun as a source of light. That was clearly the case with Schematic Art sites in north-east Spain (Hameau and Painard 2006) and with a number of statue menhirs in the southern Alps (Harrison and Heyd 2007). At the same time, more abstract drawings in Britain, Ireland, and Galicia all seem to have been orientated towards the south (Bradley 1997a: tables 9 and 29). In other cases these images were made on horizontal surfaces and seem to face the sky. This also applies to some groups of cup marks in Sweden (Coles 2000: 35). By contrast, particular designs may have been located in positions that were usually in shadow, and there are even instances in which small panels were hidden from view.

Sound was also significant. Goldhahn (2002) has suggested that this was one reason why major sites in the Northern Scandinavian style of rock art were associated with cataracts, but it seems possible that certain of the panels in the Southern tradition had special acoustic properties. A few were washed by the sea and may have been exposed to storms, while the decorated cliff at Revheim would have amplified the sounds produced by visitors gathering along its base. It is surely no coincidence that two bronze trumpets or *lurs* were deposited in the bog below the carvings (Nordenborg Myhre 2004: 106). At other sites people playing these instruments are shown in the drawings themselves.

When were these places used? Much depends on the times at which the drawings and paintings could be seen. It is important to make a distinction between the daily movement of the sun and the progression of the seasons. On a daily basis individual images might appear and disappear as the sun crossed the sky. At times they would have received direct illumination; at others, they would have been in shadow. The images were seen to most advantage in low light, and some of them might have been associated with the sunrise or the sunset. Chapter 8 suggested that certain of the Southern Scandinavian images may even have been directed towards the sun at the turning points of the year. That is not the full range of possibilities, for the carved surfaces might also have been visible by moonlight. That certainly applies to the quartz veins that feature in these panels.

For part of the year Scandinavian petroglyphs and small stone monuments could have been buried by snow and ice. Sometimes their position would also have been obscured because the sun was low in the sky during the winter. As the days became longer and warmer, they reappeared, the carved motifs enhanced by running water. For a short period ship settings and the platforms associated with them would have been seen with exceptional clarity because there was little or no vegetation. Frachetti and Chippindale (2002) have made the same point in a study of Alpine rock carvings which would have been visible over an even shorter period. Those on Mont Bégo are in an area which can be used as pasture for only three months of the year.

Prehistoric monuments emphasized similar factors, but in this case the use of architecture gave them an added emphasis. Particular parts of these buildings may have been characterized by specific kinds of images, like the paintings and sculptures in Iberian chambered tombs (Bueno Ramírez and Balbín Behrmann 2006a). Another example comes from Ireland, where there is an association between entrance passages, circular designs, and spirals (Dronfield 1996). In that case there is also a distinction between the prominent designs on the kerbs of monuments in the Boyne Valley and the more fluid pattern inside these structures, where some of the decorated surfaces were repeatedly changed (Cochrane 2005 and 2006).

Again the character of the raw material was most important. In the Irish monuments the same stones might be decorated in two quite different ways. In an initial phase they were treated as a blank canvas on which to draw. In a subsequent phase new designs were made which paid greater attention to the contours of the stones, transforming some of the orthostats into three-dimensional sculptures (O'Sullivan 1986). Sometimes the shapes, colours, and textures of these stones were also emphasized by picking (Eogan and Aboud 1990). A similar process may have been followed where the surface of the rock was masked by pigment, but in this case paintings inside the tomb were renewed. This has been recognized in the Iberian Peninsula (Carrera Ramírez and Fábregas Valcarce 2006), but it is not known how frequently it happened.

In other cases the surfaces of the stones were not embellished, but the architecture of the monuments illustrates similar concerns. Chris Scarre has shown how Neolithic tombs in north-west France, northern Germany and the Netherlands used raw materials of contrasting materials and colours. The uprights were separated from one another as if they were put on display (Scarre 2004a and b). Something similar happened in Britain, where rough stones were often paired with smooth ones in these structures (Cummings 2002). In the west of Sweden passage graves have no decoration apart from the cup marks on top of their capstones, but again they were built out of materials of contrasting colours. In this case special attention was paid to mineral inclusions visible in the surface of the rock. They resemble the abstract designs that were painted or carved inside comparable monuments in other parts of Europe (Bradley and Phillips 2008).

There are also cases in which entire styles of decoration typified particular types of structure. Thus the Neolithic houses in Orkney were embellished with linear decoration. The same designs were associated with a series of domestic artefacts, but they are also found inside the chambered tombs which took those buildings as their prototype. One source of inspiration might be the distinctive appearance of the local sandstone where it is exposed on the seashore (Shepherd 2000). Curvilinear designs, on the other hand, are associated with decorated outcrops in Britain and Ireland and are extremely rare in the domestic sphere (Beckensall 1999 and 2006). The two traditions come together in a monumental synthesis at some of the Irish tombs.

Again many of these distinctions depended on sunlight. Otherwise the pictures could only be seen with artificial illumination. Some parts of the tombs would be visible on a regular basis, but others would have been in darkness unless they were lit by torches: a process that could result in dangerously low levels of oxygen inside these buildings (Nash 2007). Only occasionally were the interiors completely visible, for, although most examples face east or south, the light would not penetrate far inside these structures unless the sun was at the correct height in the sky. It would have been difficult to align the monuments precisely, yet a significant number of tombs were lit with special intensity at the solstices. In Iberia a few of the painted and carved images might have represented the sun (Acosta 1968), but among the other elements illuminated on these occasions were the colours and textures of the raw material. Sometimes the sunlight lit the designs on the back wall of the chamber. Again they might appear in isolation or could form part of more extensive friezes extending across a series of different stones.

The movement of sunlight into the tombs had the effect of subdividing the space and of revealing some of the paintings and carvings at the expense of others. These processes have been characterized as *display*, *disclosure*, and *concealment* (Bradley and Phillips 2008). The first term refers to the visual effects that were visible from the exterior of the structure: the nature of the entrance stones, the character of the kerb, and the material used to build the cairn. *Disclosure* refers to those effects that would only be evident to someone entering the building; these experiences might well have presented themselves in a specific sequence. *Concealment*, on the other hand, describes the visual (and tactile) effects that would not have been apparent with natural lighting or to a person moving down the entrance passage. Many could only be appreciated with deliberate illumination. The darkest parts of these tombs—often the most remote—are those which may have helped to induce altered states of consciousness. Such effects sometimes occurred together with unusual acoustic phenomena, and, in combination, both would have contributed to the extraordinary character of these places.

Do such patterns extend to decorated artefacts? In fact there is little evidence, and that is precisely why monumental art provides such a useful starting point for the enquiry. Some of the images could share a common origin, but all too little is known about the places in which portable objects were used before they entered the archaeological record. Thus the Bronze Age metalwork of Southern Scandinavia features drawings of the sun not unlike those in the rock carvings of the same period. The sun also features in Iberian Schematic Art where the same motif is shared between rock paintings and

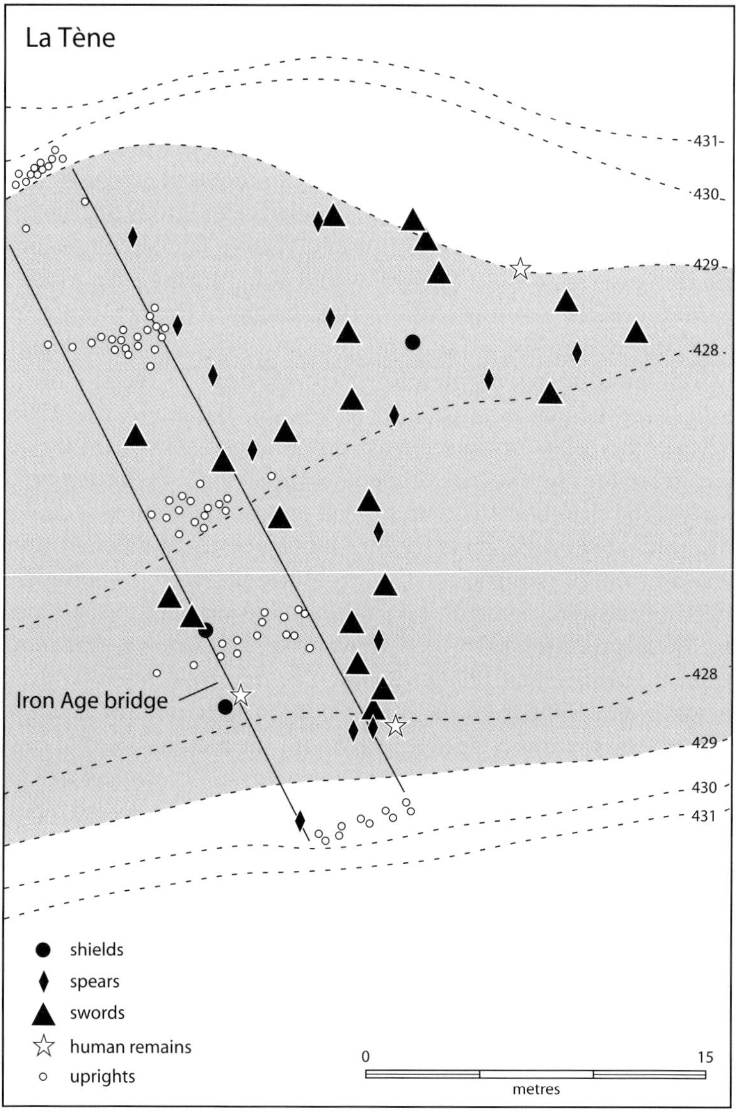

Figure 80. Iron Age timber structures and associated deposits at La Tène, Switzerland.

decorated pottery (Martín and Camalich 1982). Water is equally significant as a source of visual images. Åsa Fredell (2003) has suggested that it was depicted on Scandinavian metalwork, and this is surely true where the designs feature drawings of boats. The same idea could have been conveyed by the pictures of water birds in Celtic art (Fitzpatrick 2007), and it may be no accident that some of the artefacts that carried these designs were deposited in rivers, lakes and bogs.

In one case the relationship between Iron Age artefacts and their find spots recalls the evidence from earlier prehistory. It seems clear that La Tène and a series of related sites included wooden structures which were probably bridges (Figure 80). They were associated with deposits of weapons, tools, and human bones. It is tempting to suggest that they were places where different communities met. As people crossed the water, they made appropriate offerings. It might seem unlikely that these sites were associated with the heavenly bodies, but a number of the timber structures can be dated by dendrochronology. Chamberlain and Parker Pearson have observed that a high proportion of them were constructed, or rebuilt, in years in which there was a lunar eclipse (Field and Parker Pearson 2003: 136–48). In a way the portable artefacts support this interpretation, as La Tène metalwork features drawings of the moon (Fitzpatrick 1996).

RELATIONSHIPS BETWEEN THE IMAGES

It is possible to say rather more about the relationships between the images created in different media. There are obvious resemblances, but the differences are significant, too. Among the most important contrasts are those of scale. Chapter 4 began with a comparison between the treatment of Neolithic figurines in Eastern Europe and the histories of statues in the West. Both may have been influenced by similar concerns, but, if so, they were expressed in very different ways. On the one hand, there was a trend towards miniaturization; on the other, a predilection for the monumental (Scarre 2007a). Although the distinction is not absolute, it may have been influenced by another factor. For the most part the use of decorated figurines and other small but elaborately decorated artefacts happened in regions in which the settlement was the principal focus (Bailey 2005). In many cases sites were occupied so intensively that they developed into tells. In that sense their positions were monumentalized. The occupation sites in other regions were more ephemeral. Of course there are exceptions—a few Neolithic settlements in Western Europe were enclosed by earthworks—but in many parts of this region there was a different emphasis, and stone settings were evidently more significant. Some were embellished with non-figurative motifs, but others may have been regarded as statues of particular people, ancestors or supernatural beings. There are cases in which the miniature and the monumental came to be combined, most particularly the small 'idols' associated with Iberian passage graves, but more often designs in these two media have mutually exclusive distributions. In some areas, visual images were at their most elaborate in the domestic sphere. In others, they were created at different sites.

At a local scale the same applies to the deposits of portable artefacts—usually metalwork—which have been described as hoards or votive deposits. David Fontijn (2003) has suggested that during the Bronze Age in the southern Netherlands certain items might be associated with the settlements themselves, and others with nearby cemeteries. On the other hand, more elaborate artefacts had to be committed to the ground or deposited in water at an increasing distance from the places where people lived. Thus sickles or local types of personal ornament could be discarded among the houses; axes and spears were more appropriate further away, in streams, in marshes or along natural boundaries, while non-local ornaments and more spectacular weapons entered major rivers at a still greater remove. The same might also apply to Iron Age metalwork.

It seems possible that similar conventions applied, not just to decorated artefacts, but to the visual images created in other media. There are two possibilities to consider. The first is the situation described by Fontijn. Different kinds of images might be found with increasing distance from the domestic world. Thus in Ireland and northern Britain, it seems as if the most elaborate rock carvings were often on higher ground, or at the margins of the settled land (Bradley 1997a: chapter 6). Their special role is emphasized by the fact that their closest counterparts occur in chambered tombs. Cup-marked rocks, on the other hand, are found close to occupation sites. Again in Southern Scandinavia it seems as if the most complex images were distanced from the living sites (Nilsson 2005). Field survey in the Tagus Valley near the Spanish/Portuguese border leads to a similar conclusion. Here simple cup marks are associated with the settlements; beside the river there is a series of complex carvings; and the uplands are associated with painted caves and rock shelters. In this case the designs that occupy the most secluded locations are also associated with the dead (Bueno Ramirez, Balbín Behrmann, and Barroso Bermajo 2004).

If Fontijn's interpretation of metalwork deposits in the Netherlands suggested a way of looking at the distribution of visual images, it raises another possibility. He was concerned with deposits of Bronze Age metalwork, either as single finds or hoards. Both have close equivalents among prehistoric rock carvings (Bradley 1998a). Drawings of axes and weapons are found in north-west Spain and occasionally in the British Isles. They were also depicted in the rock art of Southern Scandinavia. Tools, weapons, and ornaments feature prominently in the rock carvings of northern Italy and southern France. They are also depicted on statues (Barfield and Chippindale 1997). There are more of these sculptures in the Iberian Peninsula where a few of the same artefacts are depicted in Schematic Art.

Occasionally the same types of objects were deposited at these sites. In the Neolithic period a hoard of stone axes are associated with a Breton menhir (Le Rouzic, Péquart, and Péquart 1923: 68–70), and during the Bronze Age a few pieces of metalwork come from the same sites as rock carvings in north-west Spain (Commendador 1995: 122–3). Such discoveries are uncommon, and there are other cases in which pictures of individual artefacts or groups of artefacts might be compared with real deposits. Thus some of the decorated stelae in the Early Bronze Age of southern Portugal represent the equipment of a single individual. Their contents are comparable with those of Argaric Culture graves in south-east Spain (Bradley 1998b). Similarly, the weapons depicted by rock carvings in Galicia bear a strong resemblance to the contents of hoards. Even their organization on the decorated surface has a certain formality, as if it represented a display of trophies; on a smaller scale, the same is true of the carvings of Early Bronze Age artefacts in England and Scotland (Bradley 1997a: 136–8). By contrast, the rock carvings in South Scandinavia often show individual artefacts which might be compared with the single finds from bogs and rivers (Malmer 1981: chapter 7; Larsson 1986). Such pictures have played a major role in dating prehistoric petroglyphs, but they may also shed some light on how portable artefacts were displayed. Again it is necessary to move between different media to set these images in context.

There are also cases in which objects are decorated with motifs that have a wider frame of reference. One of the clearest examples is provided by the *symbolkeramik* of south-east Spain. It has the same repertoire as Schematic Art (Martín and Camalich 1982). This kind of pottery does occur in settlements, but it is usually found on those enclosed by walls and has a restricted distribution within these sites. Although the decorated vessels were made in the same fabric as other ceramics, they may have played a more specialized role. The same point can be illustrated by examples from other parts of Europe. The Neolithic pottery of Orkney, for example, has some motifs in common with megalithic art. In the settlement at Barnhouse such vessels were among the smallest on the site. Residue analysis shows that they were used exclusively for the consumption of barley products and may have contained fermented drinks (Richards 2005: 291). There are further cases in which images in these media overlap. The horns of cattle feature on Neolithic pottery in north-west France, and on the reused menhirs built into passage graves (Cassen and L'Helgouach 1992; Le Roux 1992). Similarly, the distinctive idols introduced into Iberian tombs were often decorated with what appears to be a woven costume. Towards the end of their history similar patterns appear on pottery (Lilllios 2002). Such connections are not limited to ceramics. In Brittany, fine axe heads, some of them in the form of pendants, might be deposited with the dead, but they could also be portrayed in passage graves and *allées couvertes*. Others were perhaps represented by monoliths in the open air (Tilley 2004: chapter 2).

The relationship between different images might have been as important as their individual histories. There are cases in which miniature and monumental images may be found together, although they are quite rare. One is the occurrence of similar designs inside Iberian megaliths and on the idols deposited outside these buildings (Bueno Ramírez and Balbín Behrmann 2006b: 175–91). They may have been addressed to different audiences—more people may have been permitted to approach the tomb than were allowed inside it. A different situation arises in the Cyclades where Colin Renfrew (1993) suggested that the large unbroken sculptures represented deities and that the small figurines were votive offerings, destroyed as they were presented to the gods; but see Renfrew (2008) for another view. Again the visual links between them provide a clue as to how both groups were used.

Similar arguments apply to the decorated menhirs. Although they are often found singly, they can also belong to more complex settings in the open air, for example the stone alignments of north-west France (Lecerf 1999) or the horseshoe-shaped enclosures in the south of Portugal (Calado 2006). The same applies to the rows of statue menhirs in the southern Alps (Mezzena 1998). Their arrangement might have emphasized the connections between the people they represented, or even those between the communities who had erected them. The same approach can be taken to the sculptures assembled inside megalithic tombs.

THE TREATMENT OF THE IMAGES

Many of the designs were not static; they underwent changes of various kinds.

Perhaps the most drastic development was considered in Chapter 4. Stone statues, including some of the oldest in Western Europe, were levelled and broken up, and sometimes their remains were reused. The reasons for this transformation are not clear. Although these processes can be interpreted as iconoclasm, they happen in too many different contexts for this idea to be entirely convincing. Virtually the same arguments are applied to the first reused menhirs in Brittany where this interpretation seems implausible

(Cassen 2000), and to Petit Chasseur and Aosta at the very end of the tradition of megalithic art, where it probably supplies the right answer (Harrison and Heyd 2007). Moreover, there are similarities between the treatment of the first monumental images along the Atlantic coastline and the ways in which small figurines were employed in Eastern and Central Europe.

In any case the histories of these statues—whether or not they were anthropomorphic—is not unlike the processes affecting other images. It is simply that these changes were effected on a larger scale and must have required the participation of a greater number of people. Open-air rock carvings were just as likely to be reused. In northern Britain it is clear that pieces of already decorated stone were removed from their original settings and employed in burial cists. It did not happen by chance, for the motifs selected for this role were often those with counterparts in megalithic art. They must have retained their importance for a long time, as it happened after passage graves had gone out of use. Moreover, when they were taken away the parent outcrop remained significant, so that newer carvings might take the place of those that had been removed (Bradley 1997a: 138–46). The main difference is that originally the motifs commanded a view over the surrounding landscape. In their new setting they were buried under mounds or cairns and addressed exclusively to the dead.

More often the entire history of a set of carved or painted images was played out on the panels where they were made. That applies both to surfaces in the open air and to the designs inside chambered tombs. Three different processes were important. Firstly, a group of carved or painted motifs could be extended by the creation of new designs alongside those that already existed. The older panel was respected although individual elements might be elaborated or recut. The best examples of this process are found in Britain and Ireland (Bradley 1997a), but they also occur on sites in north-west Spain (Peña Santos and Rey García 1999) and in the southern Alps. In the latter area they constitute De Saulieu's 'art discret' (De Saulieu 2004). The same applies to some of the rock paintings in the south of Spain where designs in three separate styles sometimes respect one another (Fairén Jiménez 2006).

A different process is illustrated by 'art ostentatoire' where the original designs were disregarded and a new series of images was superimposed. Among open-air sites that process is most apparent in Alpine rock art (Frachetti and Chippindale 2002). It is present to a much lesser extent in South Scandinavia where it seems likely that fresh designs were placed over specific images to alter or emphasize their significance; an example in western Sweden is the addition of outside human figures to existing carvings of boats (Ling 2008: 146). Similar processes can be identified in the treatment of megalithic art. Panels could be repainted after an interval (Carrera Ramírez and Fábregas Varcarce 2006), and carvings could be superimposed on one another, or on the reused pieces introduced to the monuments from outside. At Knowth, a sequence of overlays has been recognized in the carved decoration (Eogan 1997). Their effect was to suggest a history in which the oldest designs were receding into the surface of the stone. The same may apply to the painted panels at Neolithic and Copper Age rock shelters in Iberia (Martínez García 2006).

The third process is even easier to recognize for it happens where the entire decorated surface has been pecked or flaked in order to eradicate the images. This was certainly the case with some of the menhirs in northern Italy, where the features of particular statues were destroyed (Keates 2000). The same could happen at megalithic tombs. At Newgrange and Knowth the superposition of different designs made the individual panels increasingly difficult to construe. In the end some of them were obliterated as large areas were covered by a uniform layer of picking which had the effect of enhancing the natural colour of the stone (Eogan and Aboud 1990). Only faint traces of the original panels had survived before; now this distinctive treatment concealed them from view.

In every case the important point is the same. Each of the decorated stones had a history of renewal and modification that could extend over a significant period of time. Traces of that history were still visible, so that in principle the people who carved Late Bronze Age or Early Iron Age boats on outcrops in Southern Scandinavia would have been aware of earlier drawings on the same sites, the oldest of them extending back for a thousand years. At any one time only a few motifs might have been newly made, although there is evidence that certain drawings were recut (Hauptman Wahlgren 2002) and that others might even have been altered to bring them up to date (Nordenborg Myhre 2004: chapter 6).

A comparable process applies to the comparatively rare geoglyphs: they could be elaborated, supplemented or eventually hidden from view. Some of the Scandinavian round cairns illustrate the first possibility, for they were often constructed over several phases, each of which might be characterized by a circle, or circles, of boulders. There are examples where the successive rings of stone might still be visible, and others where they were covered as they were replaced. A variant of this practice was at Sagaholm, where the decorated kerb was buried beneath an extension to the barrow (Goldhahn 1999). In the same way, there are Swedish sites at which concentric rings of boulders of the kind identified as sun symbols were completely buried beneath a mound of fire-cracked stones (Runcis 1999). Something similar may have happened at the passage graves of the Boyne Valley in Ireland, where a few of the monuments overlay settings of boulders laid out on the original land surface in the same configurations as the carvings in the tombs (Bradley 1998b: 104–9).

Similar considerations apply to the Scandinavian ship settings. As Peter Skoglund has shown, there are cases in which they were eventually buried by barrows and cairns, and others in which they were exposed on the ground surface (Skoglund 2005). The examples that were hidden from view generally occur singly, but the second group often includes several monuments laid out in relation to one another. Thus round barrows and round cairns may have been built over a single stone boat, as happened in south-west Sweden and south-west Norway, while the sites that contain several ship settings occur on the Baltic coast, and especially on Gotland where groups of vessels seem to follow the same course across Late Bronze Age cemeteries. Their sizes are more varied than the other examples, and sometimes they are organized in pairs (Capelle 1986). Where examples in Norway appear to be travelling in and out of complex circular monuments, in other cases they may have been sailing towards them (Nordenborg Myhre 2004: 217–21; Bradley and Widholm 2007). At times the stone ships are even attached to the edges of these cairns in a manner that recalls the vessels which carry the sun in the rock carvings of the same period. The cemeteries that feature complex circular monuments seem to have been used over a lengthy period, and their use could well have extended into the Early Iron Age (Storm Munch 1998; Wangen 1998). In that respect they resemble the petroglyphs.

Similar considerations apply to the decorated artefacts which may have had a long history before they entered the archaeological record. There are many instances in which fine metalwork had been altered or repaired some time before its deposition, but metal analysis raises the possibility that other artefacts were recycled for their metal content when they were taken out of circulation. Finely crafted objects appear to have been disabled, by damaging them, breaking them or even exposing them to fire (York 2002). It was only at the ends of their careers that certain pieces were employed as grave goods or votive offerings. This has been accepted for a long time and underlies the concept of 'artefact biographies'. In the light of this discussion it seems as if monumental artworks had an equally complex history

THE CONTEXTS OF THE IMAGES

Images were seldom made in isolation. The accompanied, and even aided, the performance of particular activities.

Several points need making at the outset. It is rarely possible to show that images were directed exclusively to a human audience, or even to one that was alive. Christopher Tilley (2007) has suggested that the complex designs inside the passage grave at Newgrange were intended to baffle the dead and to keep them inside their tombs. In that case the images provided protection for the living. At the same time, the three most complex designs on the kerb were meant to conceal the actual position of the entrance.

His argument recalls Alfred Gell's account of the same monument, quoted in Chapter 2. It combines two different elements: the 'hidden art' which is represented by reused stonework; and the sequence of decorated panels created after the tomb had been built. It is often suggested that the concealed designs were directed to the occupants of the tomb; these motifs might be on the backs of the orthostats or masked by successive layers of corbelling in the chamber (Cochrane 2005 and 2006). The same observations could be explained in purely practical terms, for the tombs in the Boyne Valley consumed an enormous amount of raw material which had to be brought to the site from a source twenty kilometres away. When individual monuments were rebuilt or replaced, it would have been tempting to use the stones again, especially when the original designs could no longer be seen. Most examples have been discovered by archaeologists in the course of dismantling the monuments; during the Neolithic period, the existence of these motifs may have been forgotten within a few generations. Such a pragmatic approach to the reuse of raw materials is certainly evident at Stonehenge (Cleal, Walker, and Montague 1995).

In any case there is evidence that some stones were decorated before they were incorporated into these monuments, and that others were embellished once they were in position. Afterwards they could be carved several times, until the original decorative scheme was obscured (Eogan 1997). That is a quite different process from the reuse of already decorated material, and would have created a powerful visual effect. It is here that Tilley's argument is more persuasive. It could certainly apply to Newgrange, where there is little to suggest an overall decorative scheme (O'Kelly 1982), but it is less convincing at the nearby site of Knowth (Eogan 1986). Here the kerb of the largest monument includes a series of clearly defined panels, and the internal decoration does show more signs of order. Different kinds of design are associated with particular parts of the main passage grave. Although both structures incorporated reused raw materials, there is a striking contrast between them. It seems possible that the construction of the main tomb at Knowth was organized in a different way from the work at Newgrange, and it would be interesting to know whether these two monuments had been built in sequence. Perhaps the people who constructed the principal passage tomb at Knowth had learnt from the building of Newgrange.

At the same time, the designs at the rear of the chamber at Newgrange may have been directed to the sun, which illuminates the monument at the midwinter solstice. It is a moot point whether people were allowed inside the chamber when it happened or whether this effect was directed exclusively to the dead. A similar problem arises with some of the rock carvings in Southern Scandinavia, for here the images have a dual focus. Some, like the pairs of footprints, seem to mark the positions of people observing the rising and setting sun. Other designs were illuminated by sunlight, possibly on the same occasions. Again it is not clear whether particular drawings were addressed to the sun as a source of light and warmth, or whether they were meant primarily for a human audience. At times these interpretations might even be in conflict. By gathering at the foot of a decorated outcrop people could have obstructed the movement of light, casting their own shadows across the drawings. The same problem would affect the use of megalithic tombs, where visitors to the chamber could easily block the flow of sunlight along the passage. The presence of burnt material inside these monuments suggests that they were sometimes lit by flares (Nash 2007). There is comparable evidence from the excavation of Northern European rock carvings (Bengtsson 2004).

There is another problem. So far the discussion has proceeded on the assumption that the images on natural surfaces or inside megalithic tombs were meant to be viewed in the same way as visitors inspect pictures in a modern gallery. That may not have been true. If the images were often in shadow, were the 'finished' panels the most important element, or were people more concerned to see them emerging out of the stone while it was being painted or carved? The question is impossible to answer, but it is important because different designs were often superimposed. That could have happened because the images were quick to fade. Only when the surface of the stone was newly broken were the designs especially easy to identify. The people who gathered around the base of a decorated outcrop in Scandinavia may not have been looking at an array of completed artworks; they may have been more concerned to watch them coming into being. Like those in megalithic tombs, perhaps the designs had their greatest impact while they were being formed.

In fact the emphasis on *visual* images may sometimes be misplaced and could say more about contemporary viewers of prehistoric art than the people who encountered it in the past. Maybe it was as important to touch the images as it was to see them (Lahelma 2008: 59–61). That is likely to have happened in the dark recesses of the chambered tombs. It is also suggested by the footprints that were carved in South Scandinavia, and by the handprints that feature in Iberian Schematic Art. The footprints may have played a part in guiding the movements of people across the decorated surface, in which case they could be interpreted as a kind of choreography.

Much is made of the distinction between images on vertical rocks and others that are more or less flat. It is not always explained by their visual impact. Offerings can be placed *on the designs* that were pecked into horizontal surfaces: on steeper slopes they must be placed *above or below the designs.* That arrangement is suggested by excavations in Northern Europe (Kaul 2006a). At the same time, the lighting of fires would have been influenced by similar constraints. They could have burnt at the foot of the rock where they would cast shadows on the carved and painted panels, or they would have been higher up the decorated surface where they might have had a greater impact. On some sites such fires respected the positions of the carvings; at others, they destroyed them.

It is often supposed that prehistoric architecture was employed to orchestrate public ceremonies. Megalithic tombs provide the earliest examples of this process. Few people would have been able to enter a passage grave together, while larger groups must have remained outside. These differences might be highlighted by the use of visual imagery (J. Thomas 1992). Thus the decorated kerbstones at Newgrange and Knowth have a subtly different character from the designs inside the tombs (O'Kelly 1982; Eogan 1986). Similarly the decorated idols placed outside the chambers of monuments in Spain and Portugal include miniature versions of the images painted or carved on the walls of some of these buildings (Bueno Ramírez and Balbín Behrmann 2006b: 175–91).

Natural places can have similar properties. A number of the caves and rock shelters associated with Schematic Art were very small, yet a few examples have open areas in front of them where deposits of artefacts are found. One example at El Pedroso took this process even further, for here a decorated cave had two separate chambers separated from one another by a low passage (Bradley, Fábregas Valcarce, Alves, and Vilaseco Vázquez 2005). The first was decorated with cup marks similar to those at settlements, but the small chamber at the rear of the cave was embellished with the repertoire of Schematic Art and may have contained a burial. The site was overlooked by a massive granite outcrop, and in front of it there was a terrace bounded by a wall. This created a natural arena outside the decorated cave. On excavation it produced an extraordinary number of artefacts, many of them associated with the preparation and consumption of food. Apart from the wall, the entire complex made use of the natural properties of the geology. The summit of the outcrop was like a stage, raising certain people high above an audience below. Others were hidden from view inside the cave (Figure 81). The overall effect is very similar to that suggested at the decorated cliff on the Norwegian site of Revheim, but in that case there is quite different evidence for how the site had been used. Those on the summit would have been able to observe the sun at the solstices (Vinsrygg 1980). Here the rock carvings are partly abstract and include a large spiral which a ship is entering or leaving. These people were completely cut off from those in front of the outcrop who would have encountered a different set of images. One group was *looking outwards from* the cliff edge. The other was more likely *looking at* the carved designs

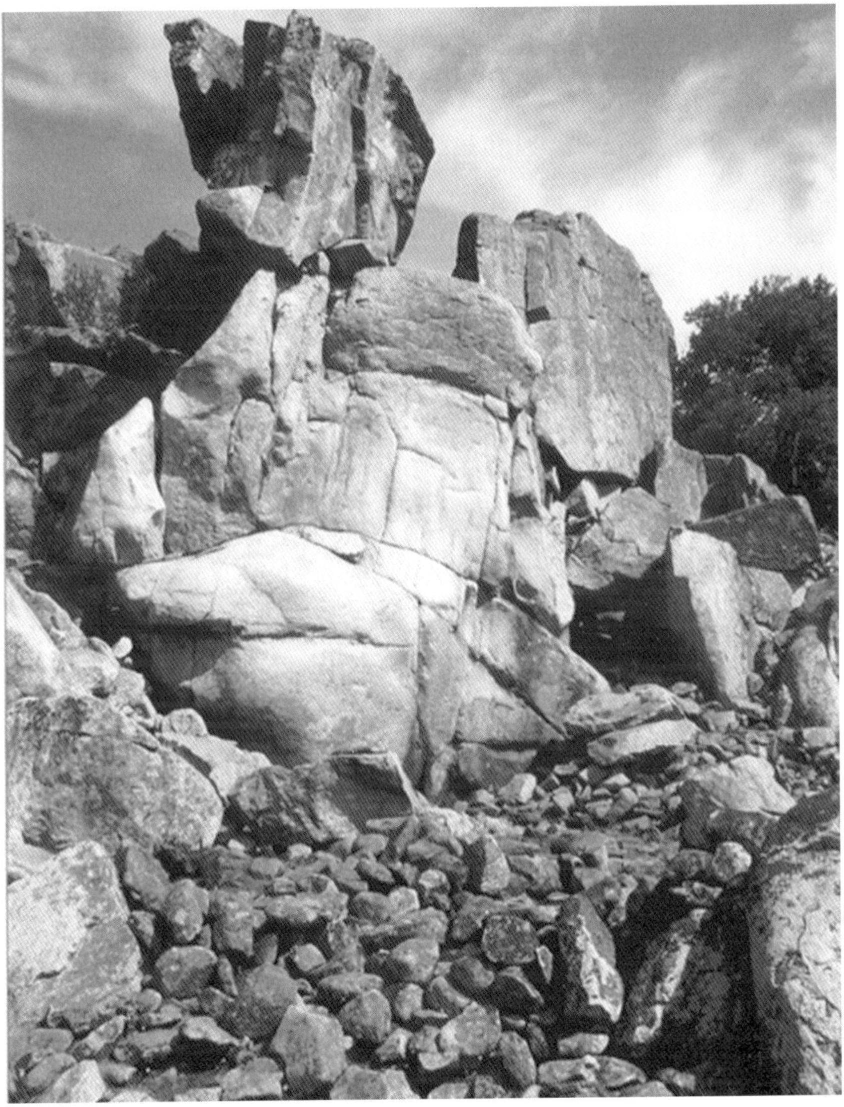

Figure 81. The Copper Age decorated cave at El Pedroso, Spain.

which seem to emerge out of hollows in the rock (Bradley, Jones, Nordenborg Myhre, and Sackett 2003).

Portable artefacts raise similar issues, although the evidence is seldom so clear cut. The use of certain artefacts was obviously restricted according to age and gender: a pattern that is demonstrated by the burial record. Thedéen (2003) has also suggested that the decorated razors of Bronze Age Scandinavia were used in life course rituals, and the same may apply to the small personal items with which they are often associated. Other decorated objects may have been made specifically for burial with the dead. This practice is well documented at Hochdorf (Olivier 1999): a site which will be considered later in this chapter.

Even closer comparisons can be made with the displays of personal artefacts associated with graves and public ceremonies. In recent years the organization of prehistoric burials has been studied in a new way. Rather than treating the contents of a grave as an indication of the wealth and status of the dead person, scholars have considered who had provided these objects and how the burial gifts were organized in the ground. They might not necessarily be the personal possessions of the deceased, so much as an idealized image of his or her roles in life. They may also have represented the relationships between the dead and the people organizing the funeral (Brück 2004; King 2004). In short, the contents of these graves were really a display to be viewed by the mourners before it was hidden from view.

In the same way, collections of fine metalwork from deposits like those at La Tène have an increasing number of counterparts on dry land; a few water deposits have even been excavated by modern methods (Field and Parker Pearson 2003: chapter 11). Again there seems to have been an emphasis on display, although there is no indication who was permitted to view such spectacles and who might have been excluded. It no longer seems as if the disposal of this material was the most important transaction—impressive as this may have been. Now it appears that large collections of metalwork, together with human remains and animal sacrifices, may have been put on display at certain specialized locations: hill forts, shrines, or even wooden bridges or causeways (Wells 2007: 471–5). There are indications that these items remained there for some time before they were discarded. It is that intermediate stage—between the use of these artefacts by the living and their role as offerings to the supernatural—that had remained elusive until recently, but now it is being recognized increasingly often. The excavation of Iron Age sanctuaries provides an indication of the numbers of objects involved (see, for example, Brunaux, Meniel, and Poplin 1985). It may be that the water finds that have commanded so much attention account for a limited proportion of the fine metalwork offered to the gods. Renewed attention to the material found on dry land is gradually redressing the balance. The collections of weapons discovered during recent fieldwork may be equivalent to the drawings of these objects found in rock art. Similarly, the ceremonies that can be postulated at some of the decorated outcrops had equivalents on other sites where artefacts are all that remain. They are the finds that have dominated studies of prehistoric art.

ANCIENT AND MODERN

This chapter began by considering the changing perceptions of ancient images that resulted from their appropriation by Modernist painters and sculptors. The associations of these designs were overlooked and their interpretation was radically curtailed. They were transformed into static artefacts that offered visual stimulus and new material for contemplation. In the course of these changes several elements were lost. The most important are described by Renfrew as *process* and *display* (Renfrew 2002: chapter 3). Both are essential to any understanding of prehistoric 'artworks'. Paradoxically, they play an equally important role in contemporary art.

In the examples quoted earlier the term *process* would refer to the way in which ancient images were related to processes in the natural world: changes in the position of the sun; darkness and light; the passage of water; the annual cycle of the seasons. They determined how and when such images could be seen and the contexts in which they were put to use. In many cases it was through the workings of nature that drawings and paintings in the prehistoric landscape were given life. They were animated by sunlight or running water, and without them they were inert. It is those features that are ignored when prehistoric art is assimilated to the Modernist canon. The argument goes even further. Interpretations of twentieth-century art depend on a complete separation between culture and nature; the 'natural' world may provide the subject matter for certain paintings and sculptures, but the galleries where they are shown are dedicated to high culture. Far from separating culture and nature, ancient artworks often combine them in such a way that the distinction is meaningless.

Process is also a useful term to describe the transformations experienced by ancient images before they reached their present form. They passed through different stages between their initial production and the ends of their periods of use. In many cases a rock carving, a painting or a statue menhir was not made as a 'finished' work; it was modified, augmented, defaced, and sometimes erased according to particular circumstances in the course of its history, and often the effects of that process could be recognized by those who viewed it. Some 'panels' of rock art may have taken a millennium to achieve their present form, and only a few images were created at any one time. Similarly, decorated artefacts might have been altered and repaired, renewed and even destroyed as they circulated in different contexts during prehistory. Again a discerning observer could recognize the traces left by those processes, just as an archaeologist can today.

At the same time, both artefacts and more monumental images seem to have been *displayed.* Indeed, there are even petroglyphs which appear to represent displays of artefacts, like the axe heads shown inside Bronze Age cists in the west of Scotland, or the hoards of weapons that were portrayed on rock carvings of the same period in Galicia (Bradley 1998a). Painted and carved designs were organized in relation to the positions of viewers who may have needed to move around them in a prescribed order. That was particularly true in the case of decorated monuments. Different kinds of images were made in different places, so that again it would be necessary to pass between them in order to appreciate their significance. Rather similar conventions determined the use of ship settings and round cairns, and the deposition of metalwork. At times different kinds of material were brought together and put in show, whether they were the contents of a grave or the components of a hoard. That was particularly true in the case of great votive deposits like that at La Tène, where the sheer variety of material is as impressive as its quantity (Reginelli Servais, 2007); and, just as certain people might have been permitted to view these collections and others might have been excluded, certain objects were appropriate as votive offerings and others probably were not. The clearest demonstration of this point is where such deposits have been excavated on dry land, for here it is possible to learn something of how such displays had been organized.

FIGURING IT OUT

Renfrew's book talks of '*The Parallel Visions of Artists and Archaeologists*'. What are those parallels, and how do they extend to the practice of prehistoric archaeology?

There are many possibilities to consider. There are artists who have been inspired by the places where archaeologists work, like Paul Nash at Avebury (Cardinal 1989). Others have been more intrigued by the procedures followed by archaeologists in the field. Thus Mark Dion has based several projects on the idea of excavation (Coles and Dion eds. 1999).

Archaeologists have sought inspiration in the methods of visual artists. The excavators of Leskernick in Cornwall wrapped and coloured granite rocks on the site to emphasize the visual effects that might have been important in prehistory (Bender, Hamilton, and Tilley 2007: chapter 13). Renfrew himself has suggested that the work of Richard Long might provide a model for prehistorians studying ancient landscapes (2002: 31–9), and the procedures used by the Boyle Family who made exact replicas of small areas of the earth's surface are very like those of excavation, with its emphasis on the precise rendering of colours and textures in the soil. When they originally exhibited their work they called themselves The Institute of Contemporary Archaeology (Arts Council of Great Britain 1986).

At times the resemblance between art and archaeology is explained by personal connections. Some of the leading pioneers in the development of field archaeology in Britain were originally trained in the visual arts, as painters, photographers, or as architectural draughtsmen. Philip Barker was perhaps the most famous example, but Mortimer Wheeler was an art student at the Slade School. Brian Hope-Taylor illustrates the same point, for surely it was their background in observation and precise documentation that encouraged such people to develop new methods in the field (Bradley 1997b).

For the most part those are instances of what Renfrew calls the *parallel visions* of artists and archaeologists. They reflect his view that contemporary art—especially abstract art—poses similar problems of interpretation to archaeological evidence, whether it takes the form of stripped surfaces or the remains of earthworks, landscapes or ancient artefacts. In that sense the two disciplines can learn from one another, because they offer a source of inspiration and suggest different ways of seeing.

There is another approach to the relationship between contemporary art and archaeology. To what extent do visual artists and archaeologists draw on a similar body of ideas? Can certain notions developed in the study of art be applied to prehistoric evidence?

Process and *display* have their equivalents among contemporary artworks. *Conceptual Art* is very much concerned with process, as it is a medium for presenting ideas, and the processes leading to its creation may be as important as the final form displayed in a gallery. It is an art that is more concerned with thought than with appearance, and sometimes it asks questions about the nature of art itself (Wood 2002).

Installation Art is a more recent development and in some respects it is related to Conceptual Art, for again it can be the expression of abstract ideas (De Oliveira, Oxley, and Petry 1994 and 2003; Bishop 2005). In this case the term is self-explanatory, for here the artworks are not single objects or images, but complex arrangements of different elements which are often drawn from the familiar world. It is their combination and juxtaposition that are most significant. They create self-contained environments that invite the participation of the viewer as he or she moves around them. There are even examples which refer directly to the processes of classification and display employed by archaeologists. Susan Hiller's work often refers to the strange assortment of artefacts in museum collections (Renfrew 2002: 100–1).

These are fashionable notions and every year they lead to controversy as the artists shortlisted for the Turner Prize display their work in London. What is their connection with archaeology? The objects that archaeologists study had histories of their own: histories which can be worked out by observing traces of use and repair (Kopytoff 1986). They had a specific point of origin, but often they moved from one location to another. They had also been used in different contexts before they were withdrawn from circulation.

Consider the Late Bronze Age swords found in the River Thames (York 2002). They were made in distant areas, and some were imported from the Continent. The raw material was often obtained by melting down other objects when they went out of commission. The sword blades show evidence that these weapons had been used in combat, and some had even been re-sharpened. When their use came to an end, a number were melted down, but others were deliberately damaged or broken, often with considerable force. Then they were placed in the water. Museum displays represent only the latest episode in a lengthy process, but when one of these weapons was deposited the audience may well have been aware of its history, and the histories of the people who had used it.

These weapons probably entered the river one at a time, and, as they did so, their biographies came to an end. This situation is rather different from the treatment of similar objects at Iron Age shrines in Gaul. At Gournay-sur-Aronde large numbers of weapons—swords, spears, and shields—were put on display around the perimeter of an earthwork enclosure, accompanied by a large collection of human and animal bones (Brunaux, Meniel, and Poplin 1985). Some may even have been nailed to wooden posts (Figure 82). Those weapons were not made by the smith as votive offerings as it is obvious that they had been used. In fact it is likely that the human remains were those of people killed in battle. The important point is that, while each object would have had its own biography, here they were brought together and put on display. That is a comparable process to Installation Art. The main difference is one of terminology, for archaeologists call such collections *structured deposits*.

If there is an overlap between some of the concepts employed by archaeologists and those used by contemporary artists, the same point can be

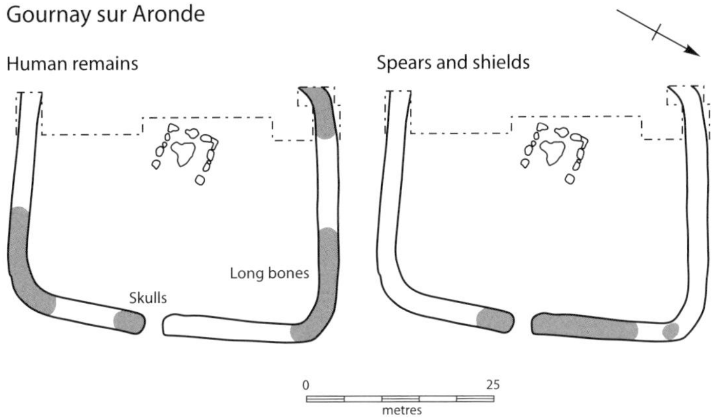

Figure 82. The Iron Age sanctuary and associated deposits at Gournay-sur-Aronde, France.

illustrated by discussing two artworks which have recently been in the news in Britain. Here they are compared with two archaeological sites.

The first examples bring together rivers and boats. Not long ago Simon Starling won the Turner Prize. Among the works he exhibited at the time was a wooden shed which attracted considerable publicity (Starling 2005: A2–A15). It had an unusual history, and the piece that was on view in Tate Britain was simply the end result of that process. Its full title was *Shedboatshed.* It came about in this way. Starling, who lives in Germany, was cycling along the River Rhine when he came across a shed which had originally been used as a guard hut on the Swiss border. He persuaded the owners to let him move it again. He took it to pieces and rebuilt it as a boat which he paddled along the river to Basel. There he reassembled the original shed. That is the work that was on display, but in practice the exhibit shown in London concerned the entire history of the structure, from its changes of site and its conversion into a boat, to its reconstruction and, finally, its display to the public. Those ideas—however zany—are similar to the biographical approach to ancient artefacts.

As seen in London, Starling's shed was simply a shed. It did it not form part of a larger installation, and yet it had once been used as a boat. A revealing comparison is with a more famous vessel: the Migration Period ship burial in Mound 1 at Sutton Hoo (Carver 2005). Even this famous vessel had a complex history, for it seems to have been dragged from the River Deben to its final resting place (Figure 83). There is no reason to suppose that it was originally constructed as a burial chamber—in that sense it was transformed. It also represented the *idea* of a boat that would convey the dead person to the Otherworld. Thus the ship was both a practical seagoing vessel

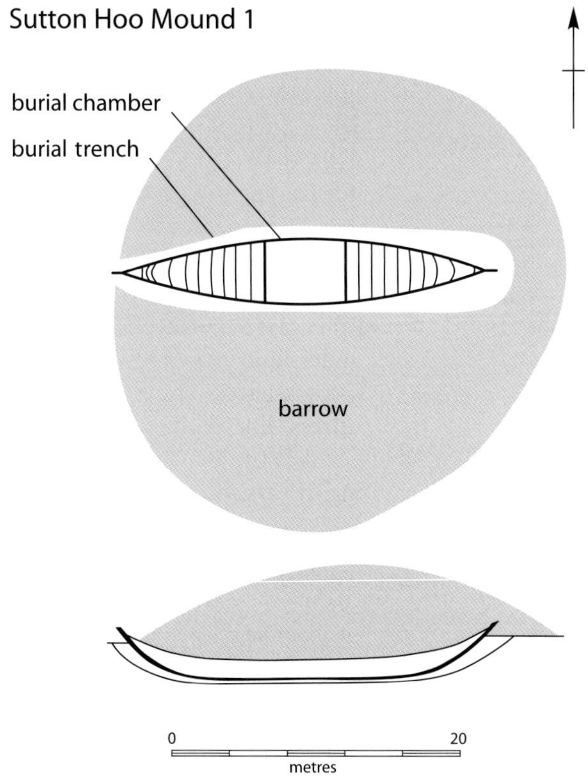

Figure 83. The ship burial in Mound 1 at Sutton Hoo, England.

which could have carried people along the nearby river, and a solid metaphor for the passage to the Afterlife just like the Bronze Age ship settings discussed in Chapter 6. Its movement from water to land is not completely different from the transformation of Simon Starling's shed, although one was conducted with a certain anarchic humour and the other in deadly seriousness.

The ship in Mound 1 at Sutton Hoo was filled with rare and valuable artefacts which would have had their own histories. More than that, individual items referred to distant places of origin and even to different systems of belief. They were brought together, laid out in the vessel in a specific order and for a while they would have been displayed to the mourners before the barrow was built. Even the placing of these artefacts might have expressed more general ideas, as Franz Herschend has suggested that the contents of ship burials were organized if they were inside a feasting hall (2001: 69–81). If so, they evoked the idea that this was not just the start of a journey; it was also a house of the dead that evoked the lifestyle of the deceased. Surely this is what Martin Carver (2000) has in mind when he compares the burial to a poem, for its separate elements carried an unusual weight of significance. Since these ideas were expressed by material forms, an even closer comparison is with Installation Art.

Simon Starling's *Shedboatshed* is also a piece of Conceptual Art. A better-known exhibit in Tate Britain was Tracey Emin's bed. This attracted considerable publicity at the time, but in this case it was not necessary to know the genesis of the display in order to understand its significance.

This is the second example. The work had the simple title *My Bed* and is catalogued in these terms as: 'Mattress, linen, pillows, rope [and] various memorabilia' (De Oliveira, Oxley and Petry 2003: 204). A recent study of Installation Art is more forthcoming. It says this:

> The British artist Tracey Emin exhibited *My Bed* unmade and rumpled after a week's illness, complete with all the paraphernalia she had used in it.. . . . In an era of superficiality this private and autobiographical emblem of the artist's everyday life was exhibited as an authentic statement about herself and her relationships.
>
> (De Oliveira, Oxley, and Petry 2003: 143)

The result may seem trivial, but the important point is that this is a carefully contrived display of items of personal significance to Emin. In that sense it is a means of self-expression of unusual directness. It is not a neutral representation. The separate items had been selected and arranged to communicate with the audience in the gallery. Outside that particular setting they would not carry the same significance, for it is their juxtaposition in this unusual installation that expresses Emin's theme of human vulnerability.

The second archaeological example features a bed of a very different kind, for in this case the person lying on it was dead (Figure 84). This is the rich Late Hallstatt burial at Hochdorf in south-west Germany (Planck, Biel, Süsskind, and Wais eds. 1985). The grave was unusually well preserved and was excavated to a very high standard. The account that follows refers to the interpretation of Hochdorf by Laurent Olivier (1999).

The burial chamber was divided into two parts. One contained the corpse, a man who was laid out on the bed with his possessions. The other part included a dismantled wagon, accompanied by large vessels for the service of food and drink. The chamber may have been lined with textiles, and drinking horns were hanging on the walls. The image recalls that of the Classical symposium, which is hardly surprising since some of the richest objects originated in the Mediterranean.

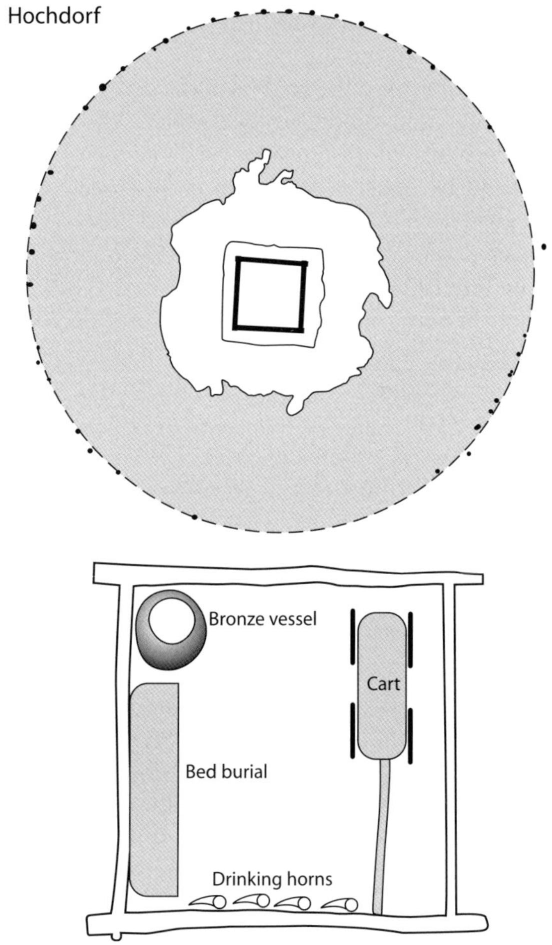

Figure 84. The Iron Age burial chamber and its contents at Hochdorf, Germany.

At the same time, the artefacts at Hochdorf evoked connections with different places. Some objects were of local origin, but others were exotic and referred to relationships with people and practices in distant areas. It may be that some of the exotic items were funeral gifts provided by allies in other communities. If so, the burial assemblage provided a kind of map of the political connections of the deceased.

Olivier also refers to the important dimension of time. Some of those artefacts had long biographies of their own, for they were already worn or damaged. Others, including the small objects which he takes to be the possessions of the dead man, were reworked specifically for the funeral and were covered in gold. All this would have taken a long time—the excavator has estimated three months—so the remains must have been preserved somewhere else. It was during this period that the body was fitted with special clothes. The construction of the wooden chamber would have taken a significant period too, and even when it was finished it was by no means easy to move the funeral gifts into their final resting place. The wagon had to be dismantled; the great metal vessels would have been difficult to manoeuvre, and in any case they could only have been filled with liquid after they had been placed in the tomb. Olivier suggests that, while all this was happening, the dead man and his accoutrements were displayed to the mourners on another site.

The important point is that this elaborate burial was not unlike the complex installations found in art galleries today. It communicated as much to the living as the dead, and, however briefly the contents of the chamber were exposed to view, this was more than an unstructured assemblage of artefacts. It was an image that would have been understood by the mourners and recalled by later generations. No doubt that image had more than one layer of meaning, but it was carefully composed by the juxtaposition and display of different kinds of objects. Ultimately it was buried under a mound and became part of prehistoric archaeology.

Perhaps there is room for dialogue between those who practise and study contemporary art and those who work in archaeology, but the implication of this discussion is that the link is at the level of interpretations—of ideas. The past may provide a source of inspiration for artists and archaeologists alike, but they have most in common when they deal with similar phenomena.

SUMMARY

Like Chapter 1, this chapter began by tracing some of the ways in which conceptions of prehistoric art were changed as it made the transition from the ancient world to the modern. It has emphasized certain of the differences between their roles in prehistoric society and their status of works of art in the present. It has traced a similar process in the translation of ancient images into twentieth century paintings and sculptures: a process that is precisely comparable to the treatment of 'ethnographic art'. One way of distinguishing between such radically different genres was by establishing which features were most obviously lost in the course of translation.

The outcome is paradoxical. There are many important differences between the roles played by prehistoric 'artworks' and the Modernist paintings and sculptures which they helped to inspire. On the other hand, the ancient images had much wider connotations. Their interrelationships are most important, and so are their histories, the combinations in which they were displayed, and the performances that must have accompanied their creation and use. These are all features that have been emphasized by contemporary artists, few of whom are influenced by images deriving from the past. Is it possible that, quite by chance, Installation Art and Conceptual Art have more in common with prehistoric archaeology than they do with the dominant trends in the Modern Movement? It is an intriguing idea with which to end the book.

References

Acosta, P. (1968), *La pintura rupestre esquemática en España* (Salamanca, Universidad de Salamanca)

Allen, D. (1971), 'The Sark hoard', *Archaeologia* 103: 1–31

Allen, J. R. (1904), *Celtic Art in Pagan and Christian Times* (London, Methuen)

Almgren, O. (1927), *Hällristningar och kultbruk* (Stockholm, Kungl. Vitterhets historie och antikvitets akademiens handlingar)

Alves, L. B. (2002), 'The architecture of the natural world: rock art in western Iberia'. In C. Scarre (ed.), *Monuments and Landscape in Atlantic Europe*: 51–69 (London, Routledge)

—— (in press), 'Signs on a rock veil: work on rocks, "prehistoric art" and identity in north-west Iberia'. In G. Cooney and B. O'Connor (eds.), *Materialitas: Working Stone, Carving Identity* (London, The Prehistoric Society)

Anderson, J. (1881), *Scotland in Early Christian Times* (Edinburgh, David Douglas)

Andrén, A., Jennbert, K., and Raudvere, C. (2006), 'Old Norse Religion. Some problems and prospects'. In A. Andrén, K. Jennbert and C. Raudvere (eds.), *Old Norse Religion in Long-term Perspectives: Origins, Changes, and Interactions*: 11–14 (Lund, Nordic Academic Press)

Arcini, C. (2005), 'Pyre sites before our eyes'. In T. Artelius and F. Svanberg (eds.), *Dealing with the Dead: Archaeological Perspectives on Prehistoric Scandinavian Burial Ritual*: 63–72 (Stockholm, National Heritage Board)

Artelius, T. (1996), *Långfärd och återkomst – skeppet i bronsålderns gravar* (Kungsbacka, Riksantvarieämbetet)

Arts Council of Great Britain (1986), *Beyond Image: Boyle Family* (London, Hayward Gallery)

Artursson, M. (2005), 'Byggnadstradition'. In P. Lagerås and B. Strömberg (eds.), *Bronsåldersbygd 2300–500 f.Kr.*: 20–83 (Lund, Riksantikvarieämbetet)

Bahn, P. (1998), *Cambridge Illustrated History of Prehistoric Art* (Cambridge, Cambridge University Press)

Bailey, D. (2000), *Balkan Prehistory: Exclusion, Incorporation and Identity* (London, Routledge)

Bailey, D. (2005), *Prehistoric Figurines: Representation and Corporeality in the Neolithic* (London, Routledge)

Ballard, C., Bradley, R., Nordenborg Myhre, L., and Wilson, M. (2003), 'The ship as symbol in the prehistory of Scandinavia and South-east Asia', *World Archaeology* 35: 385–403

Barfield, L., and Chippindale, C. (1997), 'Meaning in the later prehistoric rock-engravings of Mont Bégo, Alpes Maritimes, France', *Proceedings of the Prehistoric Society* 63: 103–28

Bartoloni, G., Bursanelli, F., D'Atri, V., and De Santis, A. (1987), *Le urne a capanne rivenute in Italia* (Rome, Bretschneider)

Baudou, E. (1968), *Forntida bebyggelse i Ångermanslands kustland* (Stockholm, Stockholms Universitet Institution förnordisk fornkunskap)

Beckensall, S. (1999), *British Prehistoric Rock Art* (Stroud, Tempus)

—— (2006), *Circles in Stone* (Stroud, Tempus)

Bender, B., Hamilton, S., and Tilley, C. (2007), *Stone Worlds: Narrative and Reflexivity in Landscape Archaeology* (Walnut Creek, Left Coast Press)

Bengtsson, L. (2004), *Bilder vid vatten* (Göteborg, Göteborgs Universitet)

Bergquist, A., and Taylor, T. (1987), 'The origin of the Gundestrup cauldron', *Antiquity* 61: 10–24

Berntsson, A. (2005), *Två män i en båt: om människans relation till havet ii bronsåldern* (Lund, Institute of Archaeology)

Bertilsson, U. (1987), *The Rock Carvings of Northern Bohuslän: Spatial Structures and Social Symbols* (Stockholm, University of Stockholm, Department of Archaeology)

Bishop, C. (2005), *Installation Art. A Critical History* (London, Tate Publishing)

Bloch, M., and Parry, J. (1982), 'Introduction: death and the regeneration of life'. In M. Bloch and J. Parry (eds.), *Death and the Regeneration of Life*: 1–44 (Cambridge, Cambridge University Press)

Boivin, N., and Owoc, M. A. eds. (2004), *Soils, Stones and Symbols: Cultural Perceptions of the Mineral World* (London, UCL Press)

Bolin, H. (1999), *Kultur-landskapets korsvägar. Mellersta Norrland under de två sista årtusendena f. Kr.* (Stockholm, Stockholm Studies in Archaeology)

Borna-Ahlkvist, H. (2002), *Hällristarnas hem* (Stockholm, Riksantikvarieämbetet)

Boujot, C., and Cassen, S. (1998), 'Tertres armoricains et tumulus carnacéens'. In Guilaine, J. (ed.), *Sépultures d'Occident et genèse des mégalithismes*: 109–26 (Paris, France)

Boujot, C., Cassen, S., and Vaquero Lastres, J. (1998), 'Some abstraction for a practical subject: the Neolithicization of Western France seen through funerary architecture', *Cambridge Archaeological Journal* 8: 193–206

Bourdieu, P. (1991), *The Love of Art: European Art Museums and their Public* (Cambridge, Polity Press)

Bradley, R. (1989), 'Darkness and light in the design of megalithic tombs', *Oxford Journal of Archaeology* 8: 251–9

—— (1990), *The Passage of Arms* (Cambridge, Cambridge University Press)

—— (1997a), *Rock Art and the Prehistory of Atlantic Europe* (London, Routledge)

—— (1997b), ' "To see is to have seen": craft traditions in British field archaeology'. In B. L. Molyneaux (ed.), *The Cultural Life of Images*: 62–72 (London, Routledge)

—— (1998a), 'Daggers drawn: depictions of Bronze Age weapons in Atlantic Europe'. In C. Chippindale and P. Taçon (eds.), *The Archaeology of Rock Art*: 130–45 (Cambridge, Cambridge University Press)

—— (1998b), *The Significance of Monuments* (London, Routledge)

—— (2000), *An Archaeology of Natural Places* (London, Routledge)

—— (2002), *The Past in Prehistoric Societies* (London, Routledge)

—— (2006), 'Danish razors and Swedish rocks: cosmology and the Bronze Age landscape', *Antiquity* 80: 372–8

—— (2007a), *The Prehistory of Britain and Ireland* (Cambridge, Cambridge University Press)

—— (2007b), 'Visions and revisions: northern influence in South Scandinavian rock art?' In R. Barndon, S. Innselset, K. Kristoffersen, and T. Lødøen (eds.), *Samfunn, symboler og identitet – Festkrift til Gro Mandt på 70-årsdagen*: 163–70 (Bergen, Universitet in Bergen)

—— (2007c), 'The shipping news: land and water in Bronze Age Scandinavia'. In D. Barraclough and C. Malone (eds.), *Cult in Context*: 210–16 (Oxford, Oxbow)

—— (2008), 'Ship-settings and boat crews in the Bronze Age of Scandinavia'. In J. Goldhahn (ed.), *Gropar och monument. En vänbok till Dag Widholm*: 171–84 (Kalmar, Kalmar Studies in Archaeology)

—— and Fábregas Valcarce, R. (1998), 'Crossing the border: contrasting styles of rock art in the prehistory of north-west Iberia', *Oxford Journal of Archaeology* 17: 287–308

—— Fábregas Valcarce, R., Bacelar Alves, L., and Vilaseco Vázquez, X. (2005), 'El Pedroso: a prehistoric cave sanctuary in Castille', *Journal of Iberian Archaeology* 7: 125–56.

—— and Gordon, K. (1988), 'Human skulls from the River Thames: their dating and significance', *Antiquity* 62: 503–9

—— Jones, A., Nordenborg Myhre, L., and Sackett, H. (2003), 'Sailing through stone: carved ships and the rockface at Revheim, southwest Norway', *Norwegian Archaeological Review* 35.2: 109–18

—— and Phillips, T. (2004), 'The high-water mark: the siting of megalithic tombs on the Swedish island of Tjörn', *Oxford Journal of Archaeology* 23: 123–33

—— and —— (2008), 'Display, disclosure and concealment: the organisation of raw materials in the chambered tombs of Bohuslän', *Oxford Journal of Archaeology* 27: 1–13

—— Phillips, T., Richards, C., and Webb, M. (2001), 'Decorating the houses of the dead: incised and pecked motifs in Orkney chambered tombs', *Cambridge Archaeological Journal* 11: 45–67

—— and Widholm, D (2007), 'The mountain of ships: the organisation of the Bronze Age cemetery at Snäckedal, Misterhult, Småland'. In B. Hårdh, K. Jennbert, and D. Olausson (eds.), *On the Road: Studies in Honour of Lars Larsson*: 246–52 (Stockholm, Almqvist and Wiksell)

Brennan, M. (1983), *The Stars and the Stones: Ancient Art and Astronomy in Ireland* (London, Thames and Hudson)

Breuil, H. (1933–5), *Les peintures rupestres schématiques de la Péninsule Ibérique, 1–4* (Lagny sur Marne, Grévin)

—— (1934), 'Presidential address', *Proceedings of the Prehistoric Society of East Anglia* 7: 289–322

—— (1952), *Quatre cents siècles d'art pariétal* (Montignac, Cenre d'étude et de documentation préhistorique)

Brox Nilsen, T. (2005), *Vedrørende en bergkunstlokalitet i Stjørdalen* (Trondheim, Norges teknisk-naturvitenskaplige universitet)

Brück, J. (2004), 'Material metaphors: the relational construction of identity in Early Bronze Age burials in Ireland and Britain', *Journal of Social Archaeology* 4: 307–33

Brunaux, J-L., Meniel, P., and Pollin, F. (1985), *Gournay 1. Fouilles sur le sanctuaire et l'oppidum*, Révue Archéologique de Picardie, numéro special

Bueno Ramirez, P., and de Balbín Behrmann, R. (2000a), 'Arte megalítico en la Extremadura Española', *Extramadura Arqueológica* 8: 345–79

—— and —— (2000b), 'Art mégalithique et art en plein air: à propos la définition du territoire pour les groupes producteurs de la Péninsule Ibérique', *L'anthropologie* 104: 427–58

—— and —— (2002), 'L'art mégalithique péninsulaire et l'art mégalithique de la façade atlantique: un modèle de capillarité appliqué à l'art post-paléolithique européen', *L'anthropologie* 106: 603–46

—— and —— (2003), 'Una geografia cultural del arte megalítico ibérico: les supeuestras areas marginales'. In R. de Balbín Behrmann and P. Bueno Ramirez (eds.), *El art prehistoric desde los inicios del siglo XX1*: 291–313 (Ribadsella, Assocació Cultural Amigos de Ribadsella)

—— and —— (2006a), 'Art mégalithique et mégalithisme: idées et interprétations jusqu'aux années 80'. In R. Joussaume, L. Laporte, and C. Scarre (eds.), *Origine et développement du mégalithisme de l'ouest de l'Europe, 2*: 733–51 (Bougon, Musée des Tumulus de Bougon)

—— and —— (2006b), 'Arte parietal, arte megalítico en la Penísula Ibérica'. In F. Carrera and R. Fábregas (eds.), *Art parietal megalítico en el nordoeste Penninsular. Conocimiento y conservación*: 153–212 (Santiago de Compostela, Tórculo Edicións)

—— and —— (2006c), 'Arte megalítico en la Península Ibérica: contextos materials y simbólicos para el arte esquemático'. In J. Martínez García and M. Hernández Pérez (eds.), *Arte rupestre esquemático en la Península Ibérica*: 57–84 (Los Vélez, Comarca de Los Vélez)

——, —— and Barroso Bermajo, R. (2004), 'Application d'une méthode d'analyse du terriroire à partir de la situation des marqueurs graphiques à l'intérieur de la Péninsule Ibérique: le Tage International', *L' anthropologie* 108: 653–710

——, —— and —— (2005a), *El dolmen de Azután* (Alcalá de Henares, Universidade de Alcalá)

——, —— and —— (2005b), 'Hiérarchisation et métallurgie: statues armées dans la Péninsule Ibérique', *L'anthropologie* 109: 577–640

——, —— and —— (2007), 'Chronologie de l'art mégalitique ibérique: C 14 et contextes archéologiques', *L'anthropologie* 111: 1–65

——, Barroso Bermajo, R., de Balbín Behrmann, R., and Carrera, F. (2006), *Megalíticos y marcadores gráficos en el Tajo internacional: Santiago de Alcántara, Cáceres* (Salamanca, Europa Artes Gráficas)

Burenhult, G. (1973), *The Rock Carvings of Götaland, Part 2* (Lund, Acta Archaeologica Lundensia)

—— (1980), *The Rock Carvings of Götaland, Part 1* (Stockholm, Stockholm University Institute of Archaeology)

—— (2001), 'Long-distance cultural interaction in megalithic Europe: Carrowmore and the Irish megalithic tradition in a western European and Mediterranean context'. In B. Werbart (ed.), *Cultural Interactions in Europe and the Eastern Mediterranean during the Bronze Age (3000–500 BC)*: 47–66 (Oxford, British Archaeological Reports)

Burrow, S. (1997), *The Neolithic Culture of the Isle of Man* (Oxford, British Archaeological Reports)

Calado, M. (2002), 'Standing stones and natural outcrops: the role of ritual monuments in the Neolithic transition of the Central Alentejo'. In C. Scarre (ed.), *Monuments and Landscape in Atlantic Europe*: 17–35 (London, Routledge)

—— (2006), 'Les menhirs de la Péninsule Ibérique'. In R. Joussaume, L. Laporte, and C. Scarre (eds.), *Origine et développement du mégalithisme de l'ouest de l'Europe, 2*: 613–35 (Bougon, Musée des Tumulus de Bougon)

Campbell, S. (2001), 'The captivating agency of art: many ways of seeing'. In C. Pinney and N. Thomas (eds.), *Beyond Aesthetics. Art and the Technologies of Enchantment*: 117–35 (Oxford, Berg)

Capelle, T. (1986), 'Schiffsetzungen', *Praehistorische Zeitschrift* 61: 1–63

—— (1995), 'Bronze Age stone ships'. In O. Crumlin-Pedersen and B. M. Thye (eds.), *The Ship as Symbol in Prehistoric and Medieval Scandinavia*: 71–5 (Copenhagen, National Museum)

Cardinal, R. (1989), *The Landscape Vision of Paul Nash* (London, Reaktion)

Carrera Ramírez, F., and Fábregas Valcarce, R. (2006), 'Datación directa de pinturas megalíticas de Galicia'. In F. Carrera Ramírez and R. Fábregas Valcarce (eds.), *Art parietal megalítico en el nordoeste Penninsular. Conocimiento y conservación*: 37–60 (Santiago de Compostela, Tórculo Edicións)

Carver, M. (2000), 'Burial as poetry: the context of treasure in Anglo-Saxon graves'. In E. Tyler (ed.), *Treasure in the Medieval West*: 25–48 (York, York Medieval Press)

—— (2005), *Sutton Hoo, A Seventh-Century Princely Burial Ground and its Context* (London, British Museum Press)

Cassen, S. (1999), 'Questions of epistemology and a working hypothesis about the engravings of the fifth millennium in western France', *Antiquity* 73: 198–205

—— (2000), 'Stelae reused in the passage graves of western France: history of research and sexualisation of the carvings'. In A. Ritchie (ed.), *Neolithic Orkney in its European Context*: 233–46 (Cambridge, McDonald Institute for Archaeological Research)

—— (2007), 'Le Mané Lud en images: interprétations des signes gravés sur les parois de la tombe à couloir de Locmariaquer (Morbihan)', *Gallia Préhistoire* 49: 1197–258

—— Audren, C., Hinguant, S., Lannuzel, G., and Marchand, G. (1998), 'L'habitat Villeneuve-St-Germain du Haut-Mée', *Bulletin de la Société Préhistorique Française* 95: 41–75

—— and L'Helgouach, J. (1992), 'Du symbole de la crosse: chronologie, répartition et interprétation'. In C-T. Le Roux (ed.), *Paysans et bâtisseurs*: 223–35 (Rennes, *Revue Archéologique de l'Ouest*, Supplément 5)

Cassen, S., and Vaquero Lastres, J. (2003), 'Le désir médusé'. In J. Guilaine (ed.), *Arts et symboles du Néolithique à la protohistoire*: 91–119 (Paris, Errance)

Chapman, J., and Gaydarska, B. (2007), *Parts and Wholes: Fragmentation in Prehistoric Context* (Oxford, Oxbow)

Chenorkian, R. (1988), *Les armes métalliques dans l'art protohistorique de l'occident Méditerranéen* (Paris, Éditions du Centre national de la recherche scientifique)

Childe, V. G. (1951), *Social Evolution* (London, Watts)

Chippindale, C., Smith, B., and Taçon, P. (2000), 'Visions of dynamic power: archaic rock paintings, altered states of consciousness and "Clever Men" in Western Arnhem Land, Australia', *Cambridge Archaeological Journal* 10: 63–101

Clark, P. (2004), *The Dover Bronze Age Boat* (Swindon, English Heritage)

Cleal, R., Walker, K., and Montague (1995), *Stonehenge in its Landscape: Twentieth Century Excavations* (London, English Heritage)

Cochrane, A. (2005), 'A taste for the unexpected: subverting *mentalités* through the motifs and settings of Irish passage tombs'. In D. Hofmann, J. Mills, and A. Cochrane (eds.), *Elements of Being: Mentalités, Identities and Movement*: 5–19 (Oxford, British Archaeological Reports)

—— (2006), 'The simulacra and simulations of Irish Neolithic passage tombs'. In I. Russell (ed.), *Images, Representations and Heritage: Moving Beyond a Modern Approach in Archaeology*: 251–82 (New York, Springer Kluwer)

Coles, A., and Dion, M. (1999), *Mark Dion, Archaeology* (London, Black Dog Publishing)

Coles, J. (1999), 'The dancer on the rock: record and analysis at Järrestad, Sweden', *Proceedings of the Prehistoric Society* 65: 167–87

—— (2000), *Patterns in a Rocky Land. Rock Carvings in South-West Uppland, Sweden* (Uppsala, Department of Archaeology and Ancient History, Uppsala University)

—— (2002), 'Chariots of the Gods? Landscape and imagery at Frännarp, Sweden', *Proceedings of the Prehistoric Society* 68: 215–46

—— (2003a), 'A measure of conviction: recording emphasis in Scandinavian rock carvings', *Antiquity* 52: 567–71

—— (2003b), 'And on they went... Processions in Scandinavian Bronze Age rock carvings', *Acta Archaeologica* 74: 211–50

—— (2004), 'Bridge to the outer world: rock carvings at Bro Utmark, Bohuslän, Sweden', *Proceedings of the Prehistoric Society* 70: 173–205

—— (2005), *Shadows of a Northern Past: rock Carvings of Bohuslän and Østfold* (Oxford, Oxbow)

—— (2006) 'Beacon on the ridge: rock carvings at Kasen Lovåsen, Bohuslän', Sweden, *Proceedings of the Prehistoric Society* 72: 319–39

Collis, J. (2003), *The Celts: Origins, Myths and Inventions* (Stroud, Tempus)

Commendador Rey, B. (1995), 'Caracterizacíon de la metallurgia inicial gallego: una revision', *Trabajos de Prehistoria* 55.2, 111–29

Cook, I., Pajot, S., and Leuchter, A. (2008), 'Ancient architectural acoustic resonance patterns and regional brain activity', *Time and Mind* 1.1: 95–104

Cooney, G. (2000), *Landscapes of Neolithic Ireland* (London, Routledge)

Coote, J. (1992), ' "Marvels of everyday vision": the anthropology of aesthetics and the cattle-keeping Nilotes'. In J. Coote and A. Shelton (eds.), *Anthropology, Art and Aesthetics*: 245–73 (Oxford, Clarendon Press)

—— and Shelton, A. eds. (1992), *Anthropology, Art and Aesthetics* (Oxford, Clarendon Press)

Crawford, O. G. S. (1957), *The Eye Goddess* (London, Phoenix House)

Crumlin-Pedersen, O., and Trakadas, A. eds. (2003), *Hjortspring: A Pre-Roman Iron Age Warship in Context* (Roskilde, Viking Ship Museum)

Cuming, H. S. (1857), 'On the discovery of Celtic crania in the vicinity of London', *Journal of the British Archaeological Association* 13: 237–9

Cummings, V. (2002), 'Experiencing texture and transformation in the British Neolithic', *Oxford Journal of Archaeology* 21: 249–61

Cunliffe, B. (2005), *Iron Age Communities in Britain*, fourth edition (Abingdon, Routledge)

Daniel, G. (1958), *The Megalith Builders of Western Europe* (London, Hutchinson)

Davidson, J., and Henshall, A. (1989), *The Chambered Cairns of Orkney* (Edinburgh, Edinburgh University Press)

De Blas Cortina, M. (2003), 'Estelas con armas: arte rupestre y paleometalurgia en el norte de la Península Ibérica'. In R. de Balbín Behrmann and P. Bueno Ramirez (eds.), *El art prehistoric desde los inicios del siglo XX1*: 391–417 (Ribadsella, Assocació Cultural Amigos de Ribadsella)

De Oliveira, N., Oxley, N., and Petty, M. (1994), *Installation Art* (London, Thames and Hudson)

——, —— and —— (2003), *Installation Art in the New Millennium* (London, Thames and Hudson)

De Saulieu, G. (2004), *Art rupestre et statues-menhirs dans les Alpes* (Paris, Errance)

Delibes de Castro, G., and Guerra Doce, E. (2004), 'Contexto e possible significando de un cuenco Ciempozuelos con decoración simbólica de ciervos hallado en Almenara de Adaja (Valladolid)', *Arqueología* 4: 117–25

Devignes, M. (1996), 'Les rapports entre peintures et gravures dans l'art mégalithique Iberique'. In J. L'Helgouach, C-T. Le Roux and J. Lecornec (eds.), *Art et symboles du mégalithisme Européen*: 9–22 (Rennes, *Revue Archéologique de l'Ouest*, Supplément 8)

Diáz-Andreu, M. (2002), 'Marking the landscape: Iberian post-Palaeolithic art, identities and the sacred'. In G. Nash and C. Chippindale (eds.), *European Landscapes of Rock-Art*: 158–75 (London, Routledge)

Dickinson, T. (2005), 'Symbols of protection: the significance of animal-ornamented shields in Early Anglo-Saxon England', *Medieval Archaeology* 49: 109–63

Domingo, I., Roldán, C., Fererro, J., and García, P. (2007), 'Nuevas aportaciones sobre el fragmento cerámico con cervidos incisos de la Cova de l'Or (Beniarrés, Alicante)', *Trabajos de Prehistoria* 64.2: 169–76

Dronfield, J. (1995a), 'Subjective vision and the source of Irish megalithic art', *Antiquity* 69: 539–49

—— (1995b), 'Migraine, light and hallucinations. The neurocognitive basis of Irish megalithic art', *Oxford Journal of Archaeology* 14, 261–75

—— (1996), 'Entering alternative realities: cognition, art and architecture in Irish passage-tombs', *Cambridge Archaeological Journal* 6: 37–72

Duval, P. M., and Kruta, V. eds (1982), *L'art Celtique de la période d' expansion* (Geneva: Droz)

Ellmers, D. (1995), 'Crew structure on board Scandinavian vessels'. In O. Olsen, J. Madsen, and F. Rieck (eds.), *Shipshape: Essays for Ole Crumlin-Pedersen*: 231–40 (Roskilde, Viking Ship Museum)

Eogan, G. (1986), *Knowth and the Passage-tombs of Ireland* (London, Thames and Hudson)

—— (1990), 'Irish megalithic tombs and Iberian comparisons and contrasts'. In *Probleme der Megalithgräberforschung*: 113–38 (Madrid, Deutsches archäologisches Institut)

—— (1996), 'Pattern and place: a preliminary study of the decorated kerbstones at Site 1, Knowth, Co. Meath and their comparative setting', In J. L'Helgouach, C-T. Le Roux, and J. Lecornec (eds.), *Art et symboles du mégalithisme Européen*: 97–104 (Rennes, *Revue Archéologique de l'Ouest*, Supplément 8)

—— (1997), 'Overlays and underlays: aspects of megalithic art succession at Brugh na Bóinne, Ireland', *Brigantium* 10: 217–34

—— (1998), 'Knowth before Knowth', *Antiquity* 7: 162–72

—— (1999), 'Megalithic art and society', *Proceedings of the Prehistoric Society* 65: 15–46

—— and Aboud, J. (1990), 'Diffuse pecking in megalithic art'. In *La Bretagne et l'Europe protohistorique: mémoire et homage à Pierre-Roland Giot*: 121–40 (*Revue Archéologique de l'Ouest*, Supplément 2)

—— and Roche, H. (1997), *Excavations at Knowth, 2* (Dublin, Royal Irish Academy)

Fabian, J. (1983), *Time and the Other: How Anthropology Makes its Object* (New York, Columbia University Press)

Fábregas Valcarce, R., and Vilaseco Vázquez, X. (2006), 'En torno al megalitismo gallego'. In F. Carrera Ramírez and R. Fábregas Valcarce (eds.), *Art parietal megalítico en el nordoeste Penninsular. Conocimiento y conservación*: 11–36 (Santiago de Compostela, Tórculo Edicións)

Fairén Jiménez, S. (2006), *El paisaje de la Neolitización. Arte rupestre, pobliamento y mundo funerario en las comercas centro-meridionales valencianas* (San Vicente del Raspeig, Universidad de Alicante)

Fett, E., and Fett, P. (1947), *Sydvestnorske helleristninger. Rogaland og Lista* (Stavanger, Stavanger Museum)

—— (1979, 'Relations West Norway – Western Europe documented in petroglyphs', *Norwegian Archaeological Review* 12, 65–107

Field, N., and Parker Pearson, M. (2003), *Fiskerton: An Iron Age Timber Causeway with Iron Age and Roman Votive Offerings* (Oxford, Oxbow)

Figenschou Simonsen, M., and Vogt, D. (2005), 'Fotsåleristninger i gravkontekst: Jong – et nytt funn fra Øst-Norge'. In J. Goldhahn (ed.), *Mellan sten och järn del 2*: 473–87 (Göteborg, Göteborgs Universitet)

Finlay, I. (1973), *Celtic Art: An Introduction* (London, Faber and Faber)

Fitzpatrick, A. (1996), 'Night and day: the symbolism of astral signs on later Iron Age anthropomorphic short swords', *Proceedings of the Prehistoric Society* 62: 373–98

—— (2007), 'Dancing with dragons: fantastic animals in the earlier Celtic art of Iron Age Britain'. In C. Haselgrove and T. Moore (eds.), *The Later Iron Age in Britain and Beyond*, 339–57 (Oxford, Oxbow)

Fleming, A. (1969), 'The myth of the mother goddess', *World Archaeology* 1: 247–61

Fontijn, D. (2003), 'Sacrificial Landscapes: cultural biographies of persons, objects and "natural places" in the Bronze Age of the southern Netherlands, c. 2300–600 BC', *Analecta Praehistorica Leidensia* 33/34: 1–393

Forge, A. (1973), 'Style and meaning in Sepik art'. In A. Forge (ed.), *Primitive Art and Society*: 169–92 (Oxford, Oxford University Press)

Fox, C. (1958), *Pattern and Purpose: A Survey of Early Celtic Art in Britain* (Cardiff, National Museum of Wales)

Frachetti, M., and Chippindale, C. (2002), 'Alpine, imagery, Alpine space, Alpine time, and prehistoric experience'. In G. Nash and C. Chippindale (eds.), *European Landscapes of Rock-Art*: 116–43 (London, Routledge)

Fredell, Å. (2003a), *Bildroar. Figurativ bildkommunikation av ideologi och kosmologi under sydskandinavisk bronsålder och förromersk järnålder* (Göteborg, Göteborgs Universitet)

—— (2003b), 'Bronze Age imagery—through water and fire', *Current Swedish Archaeology* 11: 45–63

Frey, O.-H. (1995), 'Some comments on swords with dragon pairs'. In B. Raftery (ed.), *Sites and Sights of the Iron Age*: 163–75 (Oxford, Oxbow)

Frodsham, P. (1986), 'Spirals in time: Morwick Mill and the spiral motif in the British Neolithic', *Northern Archaeology* 13/14: 101–38

García, Atiénzar (2000), 'Ojos que nos miran. Los idolos oculados entre las cuencas de los rios Júcar y Segura'. In J. Martínez García and M. Hernández Pérez (eds), *Arte rupestre esquemático en la Península Ibérica*: 223–34 (Los Vélez, Comarca de Los Vélez)

Gell, A. (1992), 'The technology of enchantment and the enchantment of technology'. In J. Coote and A. Shelton (eds.), *Anthropology, Art and Aesthetics*: 40–63 (Oxford, Clarendon Press)

—— (1993), *Wrapping in Images: Tattooing in Polynesia* (Oxford, Clarendon Press)

—— (1998), *Art and Agency: An Anthropological Theory* (Oxford, Clarendon Press)

—— (1999), *The Art of Anthropology: Essays and Diagrams* (London, Athlone Press)

Gelling, P., and Ellis Davidson, H. (1969), *The Chariot of the Sun and Other Rites and Symbols of the Northern Bronze Age* (London, Dent)

Gerdin, A.-L. (1999), 'Rösen –uttryck för makt eller platser där himmel och jord möts i det kosmiska rummet'. In M. Olausson (ed.), *Spiralens öga. Tjugo artiklar kring aktuell bronsåldersforskning*: 47–74 (Stockholm, Riksantikvarieämbetet)

Ghorghiu, D. (2001), 'The cult of ancestors in the eastern European Chalcolithic'. In P. Biehl, P. Bertemmes, and H. Meller (eds.), *The Archaeology of Cult and Ritual*: 73–88 (Budapest: Archaeolingua)

Giles, M. (2008), 'Seeing red: the aesthetics of martial objects in the British and Irish Iron Age'. In D. Garrow, C. Gosden, and J. D. Hill (eds.), *Rethinking Celtic Art*: 58–76 (Oxford, Oxbow)

Gimbutas, M. (1991), *The Language of the Goddess* (San Francisco, Harper San Francisco)

Giot, P.-R. (1987), *Barnenez, Carn, Guennoc* (Rennes, Université de Rennes I)

Goldhahn, J. (1999), *Sagaholm. Hällristningar och gravritual* (Umeå, Studia Archaeologica Universitatis Umensis)

—— (2002), 'Roaring rocks: an audiovisual perspective on hunter-gatherer engravings in Northern Sweden and Scandinavia', *Norwegian Archaeological Review* 35: 29–61

—— (2005), ' "We paint and we are proud of it" ', *Norwegian Archaeological Review* 38: 55–60

—— (2007), *Dödens hand – en essä om brons- och hällsmed* (Göteborg, Göteborgs Universitet)

Gómez Barrera, J. (2006), 'Grabados rupestres en el interior peninsular'. In J. Martínez García and M. Hernández Pérez (eds.), *Arte rupestre esquemático en la Península Ibérica*: 149–72 (Los Vélez, Comarca de Los Vélez)

Gonçalves, V. (2006), 'Quelques questions autour du temps, de l'espace et des symbols mégalithiques du centre et du sud du Portugal'. In R. Joussaume, L. Laporte, and C. Scarre (eds.), *Origine et développement du mégalithisme de l'ouest de l'Europe, I*: 485–510 (Bougon, Musée des Tumulus de Bougon)

Gosden, C. (2001), 'Making sense: archaeology and aesthetics', *World Archaeology* 33.2: 163–7

—— ed. (2001), *Archaeology and Aesthetics* (World Archaeology 33.2)

Gräslund, B. (1987), *The Birth of Prehistoric Chronology* (Cambridge, Cambridge University Press)

—— (1994), 'Prehistoric soul beliefs in Northern Europe', *Proceedings of the Prehistoric Society* 60: 15–26

Guerra Doce, E. (2002), 'Sobre el papel de la adormidera como possible viático en el ritual funerario de la prehistoria recent peninsula', *Boletin del seminario de estudious de arte y arqueologia* 68: 49–75

—— (2003), 'Drogas y rituals en el Neolítico europeo'. In P. Arias Cabal, R. Ontañón Pereod, and C. García-Moncó Piñero (eds.), *Actas del III Congresso del Neolitítico en la Península Ibérica*: 705–13 (Santander, Universidad de Cantabria)

Hallin, G. (2002), *Kummel, skepp och koksten – en studie om bosättningsområden och social struktur under bronsåldern på Gotland* (Sonla, Nykopia Global Print)

Hameau, P. (2003), 'Aspects de l'art rupestre et pariétal en France Méditerranéenne'. In J. Guilaine (ed.), *Arts et symboles du Néolithique à la protohistoire*: 137–63 (Paris, Errance)

Hameau, P. and Painard, A. (2006), 'L'expression schématique en Aragón: refléchir l'espace'. In J. Martínez García and M. Hernández Pérez (eds.), *Arte rupestre esquemático en la Península Ibérica*: 249–56 (Los Vélez, Comarca de Los Vélez)

Harding, D. (2004), *The Iron Age in Northern Britain* (London, Routledge)

—— (2007), *The Archaeology of Celtic Art* (Abingdon, Routledge)

Harrison, R., and Heyd, V. (2007), 'The transformation of Europe in the third millennium BC: the example of 'Le Petit Chasseur I + III', Sion, Valais (Switzerland)', *Praehistorische Zeitschrift* 82: 129–214

Hauptmann Wahlgren, K. (2000), 'The lonesome sailing ship. Reflections on the rock-carvings of Sweden and their interpretation', *Current Swedish Archaeology* 8: 67–96

—— (2002), *Bilder av betydelse. Hällristningar och bronsålderslanskap i nordöstra Östergötland* (Lindome, Bricoleur Press)

Hawkes, C., and Duval, P. M. eds. (1972), *Celtic Art in Ancient Europe: Five Protohistoric Centuries* (London, Seminar Press)

Helms, M. (1998), *Ulysses' Sail: an Ethnographic Odyssey of Power, Knowledge and Geographical Distance* (Princeton, Princeton University Press)

Helskog, K. (1987), 'Selective depictions. A study of 3,500 years of rock carvings from Arctic Norway and their relationship to the Sami drums'. In I. Hodder (ed.), *Archaeology as Long-term History*: 17–30 (Cambridge, Cambridge University Press)

—— (1999), 'The shore connection: cognitive landscape and communication with rock art in Northernmost Europe', *Norwegian Archaeological Review* 32.2: 74–94

Hernández Pérez, M. (2006), 'Artes esquetmáticos en la Península Ibérica : el paradigm de la pintura esquemática'. In J. Martínez García and M. Hernández Pérez (eds.), *Arte rupestre esquemático en la Península Ibérica*: 13–31 (Los Vélez, Comarca de Los Vélez)

Herschend, F. (2001), *Journey of Civilization: The Late Iron Age View of the Human World* (Uppsala, Uppsala University Department of Archaeology and Ancient History)

Hoskins, M. (2001), *Tombs, Temples and their Orientations: A New Perspective on Mediterranean Prehistory* (Bognor Regis, Ocarina Books)

Hummler, M. (2007), 'Bridging the gap at La Tène', *Antiquity* 81: 1067–70

Hyenstrand, Å. (1969), 'Gravformer och symboltecken under yngre bronsålder', *Fornvännen* 63: 185–9

—— (1984), *Fasta fornlämningar och arkeologiska regioner* (Stockholm, Statens Historiska Museum)

Ingold, T. ed. (1996), *Key Debates in Anthropology* (London, Routledge)

Jacobstahl, P. (1944), *Early Celtic Art* (Oxford, Clarendon Press)

Jellestad Syvertsen, K. 2002), 'Ristninger i graver–graver med ristninger'. In J. Goldhahn (ed.), *Bilder av Bronsålder*: 151–83 (Stockholm, Almqvist and Wiksell)

Jensen, R. (1985), 'Bronze Age settlement patterns in the Mälaren basin: ecological and social relationships'. In H-Å. Nordström and A. Knape (eds.), *Bronze Age Studies*: 133–50 (Stockholm, Statens Historiska Museum)

Johnsen, B. (2005), *The Cosmic Wedding* (Copenhagen, Frydenlund)

Johnston, S. (1993), 'The relationship between Irish prehistoric rock art and Irish passage tomb art', *Oxford Journal of Archaeology* 12: 257–79

Jones, A. (2005), 'Between a rock and a hard place: rock art and mimesis in Neolithic and Bronze Age Scotland'. In V. Cummings and A. Pannett (eds.), *Set in Stone: New Approaches to Neolithic Monuments in Scotland*: 107–17 (Oxford, Oxbow)

—— (2007a), *Memory and Material Culture* (Cambridge, Cambridge University Press)

—— (2007b), 'Excavating art: Recent excavations at the rock art sites at Torbhlaren, near Kilmartin, Mid-Argyll, Scotland', *Past* 57: 1–3

—— and MacGregor, G. eds. (2002), *Colouring the Past: The Significance of Colour in Archaeological Research* (Oxford, Berg)

Jope, E. M. (2000), *Early Celtic Art in the British Isles* (Oxford, Clarendon Press)

Jordan, P. (2003), *Material Culture and Sacred Landscape: The Anthropology of the Siberian Khanty* (Walnut Creek, Altamira Press)

Jorge, V. O. (1997), 'Questiões de interpretação da arte megalítica', *Brigantium* 10: 47–65

—— (1998), 'Interpreting the "megalithic art" of Western Iberia: some preliminary remarks', *Journal of Iberian Archaeology* (1998): 69–79

Joussaume, R., Laporte, L., and Scarre, C. eds. (2006), *Origine et développement du mégalithisme de l'ouest de l'Europe, 1* (Bougon, Musée des Tumulus de Bougon)

Kaliff, A. (1997), *Grav och kultplats* (Uppsala, Department of Archaeology, Uppsala University)

—— (2007), *Fire, Water, Heaven and Earth: Ritual Practice in Ancient Scandinavia: an Indo-European Perspective* (Stockholm, Riksantvarieämbetet)

Karlenby, L. (1999), 'Deposition i skärvtstenhögar'. In M. Olausson (ed.), *Spiralens öga. Tjugo artiklar kring aktuell bronsåldersforskning*: 115–25 (Stockholm, Riksantikvarieämbetet)

Kaul, F. (1987), 'Sandagergård. A Late Bronze Age cultic building with rock engravings and menhirs from North Zealand, Denmark', *Acta Archaeologica* 56: 31–54

—— (1995), 'The Gundestrup Cauldron reconsidered', *Acta Archaeologia* 66: 1–38

—— (1997), 'Recent finds of miniature "megalithic" art – art from the island of Bornholm and from Scania'. In A. Rodríguez Casal (ed.), *O Neolítico Atlantíco e as orixes do megalitismo*: 161–72 (Santiago de Compostela, Universidade de Santiago de Compostela)

—— (1998), *Ships on Bronzes: A Study in Bronze Age Religion and Iconography* (Copenhagen, National Museum)

—— (2004), *Bronzealders religion: studier af den nordiska bronsealders ikonografi* (Copenhagen, Der kongelide nordiska oldskirftselskab)

—— (2005), 'Bronze Age tripartite cosmologies', *Praehistorische Zeitschrift* 80: 235–46

—— (2006a), 'Udgravninger ved helleristninger', *Adoranten* (2006): 28–49

—— (2006b), 'Flere udgravninger ved helleristninger på Bornholm. En kort oversight', *Adoranten* (2006): 50–63

—— Mazarov, I., Best, J., and De Vries, N. (1991), *Thracian Tales on the Gundestrup Cauldron* (Amsterdam, Najade Press)

Keates, S. (2000), 'The ancestralization of the landscape: monumentality, memory and rock art of the Copper Age Valcamonica'. In G. Nash (ed.), *Signifying Place and Space: World Perspectives on Rock Art and Landscape*: 83–109 (Oxford, British Archaeological Reports)

Kehoe, A. (2000), *Shamans and Religion: An Anthropological Exploration of Critical Thinking* (Long Grove, Waveland Press)

King, J. (2004), 'Grave goods as gifts in Early Saxon burials (*c.* AD 450–600)', *Journal of Social Archaeology* 4: 214–38

Kirby, W. F. trans. (1907) *The Kalevala* (London, Dent)

Klindt-Jensen, O. (1961), *Gundestrupkedelen* (Copenhagen, Nationalmuseet)

König. L. (2007), 'A landscape of cairns'. In D. Widholm (ed.), *Stone Ships. The Sea and the Heavenly Journey*: 49–96 (Kalmar, Kalmar Studies in Archaeology)

Kopytoff, I. (1986), 'The cultural biography of things: commoditisation as process'. In A. Appadurai (ed.), *The Social Life of Things*: 64–91 (Cambridge, Cambridge University Press)

Kossack, G. (1954), *Studien zum Symbolgut der Urnenfelder und Hallstattzeit Mitteleuropas* (Berlin: De Gruyter)

Kristiansen, K. (1987), 'Centre and periphery in Bronze Age Scandinavia'. In M. Rowlands, M. Larsen, and K. Kristiansen (eds.), *Centre and Periphery in the Ancient World*: 74–95 (Cambridge, Cambridge University Press)

—— (2004), 'Seafaring voyages and rock art ships'. In P. Clark (ed.), *The Dover Bronze Age Boat in Context. Society and Water Transport in Prehistoric Europe*: 111–21 (Oxford, Oxbow)

—— and Larsson, T. (2005), *The Rise of Bronze Age Society: Travels, Transmissions and Transformation* (Cambridge, Cambridge University Press)

Lahelma, A. (2008), *A Touch of Red: Archaeological and Ethnographic Approaches to Interpreting Finnish Rock Paintings* (Helsinki, Iskos)

Laporte, L., and Tinévez, J. Y. (2004), 'Neolithic houses and chambered tombs of Western France', *Cambridge Archaeological Journal* 14: 217–34

Larsson, T. (1986), *The Bronze Age Metalwork in Southern Sweden. Aspects of Social and Spatial Organization 1800–500 BC* (Umeå, University of Umeå, Department of Archaeology)

Layton, R. (1991), *The Anthropology of Art*, 2nd edn (Cambridge, Cambridge University Press)

—— (1992), *Australian Rock Art: A New Synthesis* (Cambridge, Cambridge University Press)

Lecerf, Y. (1999), *Les pierres droites: réflexions autour des menhirs* (Rennes, Documents Archéologiques de l'Ouest)

Le Quellec, J.-L. (2006), 'L'art mégalithique en France: récents développements'. In R. Joussaume, L. Laporte, and C. Scarre (eds.), *Origine et développement du mégalithisme de l'ouest de l'Europe, 2*: 687–717 (Bougon, Musée des Tumulus de Bougon)

Leroi-Gourhan, A. (1965), *Préhistoire de l'art occidental* (Paris, Editions de l'art Mazenod)

—— (1982), *The Dawn of European Art: An Introduction to Palaeolithic Cave Painting* (Cambridge, Cambridge University Press)

Le Roux, C-T. (1992), 'Cornes de pierre'. In C-T. Le Roux (ed.), *Paysans et bâtisseurs*: 237–44 (Rennes, *Revue Archéologique de l'Ouest*, Supplément 5)

Le Rouzic, Z, Péquart, M., and Péquart, S-J. (1923), *Carnac. Fouilles faites dans la région* (Paris, Berger-Laverault)

Lewis-Williams, D. (1987), 'A dream of eland: an unexplored component of San shamanism and rock art', *World Archaeology* 19: 165–77

—— (2002), *The Mind in the Cave: Consciousness and the Origins of Art* (London, Thames and Hudson)

—— and Dowson, T. (1988), 'The signs of all times: entoptic phenomena in Upper Palaeolithic art', *Current Anthropology* 29: 201–45

—— and Pearce, D. (2005), *Inside the Neolithic Mind* (London, Thames and Hudson)

L'Helgouach, J. (1965), *Les sépultues mégalitiques en Armorique* (Rennes, Travaux du Laboratoire d'anthropologie préhistorique de la Faculté des Sciences)

—— (1996), 'De la lumière aux ténèbres'. In J. L'Helgouach, C-T. Le Roux, and J. Lecornec (eds.), *Art et symboles du mégalithisme Européen*: 107–23 (Rennes, *Revue Archéologique de l'Ouest*, Supplément 8)

Lilios, K. (2002), 'Some new views of the engraved slate plaques of southwest Iberia', *Arqueologia* 5: 135–51

—— (2003), 'Creating memory in prehistory: the engraved slate plaques of southwest Iberia'. In R. Van Dyke, and S. Alcock (eds.), *Archaeologies of Memory*: 129–50 (Oxford, Blackwell)

Lindgaard, E. (2006), 'Benan II. A petroglyph site in Nord-Trøndelag, Norway. A preliminary presentation', *Adoranten* (2006): 86–108

Ling, J. (2004), 'Beyond transgressive lands and forgotten seas: towards a maritime understanding of rock art in Bohuslän', *Current Swedish Archaeology* 12: 121–40

—— (2008), *Elevated Rock Art. Towards a Maritime Understanding of Rock Art in Northern Bohuslän, Sweden* (Gothenburg, Gothenburg Archaeological Theses)

Linge, T. (2005), 'Kammeranlegget i Mjeltehaugen – eit rekonstruktionjonsforslag', In J. Goldhahn (ed.), *Mellan sten och järn del 2*: 537–59 (Göteborg, Göteborgs Universitet)

Lyon Crawford, C. (2007). 'Collecting, defacing, reinscribing (and otherwise performing) memory in the ancient world'. In N. Yoffee (ed.), *Negotiating the Past in the Past*: 10–42 (Tucson, University of Arizona Press)

MacGregor, M. (1976), *Early Celtic Art in North Britain* (Leicester, Leicester University Press)

Malmer, M. (1981), *A Chorological Study of North European Rock Art* (Stockholm, Almqvist and Wiksell)

Mandt, G. (1995), 'Alternative analogies in rock art interpretation: the West Norwegian case'. In K. Helskog and B. Olsen (eds.), *Perceiving Rock Art: Social and Political Perspectives*: 263–91 (Oslo, Novus forlag)

Marstrander, S. (1963), *Østfolds jordbrukristninger* (Oslo, Universitetforlag)

Martens, J. (1988), 'Borremose reconsidered: the date and development of a fortified settlement of the Early Iron Age', *Journal of Danish Archaeology* 7: 159–81

Martín, D., and Camalich, M. (1982) 'La ceramic symbolica y su problemática', *Cuadernos de Prehistoria de la Universidad de Granada* 7: 267–306

Martínez García, J. (2006), 'La pintura rupestre esquemática en el proceso de transición y consolidación de las sociedades productoras'. In J. Martínez García and M. Hernández Pérez (eds.), *Arte rupestre esquemático en la Península Ibérica*: 33–56 (Los Vélez, Comarca de Los Vélez)

Megaw, R., and Megaw, V. (1990), *The Basse Yutz Find: Masterpieces of Celtic Art* (London, Society of Antiquaries)

—— (2001), *Celtic Art: From its Beginning to the Book of Kells* (London, Thames and Hudson)

Mens, E. (2008), 'Refitting megaliths in western France', *Antiquity* 82: 25–36

Mezzena, F. (1998), 'Le stele antropomorfe nell'area megalitica di Aosta'. In F. Mezzena (ed.), *Dei di pietra*: 91–121 (Skira: Regione autonoma Valle d'Aosta)

Milstreu, G. (1999), 'Dokumentation och registrering'. In G. Milstreu and H. Prøhl (eds.), *Dokumentation och registrering av hällristningar i Tanum* (Tanumshede, Tanums Hällristningsmuseum)

Moro Abadía, O. (2006), 'Art, crafts and Palaeolithic art', *Journal of Social Archaeology* 6: 119–41

—— and González Morales, M. (2005), 'L'analogie et la représentation de l'art primitif à la fin du XIXe siècle', *L'anthropologie* 109: 703–21

Morphy, H. (1991), *Ancestral Connections: Art and an Aboriginal System of Knowledge* (Chicago, University of Chicago Press)

—— (1994), 'The anthropology of art'. In T. Ingold (ed.), *Companion Encyclopedia of Anthropology*: 648–85 (London, Routledge)

—— (2007), *Becoming Art: Exploring Cross-Cultural Categories* (Oxford, Berg)

Morphy, H., and Perkins, M. (2005), 'The anthropology of art: reflections on its history and contemporary practice'. In H. Morphy and M. Perkins (eds.), *The Anthropology of Art: A Reader*: 1–32 (Oxford, Blackwell)

Morwood, M. (2002), *Visions from the Past. The Archaeology of Australian Aboriginal Art* (Crows Nest NSW, Allen and Unwin)

Mulk, I.-M., and Bayliss-Smith, T. (2006), *Rock Art and Sami Sacred Geography In Badjelánda, Laponia, Sweden* (Umeå, Umeå University Department of Archaeology and Sami Studies)

Munn, N. (1973), *Walbiri Iconography: Graphic Representation and Cultural Symbolism in a Central Australian Society* (Ithaca, Cornell University Press)

Myrberg, N. (2006), 'The imperative way'. In A. Andrén, K. Jennbert, and C. Raudvere (eds.), *Old Norse Religion in Long-term Perspectives: Origins, Changes, and Interactions*: 45–9 (Lund, Nordic Academic Press)

Nash, G. (2007), 'Light at the end of the tunnel: the way megalithic art was viewed and experienced'. In A. Mazel, G. Nash, and C. Waddington (eds.), *Art as Metaphor: The Prehistoric Rock-Art of Britain*: 123–43 (Oxford, Archaeopress)

Nilsson, P. (2005), 'Om boplatslokalisering inom Bråbygdens hällristningsområden', In J. Goldhahn (ed.), *Mellan sten och järn del 2*: 419–35 (Göteborg, Göteborgs Universitet)

Nord, J. (2007), 'Movements and pauses: aspects of a Bronze Age landscape'. In B. Hårdh, K. Jennbert, and D. Olausson (eds.), *On the Road: Studies in Honour of Lars Larsson*: 237–45 (Stockholm, Amqvist and Wiksell)

Nordbladh, J. (1980), *Glyfer och rum. Kring hällristningarna i Kville* (Göteborg, Göteborgs Universitet)

Nordenborg Myhre, L. (1998), *Historier fra en annen virkelighet. Forteller om bronsealder ved Karmsundet* (Stavanger, Museum i Stavanger)

—— (2004), *Trialectic Archaeology: Monuments and Space in Southwest Norway* (Stavanger, Museum i Stavanger)

Oestigaard, T. (1999), 'Cremations as transformations', *European Journal of Archaeology* 2: 345–64

—— (2007), *Transformatøren. Ildens meste i jernalderen* (Göteborg, Göteborgs Universitet)

O'Kelly, M. (1982), *Newgrange: Archaeology, Art and Legend* (London, Thames and Hudson)

Olivier, L. (1999), 'The Hochdorf "princely" grave and the question of the nature of archaeological funerary assemblages'. In T. Murray (ed.), *Time and Archaeology*: 109–38 (London, Routledge)

Olmsted, G. (1979), *The Gundestrup Cauldron: Its Archaeology, Context, the Style and Iconography of its Portrayed Motifs, and the Narration of a Gaulish Version of the Tain Bó Cuailnge* (Brussels, Latomus)

Osborne, R., and Tanner, J. eds. (2007), *Art's Agency and Art History* (Oxford, Blackwell)

O'Sullivan, M. (1986), 'Approaches to passage tomb art', *Journal of the Royal Society of Antiquaries of Ireland* 116: 68–83

—— (1996), 'Megalithic art in Ireland and Brittany: divergence or convergence?' In J. L'Helgouach, C-T. Le Roux, and J. Lecornec (eds.), *Art et symboles du mégalithisme Européen*: 81–96 (Rennes, *Revue Archéologique de l'Ouest*, Supplément 8)

—— (2006), 'La Boyne et autres sites; une revue de l'art mégalithique d'Irlande'. In R. Joussaume, L., Laporte, L., and C. Scarre (eds.), *Origine et développement du mégalithisme de l'ouest de l'Europe, 2*: 649–86 (Bougon, Musée des Tumulus de Bougon)

Paço, A. (1940), 'Places de barro de Vila Nova de S. Pedro', *Congresso do Mundo Português, Publicações.vol 1*: 235–51

Peña Santos, A., and Rey García, J. M. (1999), *Petroglifos de Galicia* (A Coruña, Vía Láctea Editorial)

Persson, P., and Sjögren, K-G. (1995), 'Radiocarbon and the chronology of Swedish megalithic graves', *Journal of European Archaeology*, 3: 59–88

Planck, D. Biel, J., Süsskind, G., and Wais, A. (1985), *Der Keltenfürst von Hochdorf* (Stuttgart: Konrad Theiss)

Powell, T. G. E. (1966), *Prehistoric Art* (London, Thames and Hudson)

Price, N. (2001), 'An archaeology of altered states: shamanism and material culture studies'. In N. Price (ed.), *The Archaeology of Shamanism*: 1–16 (London, Routledge)

Price, S. (2007), *Paris Primitive. Jacques Chirac's Museum on the Quai Branly* (Chicago, University of Chicago Press)

Raftery, B. ed. (1990), *Celtic Art* (Paris, Flammarion)

Randsborg, K. (1993), 'Kivik. Archaeology and ideology', *Acta Archaeologica* 64.1: 1–147

—— (1995), *Hjortspring. Warfare and Sacrifice in Early Europe* Århus: Århus University Press

—— and Christensen, K. (2006), 'Bronze Age oak-coffin graves: archaeology and dendro-dating' (Copenhagen, *Acta Archaeologica* Supplementum 7)

—— and Nybo, C. (1984), 'The coffin and the sun: demography and ideology in Scandinavian prehistory', *Acta Archaeologica* 55: 161–84

Rausing, G. (1984), *Prehistoric Boats and Ships of Northwestern Europe* (Lund, Gleerup)

Reginelli Servais, G. (2007), *La Tène, un site, un mythe* (Neuchâtel, Office et musée archéologique du Neuchâtel)

Renfrew, C. (1973), *Before Civilization: The Radiocarbon Revolution and Prehistoric Europe* (London, Cape)

—— (1993), *The Cycladic Spirit: Masterpieces from the Nicholas P. Goulandris Collection* (London, Thames and Hudson)

—— (2000), *Loot, Legitimacy and Ownership: The Ethical Crisis in Archaeology* (London, Duckworth)

—— (2002), *Figuring it out: The Parallel Visions of Artists and Archaeologists* (London, Thames and Hudson)

—— (2008) 'The Keros Hoard: remaining questions', *American Journal of Archaeology* 112: 295–8

Renfrew, C., Doumas, C., Marangou. L., and Gavalas, G. eds. (2007), *Keros Dhaskalio Kavos: The Investigations of 1987–88* (Cambridge, McDonald Institute for Archaeological Research)

Richards, C. (2005), *Dwelling Among the Monuments: The Neolithic Village of Barnhouse, Maeshowe Passage Grave and Surrounding Monuments at Stenness, Orkney* (Cambridge, McDonald Institute for Archaeological Research)

Rowell, M. ed. (1986), *Joan Miró. Selected Writings and Interviews* (Boston, G. K. Hall)

Ruggles, C. (1999), *Astronomy in Prehistoric Britain and Ireland* (New Haven, Yale University Press)

Runcis, J. (1999), 'Den mystiska geografin –reflektioner kring skärvstenhögar, mytologi och landskaprum i Södermanland under bronsålder'. In M. Olausson (ed.), *Spiralens öga. Tjugo artiklar kring aktuell bronsåldersforskning*: 127–55 (Stockholm, Riksantikvarieämbetet)

Sanches, M. J. (1997) *Pré-história recente de Trás-os-Montes e alto Douro* (Porto, Sociedade Portuguesa de Antropologi e Etnologia)

Sandars, N. (1968), *Prehistoric Art* (Harmondsworth, Penguin)

Santos Estévez, M. (2005), *Arte rupestre: estilo y construcción social del espacio en el Noroeste de la Península Ibérica* (Santiago de Compostela, Universidade de Santiago de Compostela)

Scarre, C. (2002), 'Contexts of monumentalism: regional diversity at the Neolithic transition in north-west France', *Oxford Journal of Archaeology* 21: 23–61

—— (2004a), 'Choosing stones, remembering places: geology and intention in the megalithic monuments of Western Europe'. In N. Boivin and M-A. Owoc (eds.), *Soils, Stones and Symbols. Cultural Perceptions of the Mineral World*: 187–202 (London, UCL Press)

—— (2004b), 'Displaying the stones: the materiality of "megalithic" monuments'. In E. DeMarrais, C. Gosden, and C. Renfrew (eds.), *Rethinking Materiality*: 141–52 (Cambridge, McDonald Institute for Archaeological Research)

—— (2007a), 'Changing places: monuments and the Neolithic transition in western France'. In A. Whittle and V. Cummings (eds.), *Going Over. The Mesolithic-Neolithic Transition in North-West Europe*: 243–61 (London, British Academy)

—— (2007b), 'Monuments and miniatures: representing humans in Neolithic Europe 5000–2000 BC'. In C. Renfrew and I. Morley (eds.), *Images and Imagination: A Global Prehistory of Figurative Representation*: 17–29 (Cambridge, McDonald Institute for Archaeological Research)

Schwab, H. (1990–2002), *Archéologie de la seconde correction des eaux du Jura, 1–3* (Fribourg, Éditions Universitaires)

Shee Twohig, E. (1981), *The Megalithic Art of Western Europe* (Oxford, Clarendon Press)

—— (1997), ' "Megalithic art" in a settlement context: Skara Brae and related sites in the Orkney islands', *Brigantium* 10: 377–89

—— (2000), 'Frameworks for the megalithic art of the Boyne Valley', in A. Desmond, G. Johnson, M. McCarthy, J. Sheehan, and E. Shee Twohig (eds.), *New Agendas in Irish Prehistory*: 89–105 (Bray, Wordwell)

Shepherd, A. (2000), 'Skara Brae: expressing identity in a Neolithic community'. In A. Ritchie (ed.), *Neolithic Orkney in its European Context*: 139–58 (Cambridge, McDonald Institute for Archaeological Research)

Shiner, L. (2001), *The Invention of Art: A Cultural History* (Chicago, University of Chicago Press)

Sjögren, K.-G. (2003), 'Megaliths, settlement and subsistence in Bohuslän, Sweden'. In G. Burenhult (ed.), *Stone and Bones*: 167–76 (Oxford, British Archaeological Reports)

Skaarup, J. (1995), 'Stone-Age burials in boats'. In O. Crumlin-Pedersen and B. M. Thye (eds.), *The Ship as Symbol in Prehistoric and Medieval Scandinavia*: 51–9 (Copenhagen, National Museum)

—— and Grøn, O. (2004), *Mollegabet III: A Submerged Mesolithic Settlement in Southern Denmark* (Oxford, Archaeopress)

Skoglund, P. (2005), 'Ideal och praktik – skeppssättningar i yngre bronsålder'. In J. Goldhahn (ed.), *Mellan sten och järn, del 1*: 324–52 (Göteborg, Göteborgs Universitet)

—— (2006), *Hällristningar i Kronobergs län. Motiv, myter och documentation* (Lund, University of Lund Institute of Archaeology)

Soggnes, K. (1995a), ' "Megalitisk kunst" i et ikke-megalitisk Norden', *Adoranten* (1995): 5–11

—— (1995b), 'The social context of rock art in Trøndelag, Norway: rock art as a frontier'. In K. Helskog and B. Olsen (eds.), *Perceiving Rock Art: Social and Political Perspectives*: 130–45 (Oslo, Novus forlag)

—— (1998), 'Symbols in a changing world: rock-art and the transition to farming in mid Norway'. In C. Chippindale and P. Taçon (eds.), *The Archaeology of Rock Art*: 146–62 (Cambridge, Cambridge University Press)

—— (2001), *Prehistoric Imagery and Landscape: Rock Art in Stjordal, Trondelag, Norway* (Oxford, Archaeopress)

Soler Díaz, J. (2002), *Cuevas de inhumación multiple en la communidad Valenciana* (Alicante, Diputación provincial de Alicante)

Sotirakopolou, P. (2005), *The Keros Hoard: Myth or Reality?* (Los Angeles, Nicholas Goulandris Foundation)

Starling, S. (2005), *Cuttings* (Basel, Kunstmuseum Basel)

Stead, I. (1985), *The Battersea Shield* (London, British Museum Publications)

—— (1996), *Celtic Art: Britain Before the Roman Conquest* (London, British Museum Publications)

Storm Munch, J. (1998), 'Gjenvisit på Gunnarstorp'. In E. Østmo (ed.), *Fra Østfolds oltid*: 143–52 (Oslo, Universitetets Olssakamlings Skrifter)

Svanberg, F. (2005), 'House symbolism in aristocratic death rituals of the Bronze Age'. In T. Artelius and F. Svanberg (eds.), *Dealing with the Dead: Archaeological Perspectives on Prehistoric Scandinavian Burial Ritual*: 73–98 (Stockholm, National Heritage Board)

Svensson, K. (1985), 'En kultplats I Dalsland', *Populär Arkeologi* 3: 29

Szabo, M. (1974), *A keleti kelta múvészet* (Skékesfehérvár, Istvan Király Múzeum)

Taçon, P., Wilson, M., and Chippindale, C. (1996), 'Birth of the Rainbow Serpent in Arnhem Land rock art and oral history', *Archaeology in Oceania* 31: 103–24

Tanner, J., and Osborne, R. (2007), '*Art and Agency* and art history'. In R. Osborne and J. Tanner (eds.), *Art's Agency and Art History*: 1–27 (Oxford, Blackwell)

Tarrete, J. (1996), 'L'art mégalithique dans le Bassin Parisien; symétrie et latéralité dans les representations du Néolithique final'. In J. L'Helgouach, C-T. Le Roux, and J. Lecornec (eds.), *Art et symboles du mégalithisme Européen*: 149–59 (Rennes, *Revue Archéologique de l'Ouest*, Supplément 8)

—— (1992), 'The Gundestrup Cauldron', *Scientific American*, March 1992: 68

Taylor, T. (1996), 'Celtic Art'. In B. Fagan (ed.), *The Oxford Companion to Archaeology*: 121–3 (Oxford, Oxford University Press)

Thedéen, S. (2003), 'Life course practices in Bronze Age landscapes of East Central Sweden', *Current Swedish Archaeology* 11: 97–118

Thomas, J. (1992), 'Monuments, movement and the context of megalithic art'. In N. Sharples and A. Sheridan (eds.), *Vessels for the Ancestors*: 143–55 (Edinburgh, Edinburgh University Press)

Thomas, N. (1999), *Possessions: Indigenous Art/Colonial Culture* (London, Thames and Hudson)

Thorn, R. (2007), 'Great rows of fire: the linearity of hearths and cooking pits in Southern Scandinavia'. In D. Gheorghiu and G. Nash (eds.), *The Archaeology of Fire – Understanding Fire as Material Culture* (Budapest, Archaeolingua)

Tilley, C. (1990), 'Claude Lévi-Strauss: structuralism and beyond'. In C. Tilley (ed.), *Reading Material Culture*: 3–81 (Oxford, Blackwell)

—— (1999), *Metaphor and Material Culture* (Oxford, Blackwell)

—— (2004), *The Materiality of Stone* (Oxford, Berg)

—— (2007), 'Architectural order and the ordering of imagery in Malta and Ireland: a comparative perspective'. In D. Barraclough and C. Malone (eds.), *Cult in Context. Reconsidering Ritual in Archaeology*: 118–33 (Oxford, Oxbow)

Treherne, P. (1995), 'The warrior's beauty: the masculine body and self-identity in Bronze Age Europe', *Journal of European Archaeology* 3: 105–45

Ucko, P., and Rosenfeld, A. (1967), *Palaeolithic Cave Art* (London, Weidenfeld and Nicholson)

Ullén, I. (1996), 'Food ethics, domestication and togetherness: a close-up study of the relation of horse and dog to man in the Bronze Age settlement of Apalle', *Current Swedish Archaeology* 4: 171–84

Victor, H. (2001), 'Bronsålderns kulthus – ett möte mellan profant och sakralt'. In H. Bolin, A. Kaliff, and T. Zachrisson (eds.), *Mellan sten och brons*: 133–52 (Stockholm, Stockholm Archaeological Reports)

—— (2002), *Med graven som granne. Om bronsålderns kulthus* (Uppsala, Department of Archaeology and Ancient History, Uppsala University)

Villes, A. (1997), 'Les figurations dans les sépultures collectives Neolithiques dans la Marne, dans le contexte du Bassin Parisien', *Brigantium* 10: 149–77

Vinsrygg, S. (1980), 'Om tidsaspekter i argarrningane'. In S. Marstrander (ed.), *Ristninger i forhistorie og middelalder. Varia 1*: 37–62 (Oslo, Universitets oldsakambing)

Waddington, C. (2007), 'Neolithic rock-art in the British Isles: retrospect and prospect'. In A. Mazel, G. Nash, and C. Waddington (eds.), *Art as Metaphor: The Prehistoric Rock-Art of Britain*: 49–68 (Oxford, Archaeopress)

Waller, S. (2006), 'Intentionality of rock-art placement deduced from acoustical measurements'. In C. Scarre and G. Lawson (eds.), *Archaeoacoustics*: 31–9 (Cambridge, McDonald Institute for Archaeological Research)

Wangen, V. (1998), 'Gravfeltet på Gunnarstorp. Et monument over dødsriter og kultutøvelse'. In E. Østmo (ed.), *Fra Østfolds oltid*: 153–71 (Oslo, Universitetets Olssakamlings Skrifter)

Watson, A. (2001), 'The sounds of transformation: acoustics, monuments and ritual in the British Neolithic'. In N. Price (ed.), *The Archaeology of Shamanism*: 187–92 (London, Routledge)

—— (2006), '(Un)intentional sound? Acoustics and Neolithic monuments'. In C. Scarre and G. Lawson (eds.), *Archaeoacoustics*: 11–22 (Cambridge, McDonald Institute for Archaeological Research)

Watson, A., and Keating, D. (2000), 'The architecture of sound in Neolithic Orkney'. In A. Ritchie (ed.), *Neolithic Orkney in its European Context*: 259–63 (Cambridge, McDonald Institute for Archaeological Research)

Wells, P. (2001), *Beyond Celts, Germans and Scythians: Archaeology and Identity in Iron Age Europe* (London, Duckworth)

—— (2007), 'Weapons, ritual and commemoration in Late Iron Age Northern Europe'. In C. Haselgrove and T. Moore (eds.), *The Later Iron Age in Britain and Beyond*: 468–77 (Oxford, Oxbow)

West, M. (2007), *Indo-European Poetry and Myth* (Oxford, Oxford University Press)

Whitley, D., Dorn, R., Simon, J., Rechtman, R., and Whitley, T. (1999), 'Sally's rock shelter and the archaeology of the Vision Quest', *Cambridge Archaeological Journal* 9: 221–47

Whittle, A. (2000), ' "Very like a whale": menhirs, motifs and myths in the Mesolithic-Neolithic transition in North-West Europe', *Cambridge Archaeological Journal* 10: 243–59

Widholm, D. (1998), *Rösen, ristningar och riter* (Lund, Acta Archaeologica Lundensia)

—— (1999), 'Rock art as part of Bronze Age funerary rites'. In J. Goldhahn (ed.), *Rock Art as Social Representation*: 65–75 (Oxford, British Archaeological Reports)

—— and Regnell, M. (2001), 'Grave monuments and landscape in South-eastern Sweden', *Lund Archaeological Review* 7: 29–49

Wigren, S. (1987), *Sørmländsk bronsåaldersbyg* (Stockholm: Stockholm University Institute of Archaeology)

Williams, H. (2007), 'Depicting the dead: commemoration through cists, cairns and symbols in Early Medieval Britain', *Cambridge Archaeological Journal* 17: 145–64

Wood, P. (2002), *Conceptual Art* (London, Tate Publishing)

Wrigglesworth, M. (2002), 'Ristninger og graver i landskapet'. In J. Goldhahn (ed.), *Bilder av Bronsålder*: 185–99 (Stockholm, Almqvist and Wiksell)

Yates, T. (1993), 'Frameworks for an archaeology of the body'. In C. Tilley (ed.), *Interpretetative Archaeology*: 131–72 (Oxford, Berg)

York, J. (2002), 'The life cycle of Bronze Age weapons from the Thames', *Oxford Journal of Archaeology* 21: 77–92

Zvelebil, M., and Jordan, P. (1999), 'Hunter fisher gatherer ritual landscapes'. In J. Goldhahn (ed.), *Rock Art as Social Representation*: 101–27 (Oxford, British Archaeological Reports)

Index